SUPER-OPTIMIZING EXAMPLES:
ACROSS PUBLIC POLICY PROBLEMS

SUPER-OPTIMIZING EXAMPLES: ACROSS PUBLIC POLICY PROBLEMS

STUART S. NAGEL

Nova Science Publishers, Inc.
Huntington, New York

Editorial Production: Susan Boriotti
Office Manager: Annette Hellinger
Graphics: Frank Grucci and Jennifer Lucas
Information Editor: Tatiana Shohov
Book Production: Donna Dennis, Patrick Davin, Christine Mathosian, Tammy Sauter and Lynette Van Helden
Circulation: Maryanne Schmidt
Marketing/Sales: Cathy DeGregory

Library of Congress Cataloging-in-Publication Data

Nagel, Stuart S.
Super-optimizing examples: across public policy problems / Stuart S. Nagel., ed
Includes index.
ISBN 1-56072-746-2
1. Policy Sciences.. I. Nagel, Stuart S., 1934
H97.S92 1999 99-051430
320'.6--dc21 CIP

6080 Jericho Turnpike, Suite 207
Commack, New York 11725
Tele. 516-499-3103 Fax 516-499-3146
e-mail: Novascience@earthlink.net
e-mail: Novascil@aol.com
Web Site: http://www.nexusworld.com/nova

Printed in the United States of America

CONTENTS

PART THREE: SOCIAL POLICY PROBLEMS

PART FOUR: POLITICAL POLICY PROBLEMS

PART FIVE: LEGAL POLICY PROBLEMS

PART SIX: CROSS-NATIONAL EXAMPLES

INTRODUCTION

Stuart S. Nagel
University of Illinois

I. WIN-WIN POLICY

Win-win policy refers to public policy that is capable of achieving both conservative and liberal goals simultaneously. Examples could be given from any field of public policy, such as economic, social, environmental, legal, or political policy. Win-win policies should be distinguished from compromises, where both sides retreat partially from achieving their goals in order to obtain an agreement.

A. As an Example, The Field of Environmental Policy

As an example, the field of environmental policy involves both conservative and liberal approaches. Conservatives emphasize the role of consumers and the marketplace in restraining business from engaging in socially undesirable activities, like pollution. The liberals emphasize the role of the government in restraining pollution. Conservatives are especially interested in the goal of economic development, which may be interfered with by governmental restraints. Liberals are especially interested in the goal of a cleaner environment, which may not be achieved so effectively by relying on selective consumer buying.

A neutral compromise approach might involve giving business firms partial subsidies to adopt antipollution devices. Doing so would involve some requirements for receiving the subsidies, but less interference than regulation and fines. Doing so would help promote a cleaner environment, but there still might be evasions by business in view of the extra expense and trouble in complying.

A win-win policy alternative instead might emphasize subsidies to universities and research firms to develop new processes (that relate to manufacturing, transportation, energy, and agriculture) that are both less expensive and cleaner than the old processes.

Those new processes then would be adopted by business firms because they are more profitable, not because the firms are being forced or subsidized to do so.

The new processes thus would achieve the conservative goals of profits and economic development, even better than retaining the present marketplace. Such a win-win policy also would promote the liberal goal of a cleaner environment, even better than a system of regulation, and without the expense of a continuing subsidy for adopting and renewing antipollution devices.

A specific example of such an environmental win-win policy has been finding a substitute for aerosol propellants and air-conditioning freon that is more profitable to manufacturers and simultaneously less harmful to the ozone layer, which protects against skin cancer. Another specific example is developing an electric car, which saves money on gasoline and maintenance, while at the same time not generating the exhaust pollution of internal-combustion cars. Developing hydrogen fusion or solar energy also may be examples of a less expensive and cleaner fuel for manufacturing processes.

B. Kinds of Feasibility

Win-win policies may be capable of achieving both conservative and liberal goals in theory, but not in practice. To be meaningful policies, they may have to satisfy various kinds of feasibility. For example, is the policy of developing solar energy for manufacturing feasible technologically? Is there sufficient funding available to subsidize the needed research if the private sector is not so willing, due to the risks, the large amount of money needed, or the long wait before payoffs occur?

Is there insurmountable political opposition from liberals who do not like government subsidies to make business more profitable? What about the opposition from conservatives who do not like government involvement in developing a research agenda? Is the program feasible administratively in terms of built-in incentives, or does it require a lot of obtrusive monitoring? Does the program violate some constitutional rights? Does the program make provision for workers and firms that might be displaced if the policy is adopted?

C. Creativity

Win-win policies may involve creativity, but developing them is becoming easier as a result of experience with the ideas. We now have many different approaches that can serve as a checklist in leading one to a win-win policy. For example, expanding the resources available can enable conservatives to have more money for defense, and liberals to have more money for domestic programs. The government sometimes can be a third-party benefactor in providing vouchers to enable both landlords and tenants, and also merchants and consumers, to come out ahead.

One also can deal with problems like abortion by getting at the causes. These causes consist of unwanted pregnancies that could be lessened through more effective abstinence programs and birth control. Thinking in terms of the goals to be achieved, rather than the alternatives to choose among, can stimulate win-win policies. So can thinking in terms of increasing benefits and decreasing costs.

Other approaches deal with early socialization of widely accepted values, technological fixes like the nonpolluting hair spray, and the contracting out of government activities to private firms (which do well as a result of both the profit motive and quality specifications in the contract). Further approaches may involve combining (rather than compromising) alternatives, developing a package with something for each major viewpoint, having international economic communities, adopting a gradual or incremental win-win policy, and arranging for big benefits on one side with small costs on the other.

Win-win policy may be especially relevant as of 1994-1995 because the Democrats control the presidency and the Republicans control Congress. That division means that neither purely liberal nor purely conservative legislation is likely to pass in view of the Republican congressional majority, the availability of the filibuster to the Democrats in Congress, and the availability of the veto to the president. It is possible that some compromise legislation might pass, such as health care without an employer mandate or required forms of health insurance. Even better would be win-win policies such as promoting real economic growth through greater productivity related to increasing labor skills, new technologies, competition, and tariff reductions.

D. Steps and Checklists

Win-win policy analysis in this context can be *defined* as handling policy problems by finding solutions that exceed the best initial expectations of conservatives, liberals, Republicans, Democrats, or whoever are the major groups sides or viewpoints in the policy dispute. Win-win is also called super-optimizing or doing better than the previous best of all major groups.

There are basically *five steps* to win-win policy analysis:

1. What are the major goals of conservatives, liberals, or other major groups who are disputing what policy should be adopted for a given policy problem?
2. What are the major alternatives of these groups for dealing with the policy problem?
3. What are the relations between each major alternative and each major goal? In their simplest form, these relations can be expressed in terms of a minus sign (relatively adverse relation) and plus sign (relative conducive relation), and a zero (neither adverse nor conducive relation).
4. What new alternative is there that might be capable of:
   a. achieving the conservative goals even better than the conservative alternative, and

b. simultaneously achieving the liberal goals even more than the liberal alternative? Whatever new alternative meets these two criteria is a win-win alternative or a super-optimum solution.

5. Is the proposed win-win alternative capable of jetting over various hurdles that frequently exist. These hurdles may be political, administrative, technological, legal, psychological, and economic in random order. Win-win solutions should also consider how to upgrade workers and firms that may be displaced by downsizing due to increased productivity, free trade, defense conversion, immigration, merit treatment, labor utilization, creativity, and related factors.

To facilitate developing win-win alternatives, it helps to have a positive can-do attitude that it can be done. It also helps to have a checklist of types of win-win alternatives that have worked in the past. Such a *facilitating checklist* of types might include the following:

1. Expand the resources.
2. Find a third-party benefactor.
3. Set higher goals.
4. Decrease the causes of the problem.
5. Re-define the problem to emphasize goals rather than alternatives.
6. Increase the benefits and decrease the costs.
7. Socialize children in widely accepted values so the problems do not occur.
8. Find a new technology.
9. Contract-out via an auction to multiple firms with societal strings attached.
10. Promote international economic communities.
11. Arrange for big benefits on one side and small costs on the other.
12. Fully combine alternatives that are not mutually exclusive.
13. Develop a multi-faceted package.
14. Adopt the win-win solution in steps, where the first step may be a traditional compromise.

For *further details* on the concepts, methods, and examples of win-win analysis, see:

1. William Baumol, *Superfairness: Applications and Theory* (MIT Press, 1986).
2. S. Nagel, *Super-Optimum Solutions and Win-Win Policy: Basic Concepts and Methods,* (Greenwood, 1997).
3. Richard Noyes, *Now the Synthesis: Capitalism, Socialism, and the New Social Contract* (Centre for Incentive Taxation, 1991).
4. Lawrence Susskind and Jeffrey Cruikshank, *Breaking the Impasse: Consensual Approaches to Resolving Public Disputes* (Basic Books, 1987).
5. For a free copy of the handout materials used in the worldwide win-win and SOS workshops, drop a note to Nagel at PSO.

Win-win analysis can be applied to handling dissident faculty as an *example*:

1. A lose-lose situation is where a department or the university seeks to destroy a dissident faculty member. The university may suffer the stigma of being enjoined for violating free speech and due process. The faculty member loses money in obtaining an injunction and subsequent enforcement.
2. A win-lose situation. This is where one side thinks it can be a winner and the other side a loser. Trying to do so often results in lose-lose situations, as in litigation, strikes, and war.
3. A win-win situation. This is where the university can try to constructively encourage the potential creativity of dissident faculty. Doing so can possibly result in new ideas, inventions, and institutions to the credit of both the university and the dissident faculty members. This is more likely to happen with administrators who have flexible democratic personalities, rather than authoritarian personalities. All administrators, however, benefit from the funding, prestige, and quality students that go to universities that are in the forefront of new ideas, inventions, and institutional arrangements.
4. The same win-win thinking can be applied to dissident citizens in a country. The analysis is also applicable to other economic, technology, social, political, international, and legal policy problems.

E. Tables and Graphs

GOALS POLICIES	Conservatives	Liberals
Conservatives	+	-
Liberals	-	+
Super-Optimum Solutions	++	++

Finding solutions where all major sides achieve better than their best expectations.

The above win-win matrix indicates that basic win-win analysis is about as simple as a tic-tac-toe table. A tic-tac-toe table has three columns made by two vertical lines. It also has three rows made by two horizontal lines. That is also true of a win-win table except it adds a fourth row for super-optimum solutions.

The first row indicates the types of goals to be achieved. The second column refers to conservative goals and the third column refers to liberal goals. The first column indicates the types of policy alternatives under consideration for achieving the goals. The second row refers to conservative policies and the third row refers to liberal policies.

A "+" sign indicates that the policy is relatively conducive to the goal in comparison with the other policies being considered. A "-" sign indicates that the policy is relatively adverse to the goal. Conservative policies usually do well on conservative goals but not so well on liberal goals) as one would expect. Liberal policies do well on liberal goals but not so well on conservative goals.

This is a classic tradeoff where adopting either of the two policies means losing some of the goals. The result is usually a compromise whereby both sides (or all major sides) lose something and gain something. Neither side is usually strong enough to impose its solutions.

A win-win or super-optimum solution involves finding an alternative that is not purely conservative, purely liberal, or a compromise. It is, however, capable of achieving the conservative goals more than the conservative policies, and simultaneously capable of achieving the liberal goals more than the liberal policies.

The SOS thus receives a "++", on both the conservative and liberal goals. In that sense, it does better than the conservative best and better than the liberal best. It should also be feasible regarding economic, technology, social, psychological, political, administrative, and legal matters.

F. An Example of the Matrix

CRITERIA ALTERNATIVES	C Economic Development	L Clean Environment
C Marketplace	+	-
L Anti-Pollution Regulation	-	+
N Compromise Regulations	0	0
SOS Improved Manufacturing, Agricultural, and Other Processes (More profitable and cleaner)	++	++

The above table applies the generic matrix to the problem of environmental protection, especially in developing nations. The main conservative goal is economic development, and the main liberal goal is a clean environment. Conservatives also endorse a clean environment but not as much as liberals. Likewise, liberals also endorse economic development, but not as much as conservatives.

The main conservative policy is to rely on the marketplace on the theory that consumers would not buy products that are causing unhealthful pollution. The main liberal policy is to rely on anti-pollution regulation on the theory that the fines, the taxes, and other penalties will cause business to reduce pollution.

The usual result consists of compromise regulations that are not as severe as liberals would like but better than nothing. The compromise regulations are not as desirable to business as no regulations, but are better than what the liberals are advocating.

A win-win or SOS solution might involve public policy designed through financial and other incentives to generate new processes for manufacturing, agriculture, transportation, and energy that are more profitable to business, but at the same time are cleaner to the environment than previous processes. Such a profitable and clean policy would be an improvement on economic development and a clean environment.

An example might include the use of vehicles and machines that use less gasoline and oil but are even more productive. Such innovations are easier in terms of technology, funding, and other considerations for some kinds of pollution. Such innovations may also have a bigger impact on some kinds of pollution. The optimum allocation of incentive money is a separate problem. The important consideration here is shifting conservatives and liberals toward such win-win solutions rather than toward relatively ineffective marketplace and regulatory policies.

G. SOS Applied to Economics

Economists (especially Keynesian economists) have argued that an expanding economy requires (or generally requires) deficit spending in order to stimulate the economy. If the government spends more than it taxes (an undesirable occurrence) then GNP goes up (a desirable occurrence).

Deficits are undesirable because they cause (1) government borrowing which raises interest rates which hurts the economy, (2) inflexibility in needed government spending because so much of the budget goes to pay interest on the debt, and (3) a class of relatively unproductive people who live off unnecessary interest paid by taxpayers. An increased real GNP is desirable because it means (1) more jobs, (2) higher wages, (3) more funds available for education and other worthwhile government programs, and (4) improved quality of life via private purchasing.

Traditional tradeoff thinking says we must accept undesirable costs to get desirable benefits. Win-win thinking says we can avoid the undesirable costs of big deficits and still have economic growth. The first graph above shows deficits turning into surpluses as of 1998. The second graph indirectly shows recent GNP growth from under $5 trillion in 1990 to over $7 trillion in 1998, at an increasing rate of growth.

This win-win occurrence comes about through improved technology, training, competition, free trade, and public policy. Those factors cause increased GNP. An increased GNP enables the government to have (1) increased revenue from income taxes, and (2) have decreased welfare costs. Those two factors lower the deficit, especially as a percent of the GNP.

Readers should not think that win-win analysis is biased against liberal economists like Keynes. For example, the Phillips Curve is associated with conservatives who say we have to suffer unemployment in order to avoid inflation. The autumn 1996 issue of Policy Evaluation shows unemployment decreasing in the 1990s to a generation low of 4.3%, and inflation simultaneously decreasing to under 1% which is almost nothing.

ENDNOTES

1. For further details on win-win analysis, see S. Nagel, *Super-Optimum Solutions and Win-Win Policy: Basic Concepts and Principles* (Quorum, 1997); S. Nagel, *Public Policy Evaluation: Making Super-Optimum Decisions* (Ashgate, 1998); S. Nagel, *Policy Analysis Methods and Super-Optimum Solutions* (NOVA Science, 1995); and S. Nagel, *The Policy Process and Super-Optimum Solutions* (NOVA Science, 1994).

Chapter 1

LAND TENURE IN PAPUA NEW GUINEA

Simon Montagu
Australia

When Papua New Guinea (PNG) gained its independence in 1975, it constitutionally (re-)established customary or traditional land tenure over the vast majority of the country. Under this tenural system, land is not held, or even perceived, as personal property. Instead, it remains under traditional 'ownership', in the sense that it is associated with a local clan, tribe or group of tribes. The claims of these groups to traditional land derive from their historical ties to the land. These ties may result from a history of using the area for subsistence farming, hunting and gathering, or related activities, or they could even come about through some traditional affiliation to an area through the spirits of dead ancestors.

In recent times, PNG has been found to contain vast reserves of a variety of important mineral resources, such as gold and copper. As a result, many foreign mining companies have shown great interest in obtaining the rights to this minerals. Under the traditional tenure system however, delineating ownership to land, and thus who receives mining royalties, has proven to be a problematic and very controversial process.

This situation has resulted in a call by the conservative business elites of PNG (and those outside the country!) to reform the land tenure system, in order to promote economic development throughout the country. Equally strong have been the calls by the liberal intelligencia of the country (and, again, from those outside of the country), who insist that PNG's unique social and cultural fabric must not be compromised in the name of economic development. This predicament is explored in the following SOS analysis.

I. THE GOALS

Table 1.1 presents a simplified SOS analysis of the PNG land tenure issue. It contains only two goals - one liberal and one conservative. The conservative goal represents the conservative elites view that PNG needs to increase its levels of economic development, while the liberal goal represents the desire of liberal elites to both restore and enhance the traditional cultural and social fabric of PNG society.

Table 1.2 expands upon this simplified analysis, presenting a more detailed evaluation of the land tenure issue. It expands upon the goals sort by the liberal and conservative interests, by adding another goal to each. Furthermore, it also includes an important, neutral goal which is of interest to both parties.

TABLE .1
SIMPLIFIED SOS TABLE:
LAND TENURE IN PAPUA NEW GUINEA

Criteria / Alternatives	CONSERV. GOAL * Increase Levels of Economic Development *Weights* C=3 N=2 L=1	LIB. GOAL * Enhance/Restore Cultural Fabric *Weights* C=1 N=2 L=3	TOTALS Conserv.	 Lib.	 Neutral
CONSERV. ALT. * Privatize Land Ownership	4	2	14	10	12
LIB. ALT. * Maintain Existing System of Traditional 'Ownership'	2	4	10	14	12
S.O.S. ALT. * Foster Local Village Enterprises * Increase Private & Village Joint-Ventures	≥3.5	≥3.5	≥14	≥14	≥14

TABLE .2
DETAILED SOS TABLE:
LAND TENURE IN PAPUA NEW GUINEA

Criteria / Alternatives	C1 GOAL * Inc. Econ Devel. *Weights* C=3 N=2 L=1	C2 GOAL * Inc. Bus. Prod. *Weights* C=3 N=2 L=1	L1 GOAL * Enchance Cult. Fabric *Weights* C=1 N=2 L=3	L2 GOAL * Stop R–U Migration *Weights* C=1 N=2 L=3	L3 GOAL * Environ. Protection *Weights* C=1 N=2 L=3	N GOAL * Admin. Feasibility *Weights* C=2 N=2 L=2	TOTALS C	 L	 N
CONSERV. ALT. * Privatize Land Ownership	5	4.5	1	2	2	3	39.5	30.5	35
LIB. ALT. * Maintain Trad. Ownership	2	2	5	4	4	3	31	49	40
* Lease Land to Private Interests	3.5	4	3	4	3.5	3	39	45	42
NEUT. ALT. * Bit of Both	3	3	3	3	3	3	30	30	30
S.O.S. ALT. * Foster Village Enterprises * Inc. Priv/Vill. Joint-Ventures	≥ 4.5	≥ 4.5	≥ 4.5	≥ 4.5	≥ 4.5	≥ 4.5	≥49	≥49	≥49

The second conservative goal portrays the belief of the conservative groups that the country needs to increase the productivity of its existing businesses. This view is based on the general premise that the economic status of the nation can be improved without additional development, if the nation's businesses work to increase their current levels of productivity.

The second liberal goal runs concomitantly with its main goal of enhancing the traditional basis of the country's society. It seeks to stem the flow of rural-urban migration, in an effort to stop many of the violent social problems that have arisen in PNG's bigger cities. This liberal position argues that through stemming the flow of young people (especially the young men) to the cities, traditional village lifestyles could not only be enhanced, but it should also have the reciprocal impact of lessening the violence and general crime committed by gangs of young men (commonly referred to as 'rascals'), discouraged by the lack of opportunity in these cities.

The neutral goal included in this detailed analysis represents an interest likely to be expressed by both parties. Both the liberal and conservative interests are likely to require that any alternative system of land tenure have a high degree of administrative feasibility with the existing political and legal framework of the country.

II. The Alternatives

The simplified SOS analysis presents two alternatives. The conservative alternative seeks to adopt a system of land tenure based on the private ownership of land, whereas the liberal alternative seeks to maintain the existing system of traditional or customary land 'ownership'.

In the detailed analysis, the number of alternatives has been expanded to four:- one conservative, two liberal and one neutral. The conservative alternative remains the same as in the simplified analysis. A second liberal alternative has been added to include the possibility of customary land owners leasing their traditional land to private interests, in exchange for some lease fee. Finally, the neutral alternative represents a middle ground position, suggesting the possibility of a system that contains a bit of both of the two original alternatives.

Both tables also present two possible SOS alternatives to the issue of land tenure in Papua New Guinea. Both alternatives suggest that land tenure should remain under the traditional system of 'ownership', which obviously fulfills the expectations of the Liberals, but both place emphasis on helping local villages establish economic ventures, thus fulfilling the goals of the Conservatives.

III. Relations Between Goals and Alternatives

In both tables, a 1-5 relational scale has been used to express the relationship 4 been the various goals and alternatives. In the simplified analysis, the replication of this scoring system has been kept very simple, using scores of 2 and 4 only. In the detailed analysis, the scores were varied in order to reflect a wider degree of variability between the goals and alternatives. This analysis uses the entire range of values, with the conservative alternative for example, scoring only a value of 1 under the liberal goal of enhancing cultural integrity, and yet managing to score a 5 for its potential to increase economic development.

Scores are also included for the SOS alternatives presented. These scores represent the threshold score needed to equal the highest combined raw score total of the conservative and liberal alternatives.

IV. Tentative Conclusions

There are several conclusions that can be tentatively derived from these two SOS analyses. Firstly, from the simplified table, it would appear that neither alternative scores higher than the other, if the goals are evaluated on the basis of having an equal weighting. If the conservative weights are applied, then naturally enough, the conservative alternative scores higher than the liberal alternative. The reverse situation applies if the liberal weights are used.

From the totals in the detailed SOS table, it would appear as though the liberal alternative is more desirable, if the two alternatives are considered on even weights. Although it loses out to the conservative alternative under the conservative weights, its total is much higher than the conservative alternative when weighted with the liberal weights.

V. What-If Analysis

Given the manner in which these two SOS tables have been constructed, it is probably more enlightening if the 'What-If' analysis is performed on the more detailed table. Having said this however, the analysis will focus on the goals and alternatives originally expressed in the simplified table, thus carrying the utility of the analysis to both of the tables (an SOS solution!!!).

This 'What-If' analysis will use a basic threshold analysis to investigate two things. Firstly it will evaluate the relational score threshold that would bring the liberal alternative up to be just as desirable to conservatives, as their own alternative. The second component will consider the relationship between the two goals. Finding this threshold value will give some indication of how important one goal is in relation to the other.

Relational Score Threshold: How much would the relational score for the Conservative goal under the Liberal alternative have to change in order to bring this alternative up to make it comparable to the conservative alternative? The equation for this has the following form:

(Conserv. alt Score for Conserv goal x Conserv weight for Conserv goal) + (Conserv. alt. Score for Lib. goal x Conserv weight for Lib. goal) = (Unknown score for Lib alt x Conserv weight for Conserv goal) + (Lib. alt. score for Lib. goal x Conserv. weight for Lib. goal).

Based on the scores in the SOS table (Table 1.2), the equation is:

$$(5x3) + (1x1) = (X \times 3) + (5x1)$$
$$16 = 3X + 5$$
$$X = 3.666$$

Thus, if the relation score for the Conservative goal under the Liberal alternative could be raised above 3.666, then this alternative would be the preferred alternative, on the basis of the Conservative weights.

Relative Weight Threshold: What is the threshold relationship between the Liberal goal and the Conservative goal? To answer this question, we have to consider the threshold value of the point where the benefits minus costs of the Conservative alternative equal the benefits minus costs of the Liberal alternative. In this particular example, these amounts are as follows:

Benefits of Conservative Alternative = 3 raw score units
Costs of Conservative Alternative = 4 raw score units
Benefits of Liberal Alternative = 4 raw score units
Costs of Liberal Alternative = 3 raw score units.

The relative weight of increasing economic development to the enhancement of the cultural fabric of PNG society can be calculated from the following expression:

$$Bc\ W1 - Cc\ W2 = BI\ W2 - C1\ W1$$

where:

Bc =	The benefits of the Conservative alternative
Cc =	The costs of the Conservative alternative
BI =	The benefits of the Liberal alternative
C1 =	The costs of the Liberal alternative
W1 =	The weight given to the Conservative goal of increasing economic development
W2 =	The weight given to the Liberal goal of enhancing the cultural fabric of PNG

For the purposes of this exercise, assume W2 to be equal to one, and thus, solve the equation for W1 :

3.W1 - 4.W2 = 4-.W2 - 3.W1
6W1 = 8-W2
W1 = 1.33

Therefore, in order for the Conservative alternative of privatizing land to become the preferred system of land tenure in PNG, then it must be agreed that the goal of increasing economic development be given at least 1.33 times the weight of the Liberal goal of enhancing the cultural fabric of the country.

Chapter 2

PROFIT SHARING AND JOB ANXIETY: MOVING PUBLIC POLICY TOWARD A WIN-WIN SOLUTION

Daniel J.B. Mitchell

Anderson Graduate School of Management, U.C.L.A. and
Department of Policy Studies and School of Public Policy and Social Research, U.C.L.A.

Interest in profit sharing as a form of flexible pay is part of a larger interest in more flexible personnel practices. The interest in flexibility, in turn, reflects a perceived increase in product-market uncertainty. Where in the past employers have offered job security - due to legal mandate or practice - increased product market uncertainty makes such job "insurance" more costly. Job security protections can be viewed as an employee option to sell labor at the going wage, even when its value to the firm has dropped. As is true of financial options, the cost increases with the variability of the value of the underlying asset. Recent political trends in the U.S. suggest that there are social costs to the flexibility in American labor markets about which mainstream politicians have little to offer.

In European and other countries, permanent unemployment seemed to rise relative to the U.S. in the late 1970s and 1980s. Some interpreted this rise as a symptom of "classical" rather than "Keynesian" unemployment and attributed the rise to a too-high real wage. This interpretation suggests that a wage push caused the increase unemployment. However, an alternative interpretation put forward in this paper is that increased product-market uncertainty made existing wage contracts more expensive and created upward pressure on pricing markups. Such an interpretation is in better accord with available data on real wages, real unit labor costs, and unemployment than the wage-push explanation.

Even in the U.S., with its comparatively low unemployment rate, unemployment durations became quite high in the 1990s, suggesting a reluctance of employers to hire. Employers shifted towards contingent workers and generally loosened the employment relationship. Neither European high unemployment nor American reductions in the quality of the employment relationship are desirable outcomes.

Profit sharing is a way of explicitly sharing product-market risk with workers. As such, it permits a more efficient employment contract to be determined than a traditional fixed wage system allows. In return for absorbing some risk, workers can be given improved job security. However, to have profit-sharing bonuses of sufficient magnitude to obtain desirable outcomes, the bonuses must be substitutes for the base wage. In a typical firm, profits are too small relative to total labor compensation to permit a substantial bonus, if such a bonus is simply an "add on" to the existing base wage. Only through substitution can this problem be overcome.

Cash profit sharing is most likely to be seen as a substitute for cash wages by workers. Yet public policies sometimes favor deferred profit sharing rather than cash. Appropriate public policy should provide encouragement to cash profit-sharing plans.

Profit sharing, and other alternative payments systems, are not new concepts. The notion of paying workers other than a time-based wage was certainly present in modern economies at their inception in the 19th century and even before. Yet there have been waves of interest in such systems during various periods; the 1980s was the most recent example. The latest wave of interest has now carried over into the 1990s.

An interesting question, therefore, is "why now?" What is there about the circumstances of the 1980s and 1990s that provoked renewed attention to alternative pay systems? A simple answer might be that economists - notably Martin Weitzman - happened to write about the advantages of profit sharing in the 1980s and that the idea passed from the academic literature to the popular.[1] Yet that response is clearly inadequate. Weitzman himself was induced to consider alternatives to the standard wage system by an American economic problem of the time, namely "stagflation." Moreover, actual high-profile experiments with profit sharing in the U.S. during the 1980s pre-date Weitzman's initial contributions, notably in the automobile industry.

My premise in this paper is that interest in profit sharing - often seen as a form of "flexible" pay - is part of a more general concern by employers and policy makers about flexibility in personnel practices. Therefore, we must ask why the employer push for flexibility developed in the 1980s in all market economies. At the most general level, my answer to that question is "increased uncertainty in the market place."

Flexibility (in pay or any other personnel policy) has value to employers *only* if future conditions cannot be predicted. In an unchanging economy, a stable equilibrium of labor practices would be achieved and there would be no need to worry about contingencies. The same practices would be optimum, period after period. Thus, if you believe that the uncertainties that appeared in the market place in the 1980s were (or are) transitory, you would predict that interest in flexibility - including the kind of pay flexibility represented by profit sharing - will diminish. I will argue that such a return to stability is unlikely and, thus, that profit sharing in particular will have special value in the future.

During much of the 1980s, and into the 1990s, the flexibility of the U.S. labor market was often touted as the key to American job creation. But the kind of flexibility that proponents had in mind was the freedom to lay off without legal or social impediments. Mainstream politicians did not question this conventional wisdom. As a result, politicians on the margin - ranging from Jerry Brown on the left to Ross Perot in the center to Pat

Buchanan on the right picked up the job insecurity issue. Unfortunately, mainstream types - even when the issue caught on - had little to say about it other than vague exhortations to improve the education and training system.

At best, education and training improvements are long-term solutions. They have little relevance to mid-career voters anxious about their jobs. And, in any case, the authorities who run the educational system are at the local level and not easily amenable to national coordination.

Ultimately, if there is a problem with the employment relationship and contract, the response of public policy needs to be focused there. Profit sharing is a more desirable way to contract in the labor market; it allows some product market risk to be absorbed by labor in the form of variable pay in exchange for more job security. When such variable pay is not part of the contract, the result is likely to be socially-undesirable labor market outcomes. These outcomes may be excessively high unemployment rates (as in some European countries) or an excessively insecure employment relationship (as in the U.S.). Regardless of the level of overall unemployment, those who have the misfortune of becoming unemployed suffer long durations of job search due to employer reluctance to hire.

Although profit sharing is a more desirable way to structure the employment contract, it needs public encouragement. Firms will not adopt enough profit sharing on their own. In part this is due to the fact that the macro-level benefits of profit sharing are external to the firm.

PREVIOUS LITERATURE

There is now a considerable literature reviewing research evidence on the impact of profit sharing.[2] In general terms, this literature finds a positive impact of profit sharing on productivity and/or profitability. However, the conclusion is not unanimous and is sensitive to model specification; in particular, simultaneous specifications do not always support a causal link running from profit sharing to some firm performance measure. There is also some evidence that profit sharing has an employment-stabilizing effect in the face of varying demand. Profit sharing research is part of a wider range of studies dealing with other forms of alternative compensation ranging from piece rates to employee stock ownership and their impact on firm performance.

The historical literature suggests that the use of particular pay systems (including profit sharing) has varied over time. It suggests that there is a strong element of historical accident and management fad in plan usage in any particular period. That is, pure efficiency considerations play only a part in determining how pay systems evolve. However, government policy - either in the form of tax incentives or mandates - can strongly affect employer compensation policy.

Generally, historical review of the literature surrounding profit sharing indicates three motivations for installation of such plans. *First,* profit sharing is seen as a possible method of alleviating labor-management tensions in the larger society, or at particular firms. A left-of-center interpretation might be that profit sharing is a social advance because it diverts income that might otherwise go to profit recipients to workers. A right-of-center view might be that by making workers into mini-capitalists, profit sharing will induce an appreciation of markets and capitalism. These various arguments for profit sharing can be characterized as *ideological*.

A *second* argument for profit sharing found in the historical literature is that profit sharing will function as a motivational device for workers. It is recognized that since profit sharing is a group plan, there is a danger of individual shirking and free riding. But steps can be taken to encourage group monitoring. Although other forms of motivational tools can be used, notably piece rates, such arrangements may create problems of quantity-over-quality and of labor-management frictions and restrictions of output when work standards must be reset. The motivational arguments for profit sharing can be characterized as the *incentive* approach.

Finally, the *third* argument for profit sharing has been that it will reduce unemployment. Weitzman's "share economy" proposal falls into this category. But the idea that profit sharing creates wage flexibility which might encourage employment can be found much earlier and was certainly present during the Great Depression of the 1930s. This argument for profit sharing can be characterized as *macroeconomic*.

Academic vs. Economic Influences on the Use of Profit Sharing

The popular and practitioner literature has moved roughly in parallel with the academic in recent years. There was much discussion in the 1980s among personnel managers of creating systems of "pay for performance." However, the academic literature was helpful in focusing the popular media, and thereby the attention of politicians, on the topic. In the U.S., the *New York Times* - which is generally seen as the premier national newspaper - dubbed the Weitzman proposal for a share economy the "best idea since Keynes" in two editorials.[3] But even before Weitzman's lucid analysis, proposals by academics - including one by this author - for widespread use of profit sharing as a macroeconomic remedy had appeared in the popular press and other non-technical sources. What Weitzman did, however, was to state a case for profit sharing in a rigorous way that would also capture the attention of professional economists.

Press Coverage and Actual Usage of Profit Sharing

Since the *New York Times* made itself a major proponent of profit sharing in 1985 with its endorsements of the Weitzman proposal, it is interesting to track that newspaper's coverage of the subject. Such coverage can be viewed as an index of popular and professional interest in profit sharing. Figure 1 shows annual citations of "profit sharing" in the *Times* in the 1980s and 1990s.[4] *Times* coverage of this topic appeared to have been rising prior to the Weitzman endorsement and seems generally to have declined after the mid 1980s.

Unfortunately, continuous, consistent data are not available. The profit-sharing coverage estimates shown on Table 1 depict a roughly parallel rise and then fall in the proportion of U.S. workers covered by profit sharing with *Times* citations.[5] Note that the first half of the 1980s (when profit sharing seemed on the rise) was characterized by two severe, back-to-back recession bottoming out in 1982. It was also a period of substantial run up in the value of the U.S. dollar on world currency exchanges that reduced American international competitiveness dramatically. In addition, there had been a marked slowdown in productivity growth during the 1970s and it was not clear as of the mid 1980s whether this problem was continuing. The latter part of the 1980s, however, was a period of employment expansion, declining value of the dollar (greater U.S. global competitiveness), and accelerated productivity growth. In addition, the stagflation problem (simultaneous high unemployment and inflation) which had worried Weitzman abated. These trends toward improved economic performance may have accounted for lessened employer interest (and popular interest) in profit sharing after the mid 1980s.

Divergent Union Trends

Figure 1 also shows annual citations of profit sharing from another information source, the *Daily Labor Report*. This specialized publication focuses mainly on the union sector and is aimed at practitioners in labor and management rather than a general audience. Its coverage of profit sharing is highly variable from year to year. However, unlike the *New York Times'* the *Daily Labor Report*'s coverage does not show a downward trend, suggesting that union sector interest in profit sharing was not declining. Figure 2, which is drawn from various sources, indicates that profit sharing's incidence rose dramatically in union contracts in the 1980s. But even with that rise, fewer than a tenth of private-sector union contracts in the U.S. had such provisions as of the mid 1990s.[6]

Considering this evidence, it is quite possible to conclude that the union and nonunion sectors diverged in their usage of profit sharing after the mid 1980s. Although private employment was generally growing, union membership in the private sector was falling for most of this period, both absolutely and relative to the overall workforce. By 1994, union contracts covered only about one eighth of private employment. Issues of job

Table 1. **Profit Sharing Incidence Among Full-Time Employees**

		Percent of Employees in Establishments with Profit Sharing Plans Whether or Not All Employees Were Covered by the Plans			
		All	Professional/ Administrative	Technical/ Clerical	Production/ Service
1981	O M-L	na	25%	26%	17%
1982	O M-L	na	25	28	18
1983	O M-L	na	27	31	23
1984	O M-L	na	28	31	23
		Percent of Employees Covered By Profit Sharing Plans			
		All	Professional/ Technical	Clerical/ Sales	Production/ Service
1985	O M-L	18%	19%	22%	16%
1986	O M-L	22	22	22	22
1988	O M-L	21	23	24	18
1988	N M-L	18	20	21	15
1989	N M-L	16	14	14	17
1991	N M-L	17	14	17	18
1993	N M-L	17	14	17	18
1990	Small	14%	15%	16%	13%
1992	Small	15	19	17	13
1994	Small	13	16	17	10

Note: O = old survey coverage: establishments of 100-250 or more workers, depending on industry.

N = new survey coverage: establishments of 100 or more employees.

M-L = medium-to-large establishments: old survey 1981-1988; new survey 1988-1991.

Small = small independent businesses with fewer than 100 workers. For 1994, only data for deferred profit sharing are available. However, in previous years, cash profit sharing has accounted for a negligible amount of coverage.

na = not available

Source: U.S. Bureau of Labor Statistics.

security and employment retention were of greater concern in the union sector and may account for a union-nonunion divergence in profit sharing trends.

Figure 1: Citations of Profit Sharing:

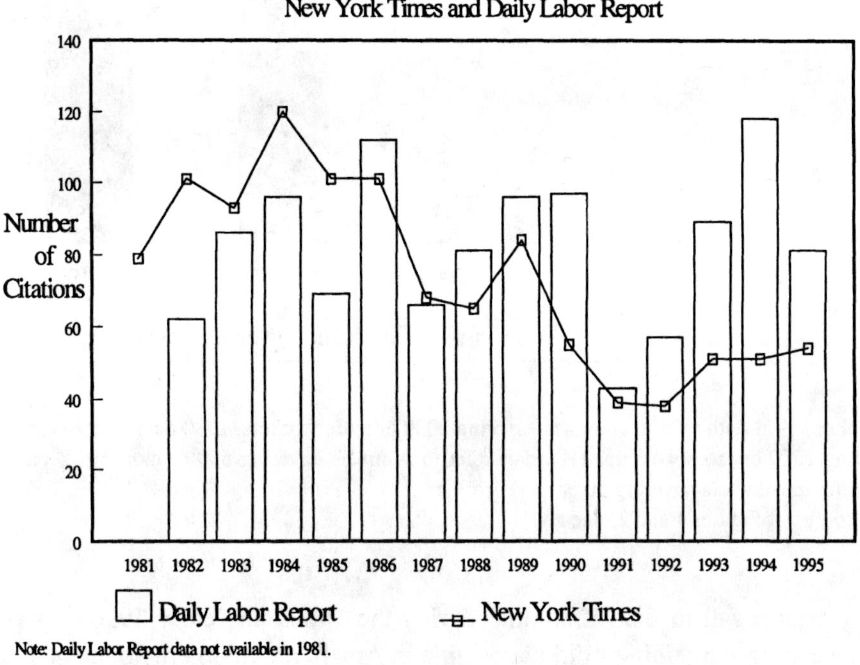

In addition, wage trends in the American union sector had deviated from nonunion over the period from the 1950s through the mid 1990s. The deviation may have suggested to unionized employers that profit sharing would have been beneficial. The continuous line on Figure 3 shows an index of the ratio of union wages under major contracts to all wages (union + nonunion) for private production and nonsupervisory workers.[7] During the first period when union relative wages fell (the 1960s), union employment in the private sector grew. But the large increase in the union wage differential in the 1970s and early 1980s seems to have precipitated a decline in union employment (also shown on Figure 3).

Figure 2: Frequency of Profit Sharing in Union Contracts

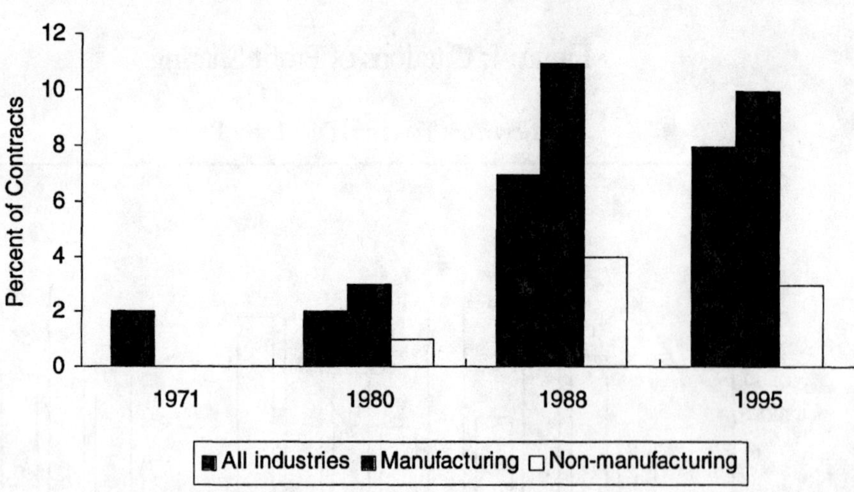

Note: 1971 data refer to contracts covering 2000 or more workers. 1980 data refer to contracts covering 1000 or more workers. 1988 data refer to contracts covering 500 or more workers. 1995 data refer to contracts covering 50 or more workers.

Source of Figures 1 and 2: See text.

Only after a fall in the differential during the 1980s and early 1990s - a period of union concession bargaining - did the decline in American union employment seem to be arrested. Given this history and relationship, it may have seemed advantageous to some unionized employers to promote profit sharing as an alternative to the pay system that previous prevailed. By having compensation set in some direct relation to firm "ability to pay," deviations between firm wage levels and those of its nonunion competitors (or potential competitors) might be avoided.

THE POLITICAL INFLUENCE

The limited evidence available suggests that the academic literature has so far proved incidental to actual usage of profit sharing in the U.S. case. Employers have tended to view profit sharing as an incentive. While some paternalistic employers may have been influenced by the ideological approach earlier in this century, such broad social notions have not had much influence on employer practice recently. Similarly, Weitzman-type arguments have not resonated with American employers. Macroeconomic benefits are not of direct concern to employers. Employers are by nature responsive to their micro-level environment. However, some of the employment-stabilizing elements of the macro approach may be attractive to employers who see some advantage in providing job security (or who may be pressed to do so by unions).

Figure 3: Major Union Wages/Average Wages vs. Union Membership: Private Sector

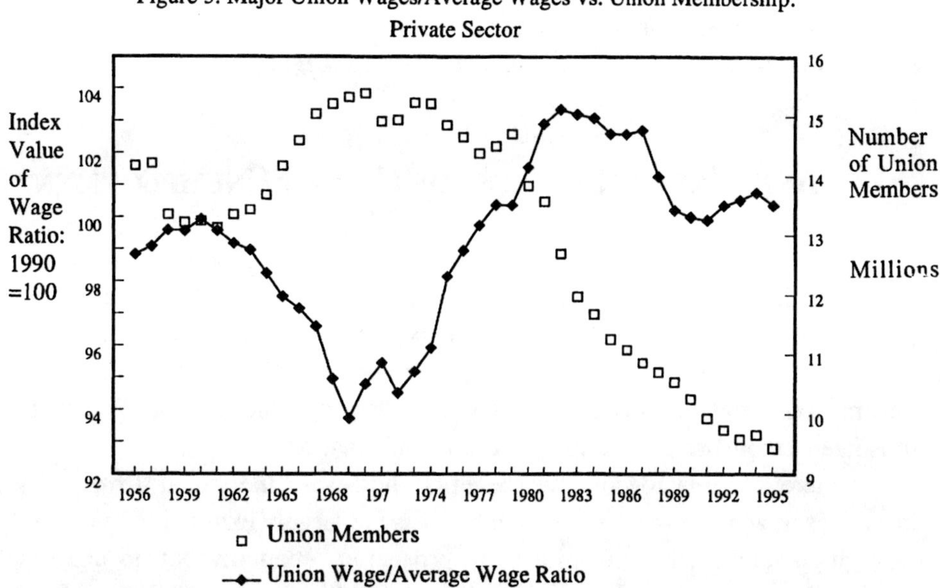

Source: U.S. Bureau of Labor Statistics. Wage data refer to production and nonsupervisory workers.

In the U.S. case, the ideological appeal of profit sharing, even when combined with Weitzman-style macro analysis, never found its way into political action. Some Democrats in Congress did suggest promoting profit sharing through tax incentives in the 1980s. There have been proposals along these lines in Congress as recently as 1994. But the Republican ascendancy in Congress in 1995 ended any such talk in the legislative arena. On the executive side, a presidential commission designated to propose changes in labor law, although identifying unemployment as an economic problem, failed to address profit sharing as a macroeconomic remedy. However, profit sharing has been endorsed by the Secretary of Labor as part of the "high road to productivity."[8]

Although the academic literature has not had much effect on actual public policy in the U.S., the British experience has been different. In the late 1980s, Britain adopted tax incentives for profit sharing (and certain other kinds of share plans), partly in response to Weitzman and partly in response to the right-of-center ideological approach. Even earlier, the French had required forms of profit sharing for right-of-center ideological reasons and later with some macroeconomic motivation as well. The fact that the profit-sharing approach can be attractive across the political spectrum internationally suggests it is one of those rare "win-win" targets for public policy. The trick is to bring that spirit to the U.S.

I will argue below that incentives for the installation of profit sharing are desirable, regardless of the motivation of the politicians who propose them. However, there is an unfortunate notion afoot that installation of profit sharing is just a hidden way of cutting wages induce hiring. Such a notion may be persuasive to those in authority who believe that current problems of unemployment are due to too-high real wages and that profit sharing will undo those wages by hidden means. But it will hardly serve to make the idea of profit sharing popular among wage earners. My argument is different: *profit sharing is a better way to allocate risk than current labor market institutions frequently allow.*

ARE WAGES THE CAUSE OF HIGHER UNEMPLOYMENT?

Economists generally find a justification for public policies to encourage profit sharing mainly through the macroeconomic channel. If profit sharing has sufficiently-desirable micro incentive effects, profit-maximizing employers will adopt it and capture the gains in higher profits. At best, government might have a role in spreading information about the advantages of profit sharing, although - as Figure 1 previously illustrated - there are private sources of this information.

If there are macroeconomic benefits, however, individual firms will not have incentives to achieve them since such benefits are largely external to the firm. Employers as a group might benefit from a more prosperous economy but no one employer can possibly have a noticeable role in achieving it. To the extent that profit sharing can reduce unemployment, some government action will be required to induce employers to adopt it.

Unemployment has been a major concern in parts of Europe and elsewhere during the 1980s and into the 1990s. A critical question, therefore, is the role of wage setting in creating the problem. One interpretation has been that real wages were pushed up too high, thus limiting job opportunities. Unemployment, according to this view, was of the "classical" rather than "Keynesian" variety. A corollary opinion was that because real wages were held in check, the U.S. was able to expand employment in this period while other countries were not.

A Simple Model of Unemployment Determination

On the surface, there is some statistical support for this view. But as I will show, the evidence quickly weakens when it is closely scrutinized. Let us review the theory of how an upward real wage push might cause a permanent rise in the level of unemployment.[9] I should emphasize that the model to be presented is of a long-run character and does *not* deal with possible variation of real wages over the short-term business cycle.

Consider an economy with a *labor market* (in which a real wage is ultimately set), a *product market* (in which a level of profitability is ultimately established), and a demand-regulating authority, say a *central bank.* The real wage is defined as the nominal wage w divided by a general price index p. Profitability is defined as a markup of prices over wage costs, i.e., p/w. The level of pressure in the market place - either labor market or product market - is measured by the unemployment rate U. Finally, the central bank can adjust the level of demand and, thus, the unemployment rate.

Given this bare-bones framework, we can imagine virtually any form of wage and price setting process ranging from classical auction markets to collectively-bargained outcomes to monopolistic wage or price determination. For convenience, I will use the terminology of bargaining in the labor market and of monopolistic price setting in the product market. However, the model is in fact quite agnostic concerning the actual arrangements of wage and price setting. That is, the actual institutions assumed will make little difference to the basic points established below.

We might expect that other things constant, higher unemployment would weaken labor's bargaining position and tend to force down the target real wage in the labor market. Downward-sloping line LL on Figure 4 illustrates this tendency. Target w/p drops as unemployment rises. In the product market, firms attempt to establish a markup above their costs. Most costs are interfirm transactions and net out, leaving profitability - as noted earlier - to be expressed as the ratio of prices to wage costs, e.g., p/w. With a softer economy, as measured by the unemployment rate, firms will be less able to achieve their profitability target. That is, target p/w will fall as the unemployment rate rises, other things equal. Figure 4 shows the relationship between the *inverse of* target p/w in the product market and the unemployment rate as upward-sloping line PP.

Only if the unemployment rate is held at U_1 by the central bank will the economy be in equilibrium in the sense of exhibiting a constant inflation rate. At lower unemployment rates ($U < U_1$), labor will attempt to raise w/p and firms will attempt to raise p/w, two mutually-incompatible objectives. The outcome of this tussle is accelerating inflation and an unsustainable wage-price spiral. At higher unemployment rates ($U > U_1$), the reverse occurs and inflation decelerates (and eventually becomes deflation). U_1, therefore, is what economists sometimes call the "natural rate of unemployment" or the "non-accelerating inflation rate of unemployment" (NAIRU).

Impact of a Real Wage Push

If labor becomes more militant, i.e., if target w/p rises in the labor market at any given unemployment rate, the NAIRU will increase. This tendency is illustrated on Figure 4 by a shift in the labor-market function to L'L' which raises the NAIRU to U_2. Given the rise in militancy, the central bank must accept U_2 as its unemployment target; attempting to hold the rate at the former U_1 level will result in rising inflation.

As I noted earlier, there is superficial support for the notion that the higher unemployment which has afflicted many countries since the 1980s is the result of some type of real wage push suggested by the shift from LL to L'L'. But we will see below that the seeming association of a real wage push and unemployment masks a more fundamental trend. And I will develop a role for profit sharing in coping with the new trend.

Figure 4: Impact of a Change in Target Real Wage on Real Wages and Unemployment

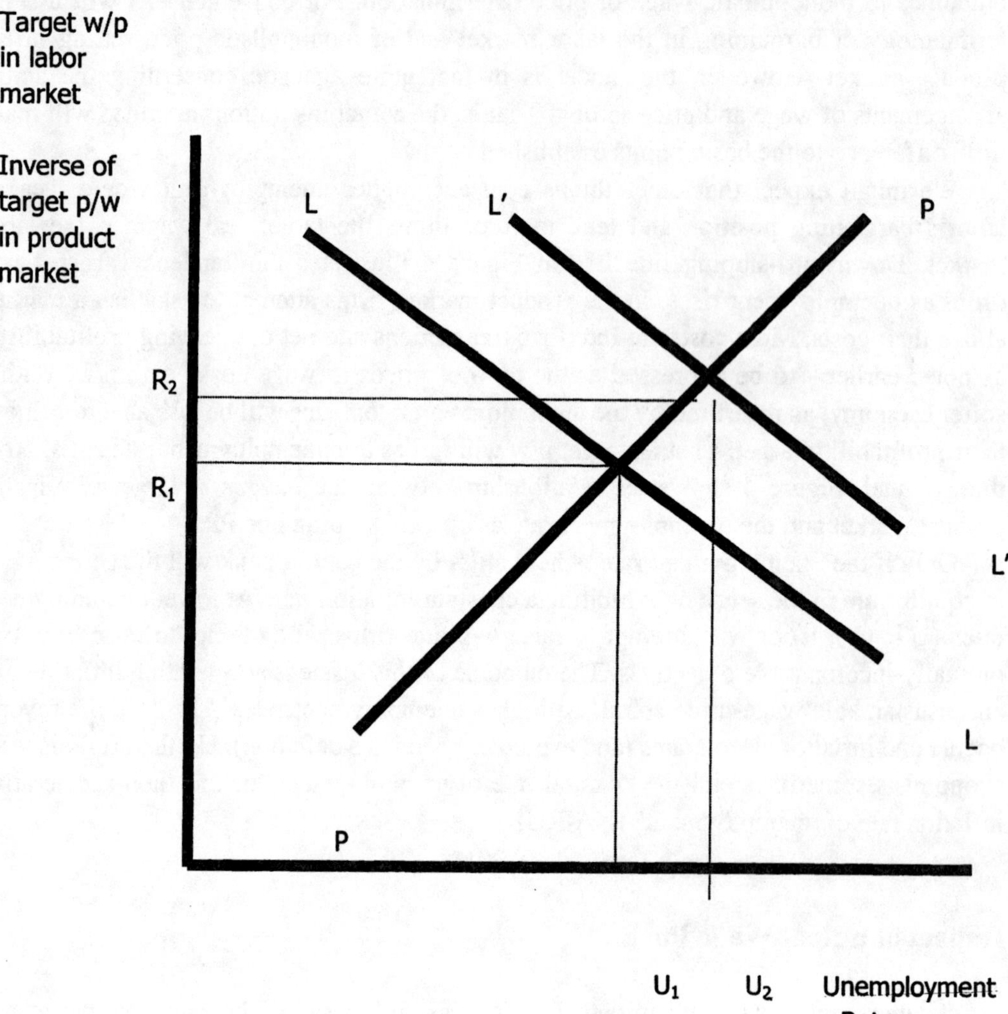

Actual Data on Wage Trends and Unemployment

Figure 5 traces the course of unemployment rates in several European countries relative to the U.S. in each year shown.[10] Figure 6 illustrates the same calculation for three non-European countries. In all cases adjusted unemployment generally exceeded U.S. levels in the 1980s and 1990s. In comparative terms, the U.S. seems to have done better than the other countries in keeping its labor force employed.

Figures 7 and 8 show the trend in real wages in the same countries over the same period, calculated using official national consumer price indexes. For the U.S., two versions of real wage trends are depicted, one using the official price index and a second adjusted calculation using a corrected consumer price index known as CPI-U-X1.[11] In every case but Canada, real wages rose relative to the U.S. during the period shown. Figure 9 thus suggests a loose association between real wage growth and unemployment; countries whose real wages rose relative to the U.S. seemed also to experience an adverse unemployment trend relative to the U.S. It was this sort of observation that convinced many that Europe in particular had experienced some kind of real wage push (classical rather than Keynesian unemployment) and that little could be done about it short of changing wage-setting institutions.

Adjusting for Productivity

In fact, this explanation is superficial. If productivity rises, unit labor costs will fall allowing for higher real wages without a squeeze on profits. Essentially, productivity growth permits a simultaneous rise in LL and PP without a change in the NAIRU intersection. To adjust for productivity, it is necessary to consider real unit labor costs rather than real wages.[12] And as Figures 10 and 11 show, most countries exhibited *declining* real unit labor costs relative to the U.S. The positive association between unemployment and real wage trends of Figure 9 vanishes on Figure 12 which substitutes real unit labor cost trends for real wage trends.

If a wage push in the sense of a shift up of the LL function did not cause the rise in unemployment, what did? Figure 13 suggests another candidate. A push for higher profitability (a higher p/w at any given unemployment rate) can be represented by a shift in the PP function to P'P'. As the figure shows, such an upward shift could raise the NAIRU. But what would account for such a shift? It is easy to point to product-market influences that could have moved PP in the opposite direction (up rather than down on Figure 13) including privatization and deregulation. However, competition and rising uncertainty in the product market inevitably affect labor-market outcomes. Below I will argue that employers are behaving as if employing labor has become more risky (costly) despite the officially-measured trends in real unit labor compensation. The result is an attempt to obtain a bigger markup over labor costs (a downward shift in the PP function) which leads to higher permanent unemployment.

Figure 5: Unemployment Indexes:

Standardized to U.S. Level in 1977: U.S. = 100

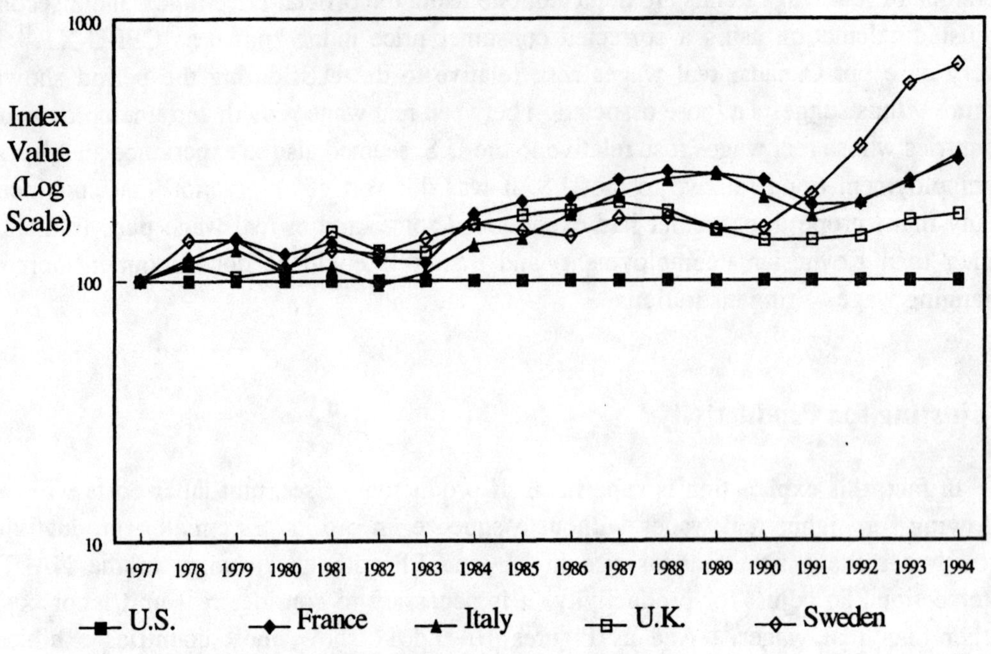

Note 1: 1994 value for U.S. adjusted to pre-1994 definition.

Note 2: Italian and Swedish values adjusted to pre-1993 and pre-1987 definitions, respectively.

Figure 6: Unemployment Indexes:

Standardized to U.S. Level in 1977: U.S. = 100

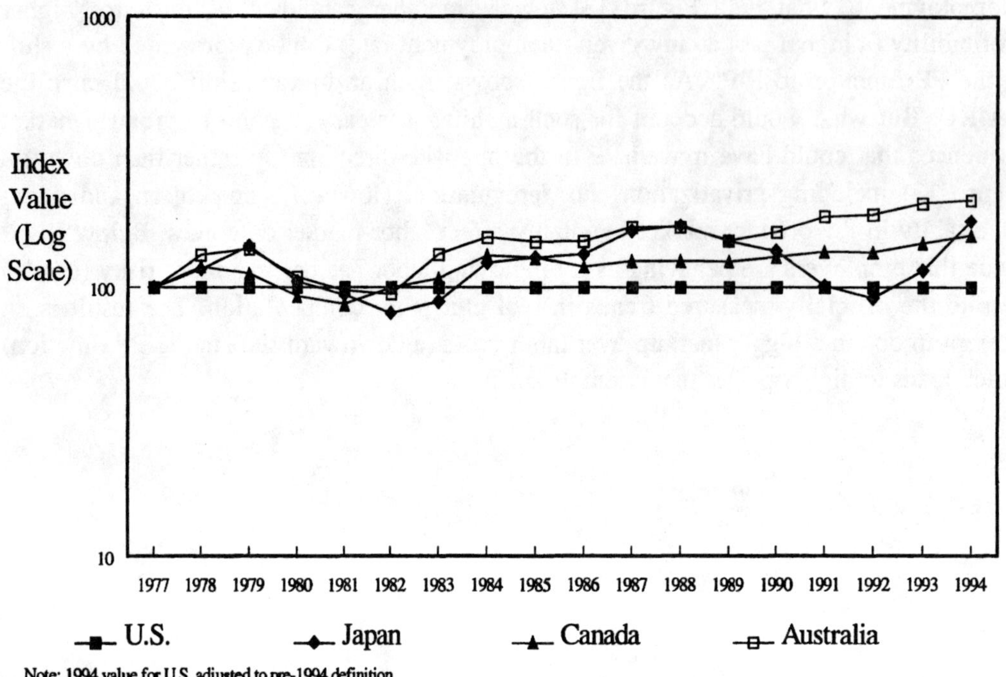

Note: 1994 value for U.S. adjusted to pre-1994 definition.

Source of Figures 5 and 6: Calculated from U.S. Bureau of Labor Statistics data.

Figure 7: Real Compensation/Employee:

Business Sector

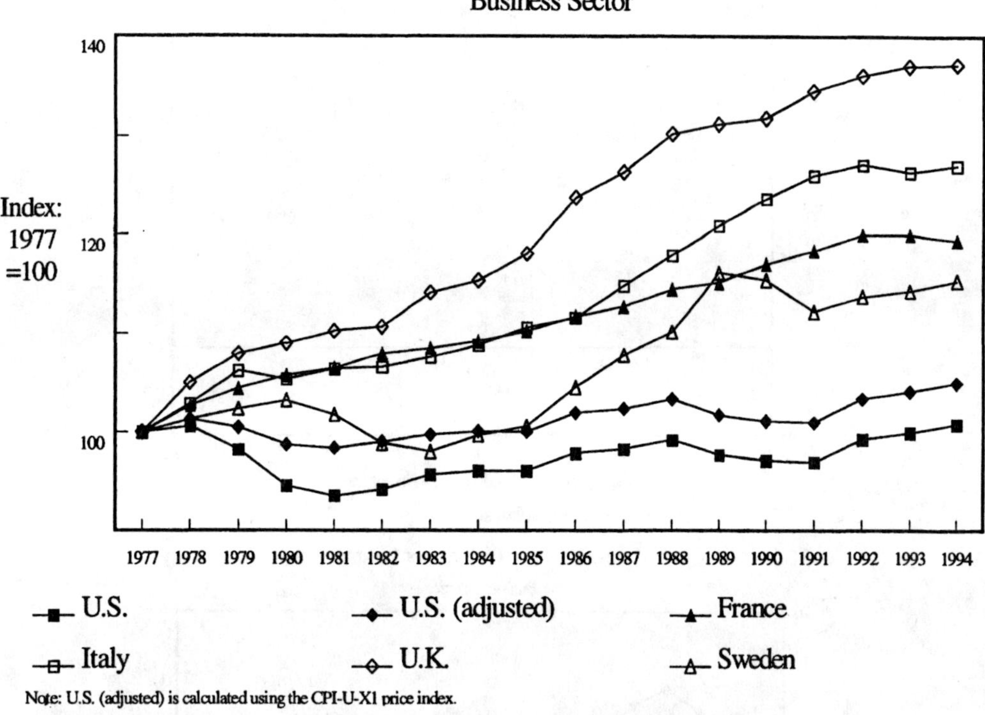

Note: U.S. (adjusted) is calculated using the CPI-U-X1 price index.

Figure 8: Real Compensation/Employee:

Business Sector

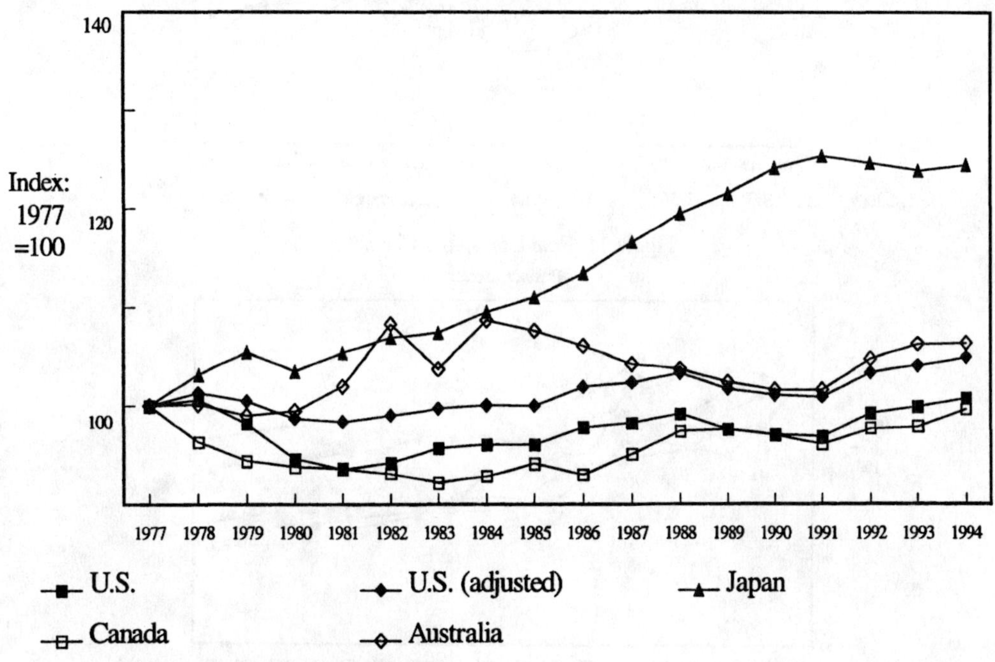

Note: U.S. (adjusted) is calculated using the CPI-U-X1 price index.

Source of Figures 7 and 8: OECD.

Figure 9: Annual Real Wage Change vs. Average Standardized Unemployment: 1977-1994

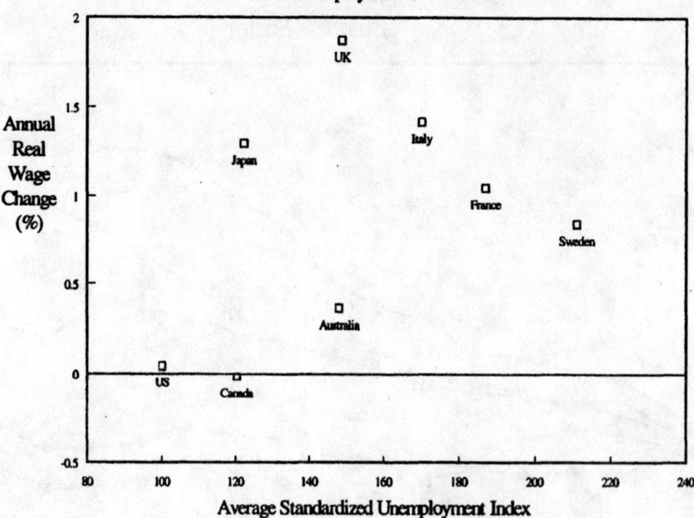

Source: OECD, U.S. Bureau of Labor Statistics.

Figure 10: Real Unit Labor Costs: Business Sector

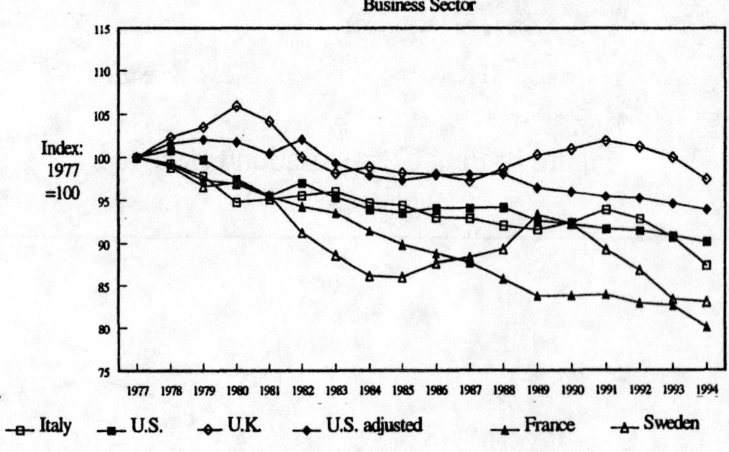

Figure 11: Real Unit Labor Costs: Business Sector

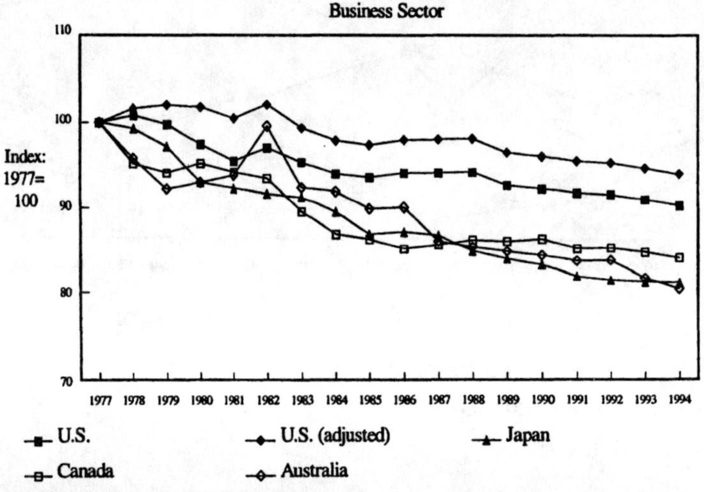

Note: U.S. (adjusted) is calculated using the CPI-U-X1 price index.

Figure 12: Annual Real Unit Labor Cost Change vs. Average Standardized Unemployment: 1977-1994

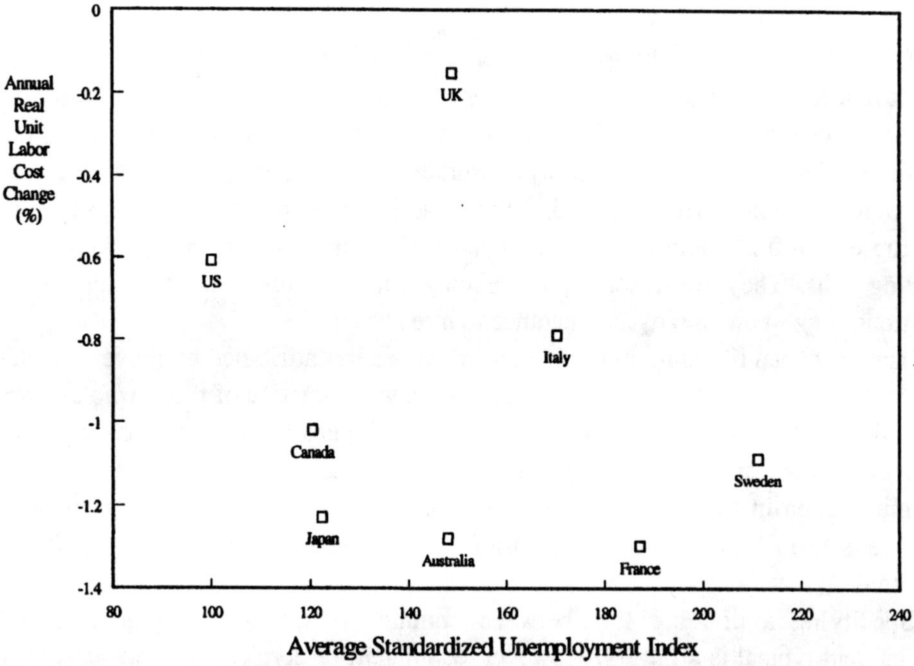

Source: OECD; U.S. Bureau of Labor Statistics.

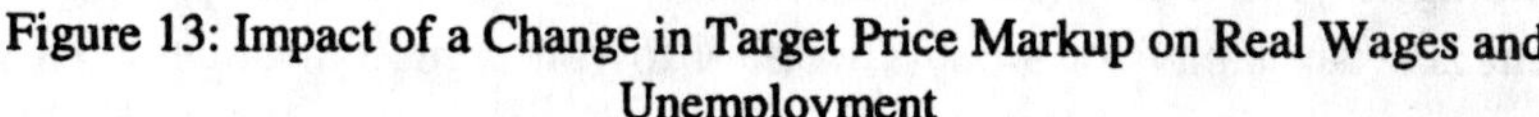

Figure 13: Impact of a Change in Target Price Markup on Real Wages and Unemployment

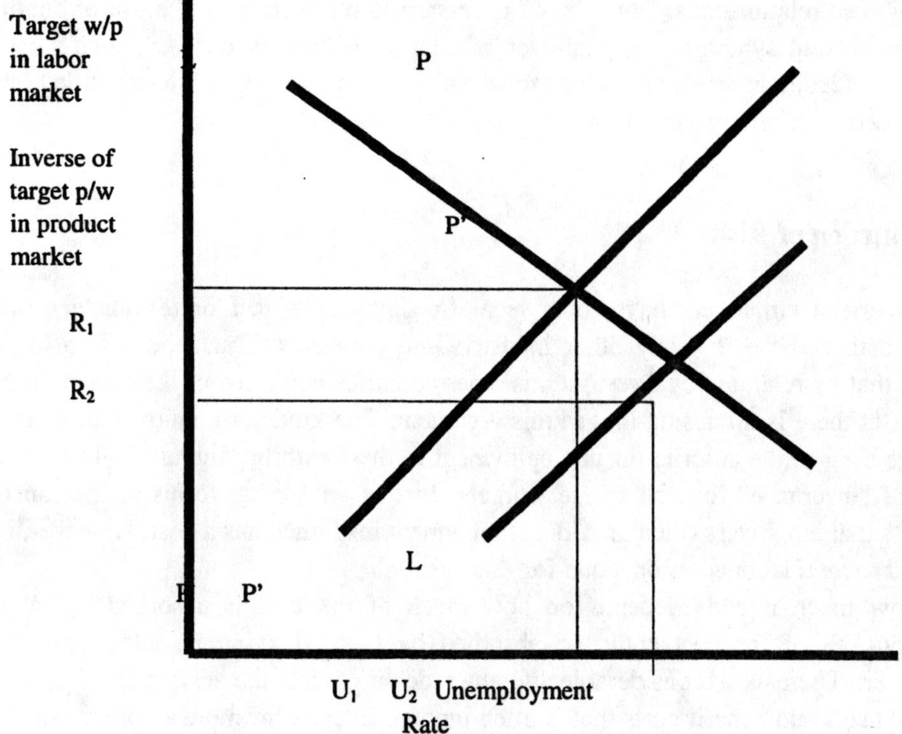

EMPLOYER DEMANDS FOR FLEXIBILITY

One of the more striking aspects of U.S. joblessness compared to that of other industrialized countries has been unemployment *duration*. Figure 14 compares the proportion of long-term unemployed (defined as being unemployed 13 or more weeks at the survey date) among all unemployed workers in five countries for which comparable data were available during 1983-93.[13] The long durations found outside the U.S. suggest that those who find themselves unemployed have been experiencing special difficulty in locating jobs. They must search for a long time. In turn, the long unemployment durations suggest an employer reluctance to hire.

The European literature in particular sometimes has attributed employer reluctance to hire to the employment protections enjoyed by law or practice of those who are working. Institutions that make it difficult to terminate employees are seen as making employers reluctant to take on new commitments through hiring. Evidence of such reluctance to commit is seen in the rise of what Americans call "contingent" employment and what Europeans term "atypical" (or "precarious") employment unless such employment is restricted by law.

Specifying a dividing line between contingent and non-contingent or between atypical and typical is arbitrary. However, contingent or atypical workers are typified by "temps" who are hired on a daily or very short term basis, sometimes through an intermediate agency. In effect, such workers are "just-in-time" people to whom the only commitment is a day's pay for a day's work. Growth in such arrangements suggests that employers are eager to avoid the costs of commitments associated with more traditional employment relationships. But it is not necessary to rely solely on the use of contingent workers to find symptoms of employer reluctance to hire. In the U.S. such symptoms include a decline in recall provisions for those who are laid off and the so-called "white-collar recession" of the early 1990s.

The Burden of Risk

American employers have more legal freedom to lay off or terminate unwanted workers than those in many other industrialized countries. Thus, the lesson has been drawn that by relaxing legal restrictions other countries could lower their unemployment rates. But there is a missing link in this argument. The kinds of employment guarantees that are seen as the culprits for unemployment in the flexibility literature are basically a form of "insurance" for risk-averse workers. Just as with other forms of insurance and benefits that employers often provide, employment insurance has a cost. However, it will not add to *total* labor costs on a one-for-one basis.

How much it adds depends on how much of the cost is absorbed by labor. In principle, all of the cost could be absorbed by labor, leaving no added cost to the employer. There is a considerable literature dealing with the absorption by labor of payroll taxes and benefit costs that is often ignored in calls for more employer flexibility as a remedy for unemployment. There is, however, an important difference between the cost of a payroll tax or a benefit such as a pension and the cost of an employment guarantee. The difference lies in the degree to which the eventual expense can be predicted. Taxes and pensions have predictable costs but in an unstable economy the cost of job security to the employer may be both significant and hard to anticipate.

To the extent that such costs are predictable, and to the extent they are not absorbed by labor, the analysis surrounding Figure 13 applies. Higher labor costs (compensation plus the implicit cost of job "insurance") will push firms to seek higher price/wage markups. Such a reaction will raise the NAIRU. In addition, note that the cost of job insurance can be viewed as analogous to an option. The worker has an option to continue selling his/her labor to the firm at the going wage even if the shadow price of that labor has fallen (due to declining product demand).

As with other options, the cost will increase with the variability of the underlying asset (in this case, the value of the worker to the firm). If firms become more uncertain about the future, the cost of providing job insurance will be perceived to have increased and function P'P' on Figure 13 will be shifted to the right, raising the NAIRU.[14] In addition, employers may behave as insurance companies sometimes do when faced with risks that are difficult to appraise; they will try to avoid writing policies rather than attempting to price them. For employers this means cessation of employment contracts that provide job security and/or reductions in hiring into positions that have security guarantees.

This interpretation of increased (but difficult-to-quantify) risk fits the facts cited earlier. Real wages have risen except in North America. But as noted earlier, a dynamic analysis requires examination of real unit labor costs which have been falling. And the NAIRUs of the countries previously reviewed seem to have risen. It appears, therefore, that firms are trying to raise target p/w to offset an increase in providing job protection, to the extent that they cannot avoid the costs by moving toward contingent workers. For whatever reason, it has not proved possible to shift the job insurance costs back to labor.

It is difficult to say exactly why the burden of the risk is not fully transferred to workers. A vertical LL function (total labor absorption) would permit p/w to rise without an increase in the NAIRU. Particularly in some European countries, one might turn to insider/outsider models to explain why - over time - a temporary rise in unemployment would become permanent. Note, however, that findings of wage rigidity and deviations from a classical supply-demand model for the labor market are hardly new. Whatever the explanation for non-absorption, it is difficult to view the upward shift of the NAIRUs outside the U.S. to be optimal social outcomes. Profit sharing could alleviate the problem by making explicit the trade off between risk sharing between employer and employee and provision of job insurance in the employment contract. I will return to that point below.

More Uncertainty to Come

As noted earlier, the U.S. has comparatively little regulation of employer freedom to lay off workers, especially in response to economic fluctuations in the product market. Thus, shifts in American labor-market structure are likely to reflect changing market forces rather than shifts in public policy. Changes observed in U.S. labor markets during the 1990s suggest that American employers have begun to exhibit the kind of reluctance to hire that earlier characterized their counterparts in other countries. In turn, these findings suggest that greater uncertainty in the market place is being anticipated.

Figure 15 illustrates two symptoms of this reluctance. First, the duration of unemployment - represented by the interrupted spells of the currently unemployed - reached very high levels by 1994 by U.S. standards. Yet the unemployment rate itself had fallen significantly from the recession peak. In the past, falling unemployment rates were accompanied by falling unemployment durations. But that relationship seems to have weakened dramatically in the 1990s.

Although there is no continuous measurement of the flow into the unemployment pool, the number of weekly new claims for unemployment insurance serves as a proxy. As Figure 16 shows, such claims had fallen to low levels by 1994. Taken together, the claims data and the duration data suggest a labor market in which relatively few individuals are becoming unemployed but those who do become unemployed have a hard time finding new jobs. That is, employers are hanging on to existing employees and showing surprisingly little interest in acquiring new ones. The unemployment rate is the product of those entering unemployment and their duration in the unemployment pool. Thus, it is quite possible for these two influences to produce both a low unemployment rate and a high duration.

There is other supporting evidence for this interpretation. Figure 15 shows that use of overtime hours in manufacturing (the only sector for which such data are available) rose to record highs by 1994. Employers were using their existing workers more intensively rather than hiring additional staff, despite the fact that by law overtime hours are paid at a 50% premium.[15] While there is no direct measure of unfilled job vacancies, there is a data series on employer help-wanted advertising. As can be seen on Figure 16, this index rose after the recession of the early 1990s. But it remained low when compared with levels attained in the late 1980s. Again, the data suggest employers were shying away from new hiring in spite of the economic expansion after 1991.

Figure 17 shows that use of employees hired through temporary help supply agencies rose steadily in the 1980s, accompanied by a rise in the relative compensation of such workers. But in the 1990s, while use of "temps" accelerated, their wages fell. Apparently, job seekers unable to find regular employment after long searches had sufficiently saturated the temporary market to drive down relative pay there.

Although relatively few workers are temps, the greater use of such forms of employment suggests a general employer search for a lesser degree of employer commitment to employees. Observers have noted a decline in employer-provided benefits such as health insurance coverage and defined-benefit pensions in the 1990s. Perhaps symptomatic of this change in the character of the employment relationship is the declining use of personnel managers within the managerial workforce shown on Figure 18. With a weaker employment relationship, firms could shift their managerial resources away from personnel departments and toward other uses.

Figure 14: Long-Term Unemployed As Percent of All Unemployed: U.S. Definitions: 1983-1993
Note: Long-term unemployed are those unemployed 13 or more weeks.

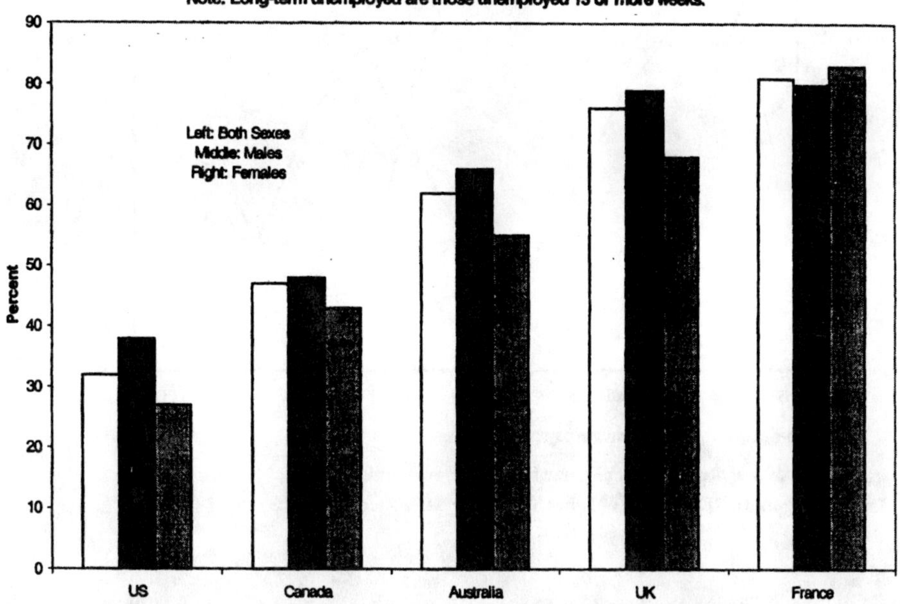

Figure 15: Unemployment Duration and Manufacturing Overtime Hours

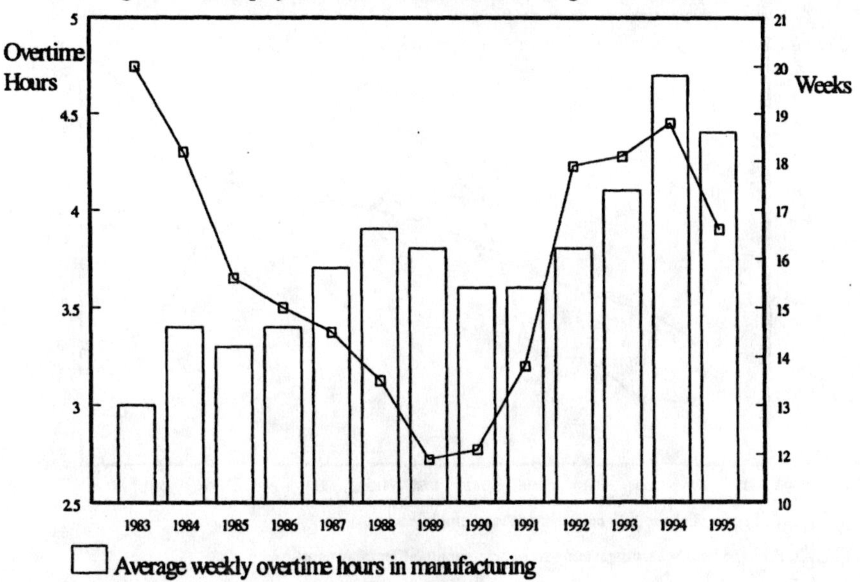

Source of Figure 15: U.S. Bureau of Labor Statistics

Figure 16: Adjusted Help-Wanted Advertising & Weekly Unemployment Insurance Claims

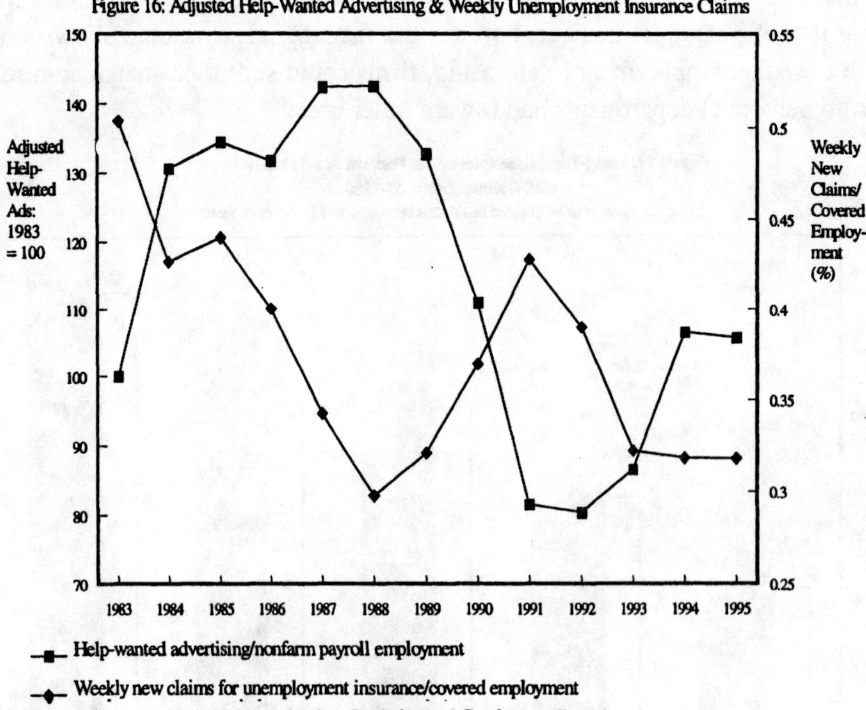

Source of Figure 16: U.S. Bureau of Labor Statistics and Conference Board.

Figure 17: Trends in Temporary Help Supply Employment 1983-1994

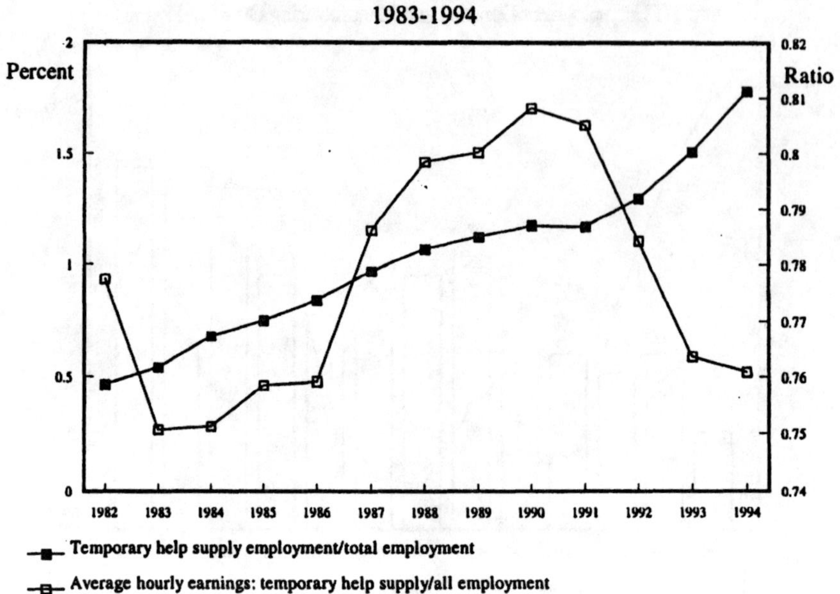

In the U.S., as in other countries, employers seem to be reluctant to hire and to commit themselves to maintaining the employment relationship. An important question, therefore, is whether current labor market trends are producing employment contracts that

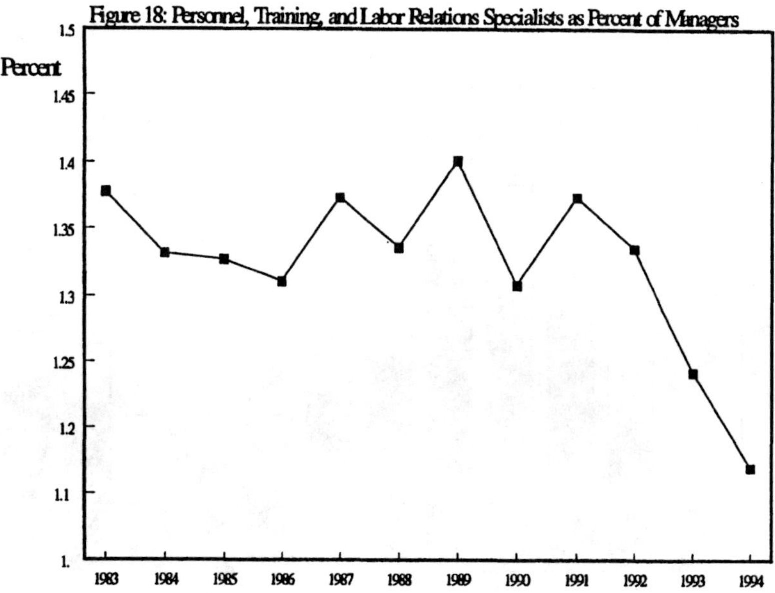

Figure 18: Personnel, Training, and Labor Relations Specialists as Percent of Managers

Source of Figures 17 and 18: U.S. Bureau of Labor Statistics.

meet employee demands for security and employer demands for flexibility. In my view, the answer is "no". Neither labor markets characterized by high levels of unemployment - as have appeared outside the U.S. - nor the erosion of the employment relationship - as has appeared in the U.S. - seem optimum. Profit sharing, however, can assist in structuring a better form of contract.

PROFIT SHARING AS A WIN-WIN APPROACH

If workers value both wages and job security and employers need flexibility to meet uncertain demand, an optimum contract is likely to reflect all of these preferences. It is likely to have a fixed wage element and a variable pay element in which the latter adjusts to changing demand levels. To some extent, the fixed wage element and the variable pay element should be substitutes (even if not perfect substitutes); pay received from the variable element adds to worker income just as does the fixed wage. In addition, if the employer is providing some degree of job security, that, too, represents a cost to the employer and a benefit to the worker.

Since such a system has a labor-demand stabilizing potential, it also has the potential to reduce the amplitude of the business cycle and the accompanying waste of economic resources. Such a potential represents an externality not captured at the micro level. That is, profit-sharing contracts will tend to be underused if pure market forces are relied upon to induce their implementation. Moreover, there may be institutional lethargy in departing from an existing pattern of employment contracts and pay systems.

Figure 19: Percent of Non-Construction Union Contracts Which Contain Lump-Sum Bonuses: Newly-Negotiated Agreements

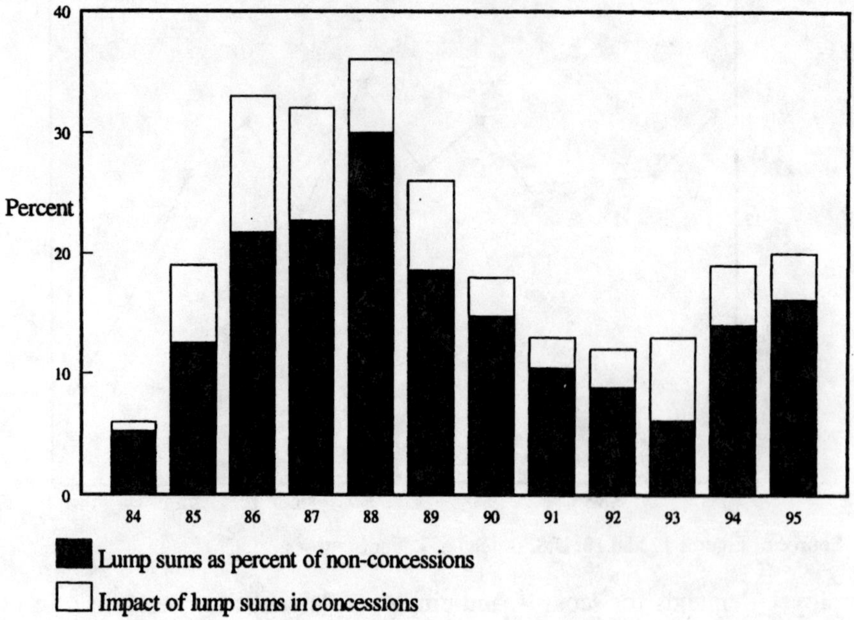

Figure 20: Impact of Lump-Sum Bonuses on First-Year Median Union Wage Settlements

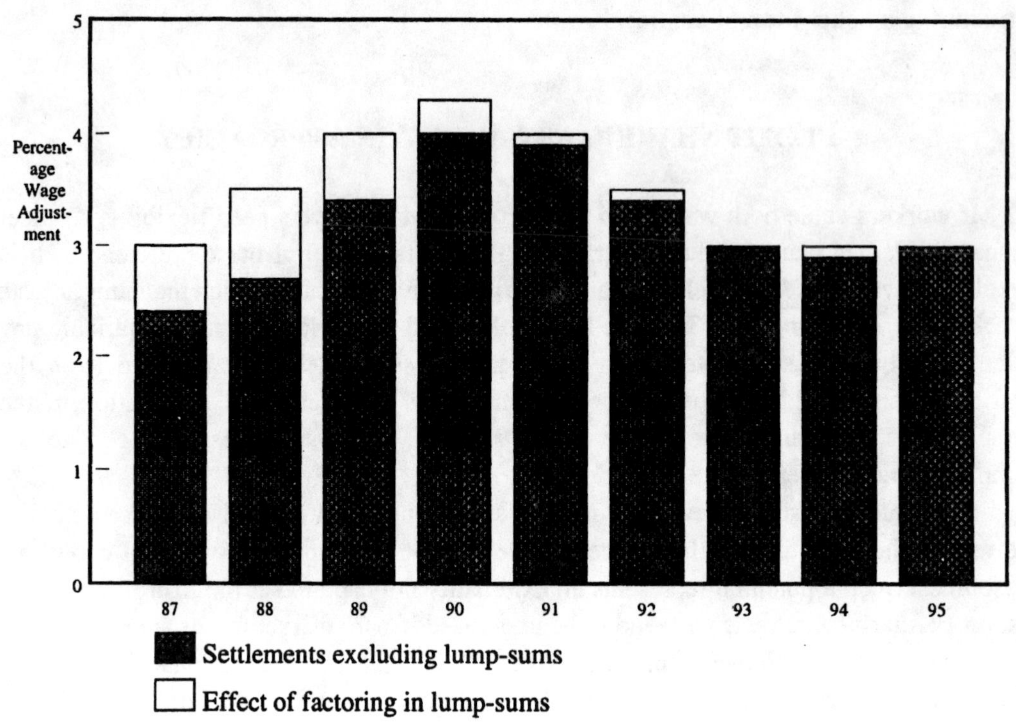

Source of Figures 19 and 20: Bureau of National Affairs, Inc.

The Union Sector

Where there are union contracts, there is available to workers an agent to monitor the variable payment and to ensure that any adjustments in that component actually follow true product demand variations. In addition, the terms of the bargain - how much job security is to be provided in return for how much risk absorption by labor - can be specified in an explicit contract. However, as noted earlier, American experience suggests that while union attitudes have shifted with regard to profit sharing relative to the pre-1980 period, there is still only limited use of such arrangements in the union sector.

It is possible, however, that unions could bargain for wages in a manner that would simulate the effects of profit sharing without formally labeling the outcome. The psychological literature suggests that workers will be more willing to accept variable pay if it is labeled as a "bonus" rather than a wage. In the late 1980s in the U.S., the use of lump-sum bonuses became common in union contracts.

Figure 19 shows the proportion of new (non-construction) contracts containing lump-sum features. There was some association of these bonuses with concession contracts (defined as contracts with no nominal first-year wage increase or with a nominal wage cut). The lower portion of the bars on Figure 19 show the proportion of new non-concession contracts that had lump sums; the upper portion of the bars represents the impact of concession contracts.[16]

As can be seen, whether the analysis includes all contracts or just non-concessions, some cyclicality appears. That is, use of lump sums peaks toward the end of the business cycle in the 1980s, declines with the recession of the early 1990s, and then shows signs of increasing in the recovery. It could be that in future business cycles, union contracts will tend to eliminate bonuses during downturns and then recreate them during recoveries. Such a practice would add a *de facto* element of variable pay to the employment contract. In this respect, use of lump-sum bonuses in the U.S. could become similar to the use of bonuses in Japan and other Asian countries; many believe that the bonus systems there function as a form of profit sharing.

Typically, however, the bonuses negotiated have not been large - on the order of 3-4% of wages of covered workers. When spread over the entire union sector (contracts with and without bonuses) - as shown on Figure 20 - the impact was to add a variation of about a half a percentage point (at most) to union wages over the cycle. And the impact would be smaller if benefits are included in the calculation of labor costs. This variation is still significant but not anywhere near the magnitude needed to smooth out employment variation over the cycle.[17] Moreover, first-year pay adjustments are more likely to be influenced by lump sums than are pay adjustments over the life of the contract (generally two to three years in the U.S.). Table 2 shows that "non-production" bonuses - which include lump sums - show no cyclical trend at all in the union sector.

In summary, the union sector has certain advantages for either formal profit sharing or *de facto* profit sharing. Workers have an agent that can monitor employer pay variation. Profit sharing usage did increase in the American union sector during the 1980s and it is conceivable that the lump-sum bonuses that also arose could evolve into some kind of implicit profit sharing. Yet the magnitudes attained privately are small. If more is to be achieved, so that macro externalities are reflected, there will need to be a tilt in public policy in that direction.

The Nonunion Sector

Nonunion employees have a disadvantage under profit sharing arrangements in not having an agent that can monitor profits and negotiate explicit trade offs between risk sharing and job security. This problem is even greater in the case of lump-sum bonuses that do not have a formal tie to profitability. There is no information on how widespread bonuses of the lump-sum variety are in nonunion settings in the U.S. Nonunion employees have long received bonuses for individual productivity. But as Table 2 shows, non-production bonuses do not account for a large fraction of pay (although more than in the union sector). There may be a slight upward trend in the bonuses shown on Table 2 but the economic impact seems negligible at such low magnitudes. As in the union sector, a push from public policy is needed.

Appropriate Public Policy

Regardless of sector - union or nonunion - profit sharing cannot reach the magnitude of bonus needed for employment stabilization and risk sharing if it is simply added on to the levels of labor compensation that would prevail absent a share arrangement. The numbers simply will not add up. For example, in the U.S. corporate profits before tax amount to about a tenth of labor compensation in a reasonably good year. Thus, if *all* profit income were given to labor in a profit sharing scheme, the bonus payment would be only about 10%.

An "add-on" plan that gave, say, 20% of profits to workers (presumably in the hopes of raising productivity) would therefore provide a bonus payment of about 2% of total compensation in a typical American corporation. On the other hand, suppose the (fixed) base wage were reduced by 10% in exchange for a scheme which over the cycle provided an offsetting 10% bonus. Under such an arrangement, workers would receive the same *average* level of pay over the business cycle in wage-plus-bonus that they received before in wages alone. However, total pay would be more variable due to the bonus component. Pre-bonus profits would double over the cycle, but workers would have a profit-sharing plan that gave them 50% of profits (and 50% of the variability of profits).

At such magnitudes, employment-stabilizing effects would be available. Surely, with a reduction in profit variability of one half, stabilizing employment would be facilitated. In addition, there might be Weitzman-style employment-expansion effects because of the lower base wage and marginal cost of hiring.

Clearly, absorption of the bonus in the base wage is important if dramatic moves toward a profit-sharing economy are to take place. *To encourage absorption, public policy should aim at promoting plans in which the bonus is seen by workers to be highly substitutable for the base wage.* Plans that put the bonus into a deferred retirement fund are less likely to promote absorption (given the absence of perfect capital markets) than those that pay cash bonuses. Thus, tax incentives should be given to cash plans that are at least as generous as those given to deferred plans.

National tax policies that only give tax preferences to profit sharing if it operates as a pension do not promote absorption. American tax policies are of this variety. The same is true of systems based on mandates; mandated deferred profit sharing does not promote absorption. Indeed, the French experience has been that mandating deferred profit sharing leads employers to discontinue cash profit sharing in order to finance the compulsory plan.

Obviously, if tax resources are to be used for encouraging profit sharing bonuses, it will be necessary for policy to specify a definition for profit sharing. Otherwise there will be a temptation simply to relabel wages as bonuses eligible for tax preferences. At a minimum, a qualifying plan must specify a formula linked to profits and that formula must stay in place for a significant period (several years). Note that with appropriate criteria written into tax law, the tax authorities may take on the missing role of a monitoring agent for workers that otherwise is lacking in the nonunion sector.

CONCLUSIONS

Interest in profit sharing among employers and policy makers since the 1980s is part of a general search for flexibility. Economic analysis of the type associated with the Weitzman proposal suggests that profit sharing as a form of flexible pay would have desirable macroeconomic properties. But these macro considerations are not reflected in private pay setting practices that are based solely on micro incentives. There is a win-win element in the profit sharing proposal; both employers and workers would benefit from a more stable economy. Thus, a role for public policy in fostering profit sharing is desirable and I advocate such an approach.

Perceived increases in risk in product markets will translate into higher unemployment if linked to an employment guarantee based on mandate or practice and if the cost of job insurance is not borne by labor. There is a need for more efficient employment contracts which balance employer and employee needs in the face of increased risk in the product market. Yet such arrangements seem to be slow in coming when left entirely to private determination, again suggesting a win-win aspect of the profit sharing proposal. An efficient contract would surely have a profit sharing element, even if that element were simply a bonus implicitly linked to profits. While there has been some move in that direction, the magnitude has been small.

Some European countries seem to be stuck with permanently high unemployment that cannot be reduced by demand measures without causing inflation. In contrast, the U.S. has achieved low unemployment but with a kind of employment flexibility that has downgraded the quality of the employment relationship. As in Europe, it has produced unusually long spells of unemployment for those unlucky enough to be jobless. On both continents it is time to move beyond vague calls for pay for performance and flexibility and move toward more concrete encouragement of profit sharing as a major element in compensation. But there is no reason the U.S. cannot take the lead.

Table 2. Non-Production Bonuses as a Percent of Total Compensation

	All	Union Sector	Nonunion Sector
1987	.9%	-	-
1988	.8	.4%	1.0%
1989	.8	.5	.9
1990	1.0	.6	1.1
1991	.9	.5	1.0
1992	1.0	.6	1.0
1993	1.1	.6	1.3
1994	1.2	.5	1.3

Source: U.S. Bureau of Labor Statistics

ENDNOTES

[1]Martin L. Weitzman, *The Share Economy: Conquering Stagflation* (Cambridge, Mass.: Harvard University Press, 1984).

[2] Detailed references are contained in a longer version of this paper available from the author. Due to space limitations, they are not included here.

[3]"The Best Idea Since Keynes," *New York Times,* March 28, 1985. Section A, p. 30; "How to Cut Unemployment, Without Magic," *New York Times*, April 25, 1985, Section A, p. 26.

[4]Data for Figure 1 were drawn from the Nexis on-line database.

[5]Data before 1985 refer to the proportion of workers in an establishment which had a profit sharing plan covering some workers. Data beginning in 1985 show the proportion of employees actually covered by a plan.

[6]Data for 1971 and 1980 were drawn from a now-discontinued series of bulletins published by the U.S. Bureau of Labor Statistics. Data for 1988 come from Contract Library and Information Service, *Characteristics of Major Private Sector Collective Bargaining Agreements as of January 1, 1988* (Cleveland: Industrial Relation Center, Cleveland State University, 1989), Table 3.9. Data for 1995 are from Bureau of National Affairs, Inc., *Basic Patterns in Union Contracts, 14th Edition* (Washington: BNA, 1995), p. 119.

---

[7]Major contracts are those covering 1,000 or more workers.

[8]Robert B. Reich, "Meet the Frayed-Collar Workers Getting the Boot," *Los Angeles Times*, September 4, 1995, p. B5.

[9]An earlier use of this model can be found in Daniel J.B. Mitchell and Mahmood A. Zaidi, "International Pressures on Industrial Relations: Macroeconomics and Social Concertation" in Tiziano Treu, ed., *Participation in Public Policy-Making* (Berlin: de Gruyter, 1992), pp. 59-72.

[10]Unemployment rates in the various countries shown on Figures 5 and 6 are converted to U.S. definitions by the U.S. Bureau of Labor Statistics. In initial year 1977, all rates were adjusted to equal the U.S. unemployment rate. Then for each year the ratio of each country's rate to the U.S. rate (multiplied by 100) was calculated. A value above 100 indicates that relative to 1977, the country's rate rose relative to the U.S. rate.

[11]The official index was afflicted by a faulty housing component until a correction was made in the early 1980s. CPI-U-X1 is an estimate made by the U.S. Bureau of Labor Statistics of values of the corrected index in the period before the correction was actually implemented.

[12]There are many technical issues about the use of real unit labor costs. If the consumer price indexes used to deflate nominal unit labor costs move with the output deflator, a rise in real unit labor costs is equivalent to a rise in labor's relative share of output which might be interpreted as a profit squeeze. If the production of business output were well described by a Cobb-Douglas production function, and if wage and price setting were perfectly competitive, such a squeeze could not occur since, by definition, the share of labor would be constant. However, such conditions do not well describe modern economies which can exhibit changes in labor's share over time.

[13]The data were drawn from Constance Sorrentino, "International Unemployment Indicators, 1983-93," *Monthly Labor Review*, vol. 118 (August 1993), pp. 31-50.

[14]Suppose the LL relation is approximated in the relevant range by the equation $w/p = aU^{-b}$ and the PP relation is approximated by $p/w = cU^{f}$, where all variables (p, w, U) and parameters a and c are positive and where parameters b and f are negative. It can be shown that $dU/dc = -U/[c(b+f)]$. Suppose b and f are set at values such that a 1 percentage point rise in unemployment (from, say, 5% to 6%) leads to a target drop of w/p or p/w of 1%. A boost in the value of c sufficient to raise target p/w by 10% will raise the unemployment rate about 4 percentage points (from 5% to 9%).

[15]It does not appear that a labor shortage could be the cause of this tendency. Although labor market tightness varied regionally, the overtime phenomenon appears even in areas of soft markets. Thus, in California - which had an above-average unemployment rate in 1994 due in part to declining aerospace and defense employment - the same high overtime usage occurred.

[16]The full height of each bar is the proportion of all (non-construction) contracts with lump sums. The lower portion of the bar is the proportion of all non-concessions with lump sums. Hence, the difference (the upper portion) is the impact of concession contracts.

[17]During the recession of the early 1990s, the employment-to-population ratio in the U.S. dropped about 3% from peak to trough. Thus, in principle a 3% reduction in a hypothetical bonus could have eliminated the cyclical employment drop, assuming it could have been carefully spread around all firms and workers. Comparable figures for Canada and Australia were 7% and 6%, respectively. Half a percentage point is far from these magnitudes which are themselves underestimates due to workforce and enterprise diversity.

Chapter 3

POLICIES AND STRATEGIES OF INTERNATIONAL ORGANIZATIONS IN COMBATING CHILD LABOR IN INDIA: A WIN-WIN ANALYSIS*

Rupa Chanda
Indian Institute of Mangement, Bangalore, India
and
Rekha Datta
Monmouth University, New Jersey

Few problems confronting humanity are as baffling and as complex as that of child labor. The most common cause for child labor is poverty. Poor families depend on the income of their children who may be as young as five. This is compounded by the lack of access to education.[1] How to combat child labor is a complex problem. Most countries have legislation seeking to prevent child labor. In practice, however, these are not always implemented and many developing countries continue to put their children to work. There are several challenges that developing countries encounter in the area of combating child labor. These include poverty, lack of access to basic and vocational education, cultural acceptance of norms such as apprenticeships and bonded labor etc.

At what age can children work? The minimum age at which a child can work in a salaried position is a much debated one. In 1973, the ILO convention 138 on Minimum

---

* This chapter is based on information gathered from the United Nations System in India. The section on the activities and views of the various UN agencies in the area of child labour are excerpted from an ILO report titled, "UN System in India: Position Paper on Child Labour." This Report was prepared for the United Nations System's Operational Acivities for Development in India, ILO Area Office for India and Bhutan on behalf of the UN system in India, New Delhi, 1998. The authors are grateful to the UN system for sharing valuable information and for suggestions and comments which helped shape this chapter. The views expressed here are solely those of the authors and not of theUN System/ ILO. The authors also wish to thank Mr.M.P. Joseph of the ILO Office in New Delhi for his help and Stuart S. Nagel and the Policy Studies Organization for providing the useful framework of Win-Win analysis.

age for employment provides: "The minimum age ... should not be less than the age of compulsory schooling and, in any case, shall not be less than 15 years." [2]

According to one estimate, there are 120 million children between the ages of 5 and 14 working full time. Most of them are in developing countries. The number is higher when secondary activities are included.[3] India accounts for the largest number of child workers in the world. According to the 1991 census estimates, about 13 million children between the ages of 5 and 14 are engaged in child labor. This figure is considerably lower than other estimates of child labor in India which range from 40 million to over 100 million.[4]

Child labor occurs in many countries, developed and developing alike. But it is more widespread in the developing world. In today's interdependent world, a problem like child labor transcends national boundaries. As such, it becomes critical to see how international agencies cope with the issue and the challenges they encounter from national governments in doing so. This chapter examines the role of international organizations such as that of the United Nations system in implementing programs and policies to combat child labor in India.

Child Labor in India: The Setting

Accurate data on child labor is difficult to obtain. Quite understandably, many governments downplay the extent of child labor. This is true in the case of India as well. Noted social scientist Myron Weiner explains in his 1991 study on child labor in India: "Given the uncertainties of definition and the complexities of remuneration, it is no wonder that estimates of child labor vary so greatly in India....The official National Sample Survey of 1983 reports 17.4 million child laborers, while a study by the Operations Research Group of Baroda, sponsored by the Labor Ministry, concluded that the child labor force was 44 million, including children paid in kind as well as cash."[5] As in the international context, the total magnitude of child labor in India is very difficult to estimate. As already stated, the latest census indicates that some 13 million children between the ages of 5 and 14 are engaged in child labor.[6] Other estimates of child labor in India show the range from some 40 million to over 100 million. These higher numbers may be correlated with the number of children not attending primary schools. Over 80 percent of child labor in India is found in the rural sector with the remainder in the urban informal sector. About 2 million or so children are believed to be engaged in hazardous employment.

The rural child labor force is mainly engaged in agriculture and its allied activities, and in household chores. In the urban informal sector, child labor is found in small scale cottage industries, in tea stalls, restaurants, workshops, factories, domestic servants, and on streets. In the non-agricultural sector, child labor is found in many activities such as in the:

carpet industry in the Mirzapur-Bhadohi belt of UP
match and fireworks industry of Sivakasi, Tamil Nadu
diamond cutting industry of Surat
glass industry of Ferozabad
pottery industry of Khurja
brassware industry of Moradabad
tea plantations of Assam and West Bengal
silk weaving industry of Varanasi
sports goods industry in Meerut and Jullunder

State-wise, child labor is predominant in the states of Uttar Pradesh, Bihar, Madhya Pradesh, Andhra Pradesh, Orissa, Karnataka, and Tamil Nadu, and is mainly found in poor areas, and among the most disadvantaged and marginalized groups in society.

There is a deep-rooted view in Indian society that child labor is caused by poverty and that elimination of child labor is not possible without first eradicating poverty. Thus, child labor is an accepted socio-economic reality that is perpetuated by traditional attitudes and also institutionalized in practice in many parts of the country. However, as in the international context, some major causes of child labor are the exploitation of poverty made possible by unequal access to principal productive resources and assets, the lack of education, and societal attitudes.

Of late, a consensus is gradually emerging in Indian society on the importance of these factors and thus on the strategies required to eliminate child labor. Compulsory and universal primary education is increasingly being recognized as the most relevant instrument to combat child labor, along with strategies for income generation, empowerment of women, enforcement of child labor laws and minimum wage legislation, and overall convergence of social services on families with child labor.

One of the most common forms of child labor in India is *bonded* labor. Usually when a person or a family needs a loan and has no asset to stand as security, they pledge their labor or that of their children as security against a loan. In most such cases, when the debt becomes too high, it is transferred from one generation and children are "loaned" as repayment of loans. Because of the high amount of the loan, the service or "labor" that was originally pledged usually increase with time and the children remain bonded sometimes for life. The service time also increases arbitrarily when the moneylenders punish their "slaves" by increasing the time they have to serve because they have either been slack or slow in their work or have disobeyed them. Bonded labor is widely used in many industries. It is especially widespread in the carpet industry. 85% of India's carpet exports come from Uttar Pradesh in northern India. Children between ages six to nine were reportedly employed in the weaving looms in Uttar Pradesh and other parts of India.[7]

The fireworks industry in Sivakasi in the southern state of Tamil Nadu also employs large numbers of children, sometimes very young. More than a decade ago, it was estimated that 45,000 children between the ages of 3 ½ and 15 were employed in the match industry. Children as young as 3 ½ years were picked up in buses very early in the morning and sent to work in match factories. Accidents are common in fireworks factories and there have been several reports of accidents and evidence "of children being roasted alive." Poverty is a major cause for the large concentration of child labor in such areas. There is also a complex mix of economic and social constraints that contribute to the perpetuation of the problem. The fireworks industry is owned by the Nader caste which capitalizes the fact that the region is barren and drought prone. They prevent the spread of agriculture in the area so the people are forced to depend on the fireworks industry as a means of livelihood. Thus whereas child labor is common in farmlands, where children help out in the farms, children in this region have no other alternatives other than working in the fireworks factories.[8]

The Indian constitution bans the use of child labor in factories and mines. For instance, Articel 24 prohibits the use of children for work in factories and mines. Under Article 45, the state shall try to provide children up to the age of 14 with free and compulsory education. In addition to these and other constitutional guarantees, several laws sought to protect the underage children in factories and mines. These included the Labor Act of 1951, the Mines Act of 1952, and the Factories Act of 1954. The 1979 Committee on Child Labor appointed by the government to review the status of children concluded that despite the legislation and constitutional prohibition on using child labor under certain ages and in hazardous employment, the government had not enforced legislation banning child labor. More recent efforts by the government to prohibit child labor have not been very effective either. For example, the Child Labor Act of 1986 does not deal with the causes of child labor but only with its consequences.[9] Also, it makes recommendations about not using children in hazardous employment without clearly defining what constitutes hazardous. This means that many employers continue to employ children in various industries and work long hours in unsanitary and unhealthy conditions without violating the law.

Administrative shortsightedness and unwillingness to deal with the problem was exacerbated with the social and economic pressures by families which have to send their children to work for economic reasons.[10] Furthermore, the government has passed several laws dating back to the inception of the constitution prohibiting the use of child labor in factories but not in agriculture or the informal sector, including domestic helpers, cottage industries and restaurants. Leading social scientists have repeatedly argued for compulsory primary education. They argue that "No country has successfully ended child labor without first making education compulsory. As long as children need not attend school, they will enter the labor force. But Indian officials and politicians reject compulsory education, arguing that poor families need the labor and income of their children."[11]

Given the magnitude of the problem and the relative ineffectiveness of the government, many nongovernment organizations and collaborative efforts by the government and nogovernment agencies are becoming more prevalent in recent years.[12] Many organizations are focusing on eradicating child labor by mobilizing community participation for universal primary education.[13] Draft papers and background notes of NGOs often shed light on various aspects of the national initiatives on child labor, the existing legislation, national projects (like the NCLPs-National Child Labor projects and the Child Labor Action and Strategy Program and the ILO's IPEC program -International Program on the Elimination of Child Labor). One such paper is C.J. George's "Child Labor: The Inadequate Responses and Prevalent Myths," Terre de Hommes, (an NGO), which came out in January 1996. It looks at legislation to deal with bonded child labor, the work of local activists, different approaches that have been taken to address the problem including outright abolition, and compulsory primary education. Such efforts attempt to complement the gaps still to be overcome by legislation alone. Community activism has proven to be very effective in the drive toward eradicating child labor.

THE UN SYSTEM AND ITS VIEWS ON CHILD LABOR[14]

The United Nations and its affiliate agencies such as UNICEF and the International Labor Organization are at the forefront of the movement to eradicate child labor. When we examine the role of the UN in eradicating child labor in India, we find that it is broad and comprehensive.[15] There is a common concern for the problem, either in terms of protecting the child directly from exploitation, or from the adverse consequences of such exploitation, or from the factors leading to such exploitation.

The UN system's comprehensive view of child labor is well reflected in some of the UN agencies' definitions of child labor. For instance, according the UNICEF, any child who is out of school is a child laborer or a potential child laborer. UNIFEM views child labor as any work that prevents children from enjoying their childhood. UNESCO's perspective on child labor is in terms of a group with special needs. The UN system's holistic view of child labor is also reflected in the agencies' recognition of the complex range of demand and supply factors that give rise to child labor. The 1996 ILO publication, *Child Labor: Targeting the Intolerable* highlights numerous factors such as lack of education, societal attitudes and norms, inequities in economic and social conditions, and economic motivations as contributing to child labor. Likewise, the UNICEF report, *The State of the World's Children, 1997* presents the issue in all its complexity discussing its various causes and solutions and exposing several myths which exist on child labor.

A. Programs and Projects Initiated by the UN Agencies

There are many UN agency-supported programs specifically on child labor which are implemented by the government and by NGOs. These relate mainly to the ILO and UNICEF. Some of these programs are discussed below.

I. ILO and Programs to Eliminate Child Labor

In 1992, the ILO has introduced **the International Program on the Elimination of Child Labor (IPEC)** . It is a major initiative and the main UN program targeted specifically at this issue. The ILO implements them through various Action Programs. The program aims at progressively eliminating child labor. It also emphasizes on making the agencies and the public aware of its negative effects. As of 1997, 121 agreements were signed for implementing Action Programs under IPEC in India. Most of these programs are implemented through NGOs.

The programs that IPEC has launched are comprehensive and far-reaching. For instance, the Action Programs focused on the setting up of nonformal education centers, drawing local working children into these centers and often supplementing the basic curriculum with low level vocational skills, supplementing the diet of the children, providing health care, and conducting awareness-raising campaigns for the children, their parents, the community, and employers.

Since 1993 there has been a change in focus of the programs. They shifted from providing welfare inputs to combating child labor at the local level through community support and involvement. There was more emphasis on ensuring sustainability of these initiatives. During this second phase, preventive strategies have also been included, such as enrolling children into schools before their entry into the labor force, mainstreaming children into formal schools, and providing follow-up assistance to prevent dropping out.

In addition, IPEC and Indian agencies have launched joint initiatives to combat child labor. They have established links with many new partners, including trade unions such as the Indian National Trade Union Congress (INTUC), Bharatiya Mazdoor Sangh (BMS), Centre of Indian Trade Unions (CITU), the All India Trade Union Congress (AITUC), and the Bharatiya Mazdoor Sangh (BMS). They have also sensitized the National trade union leaders about the nature and magnitude of the problem of child labor under Action Programs. Between 1992-95, at least five nation-wide trade unions have taken a stand against child labor within and outside their organizations. They have made efforts to educate their workers about child labor and are influencing the central and state governments to intervene against this problem. IPEC has also involved national employers' organizations such as the Federation of Indian Chambers of Commerce and Industry (FICCI), the Confederation of Indian Employers (CIE), and regional employers' organizations such as the Punjab, Haryana, and Delhi Chambers of Commerce and Industry (PHDCCI) in combating child labor in India.

Training inspectors is an essential step in the process of eradicating child labor. IPEC has provided support to the government through training programs for labor and factory inspectors. Under these programs, inspectors have been sensitized about the negative impact of child labor on the development of children and on the society and economy as a whole. These training programs have had a significant impact on the law enforcement machinery in the country.

To be sure, IPEC has played an important role in developing the institutional capacity of training and research institutions in combating child labor. Under its Action Program with the Central Board of Workers' Education (CBWE), educational modules were developed and introduced on child labor into all the CBWE's workers' training programs with a reach of 1,50,000 workers per year. As one of its projects, the program improved the library and made it the focal point for distributing information about child labor. This strengthened the CBWE cell on women and children . Many workshops on awareness raising and sensitization have also been conducted through institutes such as the National Institute of Rural Development and the National Safety Council which have been important for capacity building in the country.[16]

Another very important project that the ILO has implemented is the **Child Labor Action Support Project (CLASP)**. This was a three year project supporting 9 specified National Child Labor Projects. Its objectives were to enhance the central government's policy, its planning and implementation capacity, and its ability to support ongoing and future projects by state governments and NGOs. CLASP also aimed at mobilizing community-wide support against child labor and at facilitating a more efficient use of government resources. The goal was to enable a more rapid abolition of child labor in accordance with the ILO's Minimum Age Convention Number 138 of 1973.

II. UNICEF and Programs on Child Labor

UNICEF has a long history of cooperation with the Government of India. Since the country's independence in 1947, it has supported programs for women and children. While UNICEF's interface with the government is through the Department of Women and Children, its various program sections have regular working contacts with the Ministries/Departments of Education, Health, Rural Development, Urban Development, Welfare, and Information and Broadcasting. UNICEF's cooperation with the Ministry of Labor on the issue of child labor began in 1983.

Since then, it has been involved in a variety of activities concerning the elimination of child labor. Its main emphasis in this area has been on the prevention of child labor through primary education and other actions. UNICEF has also provided support to the setting up the child labor cell within the National Labor Institute as well as provided financial and technical assistance for the training of factory and labor inspectors, government officials, and NGOs, for the organization of meetings and workshops, and for studies on street children in various cities and child labor in various occupations. UNICEF field offices located in 10 states have supported state level workshops on child labor in almost all the states. In several states, UNICEF has also supported studies to compile state profiles of child labor which have been important for creating awareness about the issue and generating actions by the state governments and NGOs.

UNICEF has focused on the 13 states that have the highest incidence of child labor in the country. These include Andhra Pradesh, Tamil Nadu, Uttar Pradesh, and Bihar. In Andhra Pradesh, it has supported state level studies on child labor, orientation workshops for government officials, meetings of trade unions, innovative NGO projects, and efforts for the convergence of programs. In Uttar Pradesh, UNICEF provided supplementary funds for an initiative focusing on the elimination of child labor in carpet weaving in the three main carpet weaving districts. In Bihar, UNICEF initiated a UN interagency effort to assist the Bihar government in developing a strategy for the prevention and elimination of child labor. In Tamil Nadu, the state government and a UNICEF task force formulated a plan of action for the elimination of child labor in Sivakasi.. Also, in the context of the state government's **Child Labor Action Support Scheme (CLASS)** in North Arcot district, aimed at eliminating child labor in the beedi rolling industry, UNICEF provided technical inputs and seed capital for sensitization, education, and training, supported the district administration in developing an elimination strategy, and helped bring out a video on the project.

More recently, UNICEF has been involved in the area of child prostitution and trafficking. In 1996, it supported 6 regional workshops on this issue and is now working with the National Human Rights Commission to coordinate policy action and do advocacy work in this respect. In 1995, along with some other organizations, UNICEF organized a national consultation on child prostitution and will be part of a working group in this area.

UNICEF has also played an important role in the Rugmark labeling initiative. Rugmark Foundation is a joint international initiative which began in 1992. It involves the UNICEF, the Indo-German Exporter Promotion Program, carpet manufacturers, and NGO' such as the South Asian Coalition on Child Servitude(SAACS). Rugmark has become a very effective mechanism to monitor, control, certify anf label carpets that are made without using child labor.[17] This was initiated to threats from industrialized countries of sanctions on imports of goods made with child labor. Thus, UNICEF along with Rugmark, has helped to develop an inspection system to ensure that Indian carpets are child-labor-free. UNICEF is a board member of the Rugmark Foundation which supervises this system and it also manages the rehabilitation funds collected under this scheme.[18]

III. Other UN-Supported Programs with Bearing on Child Labor

There are UN agency programs that are not directly concerned with child labor but include the issue as a component within the overall program, or have an indirect impact in this area through some of their activities. Some of these are:

(1) The **UNDP's South Asia Poverty Alleviation Program**, currently being implemented in three districts, focuses on institution building at the grass roots level, and includes child labor among several other issues. In Andhra Pradesh, under this program, UNDP is supporting the MV Foundation in various activities that have bearing on child labor. These include social mobilization, development of community infrastructure including schools, and training of teachers and volunteers. Similar social mobilization initiatives are being considered in Madhya Pradesh, with a focus on getting children out of work and into schools through community involvement and infrastructure building.

(2) The **UNDCP program for street children** focuses on children involved in drug and substance abuse. Its aim is to provide these children with access to services and information to reduce their vulnerability to drug-related risks. Although there is no direct focus on working children, since many street children are employed in ragpicking, peddling, and other activities that make them prone to drug and substance abuse, the program necessarily touches upon child labor. It addresses their working conditions on the street and tries to prevent some of the adverse consequences of such work on their health and well-being.[19]

(3) **UNESCO's Learning Without Frontiers (LWF)** program which is to be implemented in six selected districts of three states in India, also has bearing on child labor. It targets the unreached and the disadvantaged who have no formal access to education, be it in the geographic, social, or economic sense. It aims to provide them with innovative and alternative learning opportunities at the basic and primary level, and in this context to strengthen community institutions and facilitate transition to formal schooling utilizing open schooling and distance education where appropriate. The campaign approach for literacy and neoliteracy programs is also supported. Since child workers are often among the marginalized and disadvantaged, the LWF program's activities have implications for child labor.[20]

(4) The **UNFPA's support to the government of India's adult literacy program** includes the preparation of booklets and materials for literacy campaigns targeting the 9-15 age group. Many of the latter group are previously or presently child laborers.

(5) **UNIFEM's Entrepreneurship development programs for women** such as its sericulture project in Udaipur and fisheries project in Orissa are explicit about the positive impact on the child's well-being from an improvement in women's status in the community.

(6) **WHO's projects on street children** include running informal courses on health awareness for this target group with the help of NGOs. They also aim to develop minimum standards of quality for services provided to street children.

(7) **UNAIDS' activities on child trafficking** include assisting the government to obtain information regarding this problem. They also include facilitating the National Aids Control Organization's role in strengthening State AIDs cells and in working with NGOs on social mobilization and advocacy concerning HIV/AIDS.

(8) The World Bank's sericulture project in Karnataka, cofinanced by the Swiss Development Corporation and implemented by the state government, made a conscious effort to replace child workers in the silk industry with other means of production.

B. Joint UN System Initiatives in India Relevant to Child Labor

There are several joint initiatives within the UN system in India that have relevance to child labor and its elimination. Some take the form of cofinancing arrangements with allocation of responsibilities across the partner agencies. Others involve funding by one agency and implementation by another. Some others are very informal in nature and based only on exchange of information and expertise. A few of these joint initiatives are highlighted below.

(1) The **Joint UN System Support for Community-Based Primary Education** is a collaborative effort including UNICEF, UNDP, ILO, UNESCO, and UNFPA. It is proposed to be implemented in selected blocks of districts in the states of Rajasthan, UP, Bihar, Madhya Pradesh, Maharashtra, Karnataka, Orissa, and Andhra Pradesh. The aim of the program is to provide support to ongoing government efforts on universal elementary education and to make primary education more accessible and effective for primary school-age children, especially girls and children from deprived and disadvantaged communities or groups.

The general objectives of this program are to:

enhance capacity for community participation in effective school management;
improve the performance of primary school teachers;
improve the social conditions that affect attendance and performance of school age children in selected districts through integrated social sector development programs.

Of significance to child labor is the fact that one of the criteria for selecting districts is their designation as a child labor area. Also, since this program targets the most disadvantaged and backward groups, it necessarily also covers child workers who are often from the marginalized and deprived groups in society.

(2) The **UNICEF-ILO protocol** has direct bearing on child labor. It is based on the recognition that the ILO and UNICEF have complementary and mutually supportive roles to play in the progressive elimination of child labor and protection of working children. The framework for cooperation between the two agencies includes: regular consultations and coordination of policies regarding priority categories of child labor; encouraging member states to ratify and implement international standards; collaboration on research and exchange through regional and subregional workshops as well as development of methodologies for assessing and improving the condition of working children; and technical cooperation especially in field activities of the two agencies.

(3) Under the UNDP's **South Asia Poverty Alleviation Program,** UNICEF has supported initiatives with bearing on child labor in Mehboob Nagar district of Andhra Pradesh.

(4) ILO and UNESCO have a **Joint Convention on the Status of Teachers** and a collaborative unit in Geneva to implement its recommendations. Enhancing the quality of teachers as a vital human resource has significant implications for school effectiveness and thus student participation and retention.

(5) In the **prevention of child trafficking,** UNAIDS has provided technical inputs to the UNICEF in the latter's advocacy work and regional initiatives in this regard.

(6) In the health area, UNDCP in conjunction with UNICEF and others (ODA, Ministry of Health) has helped carry out a survey on the behavioral and health aspects of children involved in drug abuse and HIV/AIDS.

(7) UNDCP is cooperating with the ILO for the prevention of drugs at the workplace.

(8) UNAIDS is working with UNICEF, UNESCO, and WHO to put HIV/AIDS-related information into the school curriculum. With funding from the various co-sponsors, UNAIDS is assisting NGOs to mainstream STD/HIV/AIDS into their activities and helping to provide targeted interventions for HIV/AIDS to prevent risk behavior in the general population as well as defined groups such as sex workers, mobile populations, and migrants.[21]

CONCLUSION

Like in many other parts of the world, child labor has become a serious and widespread problem in India. It is all the more problematic because even though there is widespread concern about child labor, not everyone agrees on the solution. Especially in a poor country like India where a majority of the population is struggling to remain above the poverty line and where a large portion of the workforce is engaged in agriculture, engaging children in family farms and businesses seem the only feasible alternative to many. Instead of going to school, millions of children go to factories and farms instead every morning.

As already stated, making education compulsory has been suggested as a solution to ending child labor. In spite of several pleas, the government is reluctant to make compulsory education a priority. There is vested interest from many who use and employ child labor for their gains, and the government needs to be more forthright about its role if it is serious about eliminating child labor.[22] Researchers and analysts have made several recommendations about the impact of education in eradicating child labor. Among them are suggestions that the entire primary education system needs to be overhauled. Compulsory primary education has met with resistance in the past and the government has conveniently used it as a rationale not to implement it because the argument has been that poor families may need to put their children work in order to survive economically.[23]

In the absence of government initiative, international pressures, public awareness, and non-governmental organizations' efforts are going far in ensuring the steady consciousness about the cruel practice of using child labor to cut costs, pay low wages, and ensure higher productivity. One such enterprise is Rugmark Foundation, which was founded in India in 1994 and has extended to Nepal. It gives licenses to companies to use their log that no child labor was used in the manufacture of the carpets carrying the logo. In return, the companies have to comply with surprise inspections and other codes that ensure hat child labor was not used in the manufacture of the carpets.[24] Individual success of Rugmark notwithstanding, it is a step in the direction of using public pressure and individual and group initiative to bring about changes in people's attitude toward child labor. Similar ventures are now in operation in other South Asia countries such as Nepal and Bangladesh as well as countries such as Brazil.

The structure of the labor market will also determine whether eradicating child labor will meet with a whole lot of resistance. In markets where wages are flexible, employers will tend to hire children at lower wages. Where minimum wages are firmly determined and practiced, employers will tend to hire adults who can deliver more with the same wages. Thus stabilizing wages may go a long way in eradicating child labor, especially in developing countries.

In the changing environment of globalization of the market, many developing countries are finding it almost imperative to engage in structural adjustment progarms to compete as well as to qualify for various kinds of financial assistance from international lending agencies such as the World Bank and the IMF. Structural adjustment programs have also had an impact on child labor.[25] Economic liberalization has attracted more foreign investment and the demand for labor has increased, making it easier for many industries to hire children at lower costs and meet the demands of increased production.

NOTES AND REFERENCES

1 This information is from N. Burra, *Born to Work: Child Labor in India*, New Delhi, 1995; UNICEF, *The State of the World's Children 1997*, NY, 1997; and ILO, *Child Labor: Targeting the Intolerable, Geneva*, 1996.

2 *General Survey of the Reports relating to Convention 138 and Recommendation No.146 concerning Minimum Age, Report III (Part 4 B),* Geneva: International Labor Organization, 1981, p.73.

3 ILO, *Child Labor: Targeting the Intolerable*, Geneva, 1996.

4 Chaudhuri, *A Dynamic Profile of Child Labor in India, 1951-1991*, ILO, New Delhi, 1996. Other sources that are useful inclde R. Kanbargi (e .), *Child Labor in the Indian Sub Continent: Dimensions and Implications, 1991.*

5 Myron Weiner, *The Child and the State in India: Child Labor and Education Policy in Comparative Perspective* (Princeton, NJ: Princeton University Press, 1991), pp.20-21.

6 Chaudhuri, *A Dynamic Profile of Child Labor in India, 1951-1991*, ILO, New Delhi, 1996.

7 Pharis Harvey and Lauren Riggin, *Trading Away the Future: Child Labor in India's Export Industries* (International Labor Rights Education and Research Fund, 1994), 53; B.N. Junyal, *Child Labor in the Carpet Industry in Mirzapur-Bhadohi* (New Delhi: ILO, 1993), 13. *Human Rights Watch, Children Rights Project*, Sept 1996 looks at bonded child labor in India, why it exists, domestic and international legislation on bonded child labor in various industries where it is found, Indian

government programs and their failure to address the problem, alternative solutions and recommendations to the government.

8 Christine Whitehead, "The Economics of Children at Work," *New Statesman*, 12 December 1986, p.19.

9 Fernandes, "A Critique- Towards Amendments/Restructuring of the Child Labor (Prohibition and Regulation) Act of 1986", draft paper, 1996.

10 For a review of the legislative history in India regarding child labor, see Weiner, 1991, chapter 5.

11 Myron Weiner, "Suffer the Children," *Far Eastern Economic Review*, 7 February, 1991, p.26. Also Weiner, *The Child and the State in India* (Princeton University Press, Princeton, NJ, 1991).

12 H. Bertsch and E. Schalegger, "Seri 2000 - Concept paper for a collaborative seri-development program between government of India and non-governmental private sector institutions and firms and the Swiss Agency for Development and Cooperation, 1997-2002", Beme, May 1996. This paper looks at the sericulture industry in India and makes references to the consequences of developing this industry for child labor. Also, "Campaign Against Child Labor," Position Paper on Child Labor, 1997. This paper looks at the causative background for child labor from a socioeconomic perspective, the rural and urban features of child labor, definitional issues, and the work of CACL.

13 Dr. V. Dhagamwar, "Eradication of Child Labor through Social Mobilization for Primary Education", Report on two organizations, 1995.

14 The programs and projects initiated by the UN system and the ILO are exerpted from the ILO Report "UN System in India: Position Paper on Child Labour," 1998.

15 The reference here is to all the UN agencies with whom discussions were held for this paper.

16 For further details on IPEC, see M.P. Joseph, *IPEC in India, 1992-95: Looking Back*, 1996.

17 More details, see Martine Kruijtbosch, *Rugmark: A Brief Resume of Concept to Reality for Visual Guarantee of Carptes Made Without Child Labor* (New Delhi: SAACS, 1995).

18 The funds are mobilized by implementing a levy of 1-2 percent on the export value of the carpets. This is used to rehabilitate children released from the carpet industry.

19 UNDCP is at present also supporting a project on the Rehabilitation and Prevention of Drug Abuse at the Workplace. The project is being instituted by the ILO and the government counterpart agency is the Ministry of Welfare. While the focus is not on child labor per se, the preventive measures have an impact on the working conditions of children, their health, and on community awareness of these problems.

20 Important components of the program are formal schooling, income generation, environmental awareness, generation of employable skills, coordination and mobilization of ministries, departments, the community, NGOs, donor agencies, the business sector, and key individuals, and local capacity building. Many of these activities have significance for the elimination of child labor.

[21] There was also an interagency group consisting of UNICEF, ILO, and UNESCO to work on child labor in Bihar. The goal of this joint initiative was to enable the agencies to play complementary roles in the area of education rather than running parallel programs. However, it did not make much headway.

[22] M. Weiner, "Child Labor in India, Putting Compulsory Primary Education on the Political Agenda", *Economic and Political Weekly*, Nov 9-16, 1996.

[23] K. Charnaraj, "Chalking in Change", in *Humanscope*, July 1996. This study talks about the need for structural change in primary education to eliminate child labor and provides views on the important role played by education in this process.

[24] International Labor Rights Education Fund, "Rugmark Label Gathers Support amidst Carpet Industry Violence" in *Workers' Rights News*, August 1995. This article talks about steps being taken in the carpet industry to cope with trade based pressures on carpet exports made with child labor.

[25] M. Swaminathan, and V.K. Ramachandran, look at "Structural Adjustment Programs and Child Welfare", Indira Gandhi Institute of Development Research, August 1993.

Chapter 4

METHOD OBSTACLES IN SOS ANALYSIS: TROPICAL RAINFOREST MANAGEMENT

Simon Montagu,
Australia

In recent times, many tropical countries have had to deal with the vexing issue of what is the most appropriate use for their tropical rainforests. On one hand, these areas represent a valuable economic resource, capable of supplying timber for both domestic and international markets. On the other hand, rainforests are thought to be one of the Earth's most ecologically important ecosystems, and thus worthy of long-term protection.

This issue will be addressed in the following SOS analysis. It will be used to highlight some of the ways of overcoming the methodological obstacles involved in undertaking an SOS analysis.

The SOS analysis is presented in a simplified form in Table 1. This table shows that their are two main goals and alternatives involved, representing each of the two main positions - liberal and conservative. The liberal goal seeks to maximise the levels of protection that are placed over the rainforests, while the conservative goal seeks to maximise the levels of profits that can be drawn from these forests. The liberal alternative therefore proposes that the use of the forest be subject to greater levels of official regulation, while the conservative alternative proposes the continuation of the unregulated use of the resource.

A potential SOS alternative to this issue is also offered. This alternative, by definition, seeks to better the expectations of both parties simultaneously. To this end, the SOS alternative proposes that 'eco-tourism' ventures be established within the rainforests. Such ventures have the potential to not only provide good returns on investment, but are also far less a destructive use of the forest than continued logging and clearing for farming.

It should be noted that the relation scores presented in Table 1 are represented in two distinctly different forms. On the one hand, the liberal goal is scored in terms of the hectare-amount of forest that can be preserved through each of the alternatives, and is expressed in hectares saved per annum. On the other hand, the conservative goal is scored in terms of the dollars of return that the alternatives can provide. It is expressed in $ per hectare per annum.

Table 1. Simplified SOS Table: Tropical Rainforest Management

Criteria / Alternatives	CONSERV. GOAL * Maximise Return on Investment. ($ made/ha/yr) *Weights* C=3 N=2 L=1	LIB. GOAL * Maximise the Level of Environ. Protection (ha saved/yr) *Weights* C=1 N=2 L=3	TOTALS Conserv.	Lib.	Neutral
CONSERV. ALT. * Unregulated Resource Usage	4 $1,000 *91%*	1 5,000 ha *20%*	?	?	?
LIB. ALT. * Regulated Resource Usage	2 $100 *9%*	4 20,000 ha *80%*	?	?	?
S.O.S. ALT. * Sustainable Resource Use: "Farm" the forest * Eco-tourism	?	?			

Notes:
1. No. in the top left corner is the relational score using the 1-5 scale
2. Percentage in the lower right corner is the part/whole percent value

I. Multi-Dimensionality of Goals

The significance on these scores being in different and incommensurate units is that it makes comparisons between the goals and alternatives (based on the raw scores alone) difficult. To highlight this fact, Table 2 presents information regarding the incremental costs and benefits of both of the alternatives shown in Table 1. This table shows that, because of the incommensurate relational scores, the overall value of each alternative (as determined by calculating the benefits - the costs of each alternative) can not be evaluated.

Table 2 Benefit-Cost Analysis using the Raw Scores

	Benefits	Costs	Benefits-Costs
Conserv. Altern.	$900	15 000 ha	?
Liberal Altern.	15 000 ha	$900	?

This part of Question III investigates some of the ways of overcoming the problem of the multi-dimensionality of goals. There are about seven different approaches to resolving this methodological obstacle. These are:

1. Raw Score Increments
2. Weighted Raw Scores
3. Part/Whole Percentages
4. Paired Comparison Monetizing
5. Economic Monetizing
6. 1-5 Scale
7. Reducing Problem to Only One Variable

In the case of tropical rainforest management, three of these methods are particularly useful. Each of these will be discussed in turn.

A. Part/Whole Percentages:

One means of converting the incommensurate raw scores into a common unit of measurement is to reduce the individual scores for each goal into a proportional fraction of the total combined score for that goal. Thus, in this example, the conservative goal score for the conservative alternative can be expressed in terms of the percentage that $1000 dollars represents of a total for that goal of $1100 ($1000 + $100). Each of the part/whole percentage values are shown in Table 1, in the lower right corner of each score-cell.

Having now expressed the relationships between the goals and alternatives in a common unit of measurement, the alternatives can be analysing in order to see which is the most preferred. This analysis considers which of the alternatives achieves the highest value, when the incremental costs of the alternative are subtracted from its incremental benefits. Table 3 below summarises this analysis.

Table 3 Benefit-Cost Analysis using Part/Whole Percentages

	Costs	Benefits	Benefits-Costs
Conserv. Altern.	82%	60%	22%
Liberal Altern.	60%	82%	-22%

Based on this analysis, and assuming that the each of the goals represented in the SOS table are of equal weight, then it can be concluded that the conservative alternative is the preferred alternative.

B. 1-5 Scale:

The 1-5 Scale resolves the problem of goal multi-dimensionality by reducing the relational scores to a common, simple relativistic scale. The five numbers of the scale represent the following:

1 = Alternative is highly adverse to goal
2 = Alternative is mildly adverse to goal
3 = Alternative is neither conducive, nor adverse to goal
4 = Alternative is mildly conducive to goal
5 = Alternative is highly conducive to goal

These 1-5 scores for the tropical rainforest management example are shown in Table 1 in the top-left corner of each of the score-cells.

Once again, expressing these relational scores in a common format allows for the comparison of the alternatives. This analysis is summarised in Table 4 below.

Table 4 Benefit-Cost Analysis using the 1-5 Scale

	Benefits	Costs	Benefits-Costs
Conserv. Altern.	2	3	-1
Liberal Altern.	3	2	1

On the basis of this analysis, and once again assuming that both of the goals presented in the SOS table are of equal weight, the liberal alternative is the preferred alternative.

Weighted Raw Scores:

The weighted raw scores approach seeks to determine a relationship between the two raw score systems used. It tries to determine, firstly, which of the goals is the most preferred, and then secondly, by how much (in terms of the units of the lesser goal) this goal is preferred. Once this relationship is known, then the preferred goal can be expressed in terms of the units of measurement used for the lesser goal.

In the case of the tropical rainforest issue, we can use this approach if we choose for example, to let the conservative goal be the preferred goal, and assume that each dollar made in profits is equivalent in value to 1000 ha of rainforest that would otherwise be saved. Using this ratio, the benefit cost relationship that is shown in terms of raw scores in Table 2, can be reexpressed in terms of this weighted raw score system. Having it in this form allows for the direct comparison, and hence, evaluation of the alternatives. This information is summarised in Table 5.

Table 5 Benefit-Cost Analysis using Weighted Raw Scores

	Benefits	Costs	Benefits-Costs
Conserv. Altern.	90 000 ha	15 000 ha	75 000 ha
Liberal Altern.	15 000 ha	90 000 ha	-75 000 ha

Not surprising, this scoring system, which is heavily weighted toward the conservative alternative, allows it to come out ahead of the liberal alternative.

II. Multiple Missing Information

It is often the case that the relationships between the goals and alternatives are not known sufficiently. This situation obviously has a flow-on effect on the determination of benefits and costs, and hence therefore, the analysis of the various alternatives proposed. This part of Question III will investigate some of the approaches of dealing with this missing information.

There are seven ways of dealing with missing information. These are:

1. Threshold Analysis
2. Best-Worst Analysis
3. Graph Analysis
4. 1-5 Scale Analysis
5. Find the missing information!
6. Convergence Analysis
7. Trial and Error Sensitivity Analysis.

Of these, there are two that are particularly relevant to the issue of tropical rainforest management. These are discussed in turn.

A. Threshold Analysis:

Threshold analysis is useful at solving the problem of missing information, because it reduces the problem from being one of finding what the absolute value of the missing information is, to one of whether this information is above or below a certain threshold score. This approach is particularly useful when only one piece of information is missing.

If we use the 1-5 scale to score the relationships between the goals and alternatives expressed in Table 1, and if we have the information on costs and benefits that is displayed in Table 4, then we can assume for the moment that we are uncertain as to the actual costs of the conservative alternative. Table 6 displays this information.

Table 6 Benefit-Cost Analysis with One Piece of Missing Information

	Benefits	Costs	Benefits-Costs
Conserv. Altern.	2	X	?
Liberal Altern.	3	2	1

Rather than search for the absolute value of this cost, we can calculate the threshold point where the benefits minus costs of the two alternatives are equal, and then use this information to decide whether the costs of the conservative alternative fall above or below this threshold. This information therefore tells use which is the preferred alternative, depending on whether we choose the costs of the conservative alternative to be above or below the threshold value.

The threshold value can be determined using the following equation:

Bc -Cc = BI-C

where:

BC = Benefits of the Conservative Alternative
X2 = Unknown costs of the Conservative Alternative
X3 = Unknown Benefits of the Liberal Alternative
C1 = Costs of the Liberal Alternative

Substituting in the values in Table 6 reveals that we have an equation with two unknowns:

2-X2 = X3-2
4-X2 = X3

Obviously, in this form, the equation represents a straight line. Therefore, all we need is two points in order to plot this line. The intercepts are the easiest to calculate:

IF:
4-X2 = X3
THEN:
when X3 = 0, X2 = 4; and
when X2 = 0, X3 = 4.

This line therefore looks like that shown in Figure 1:

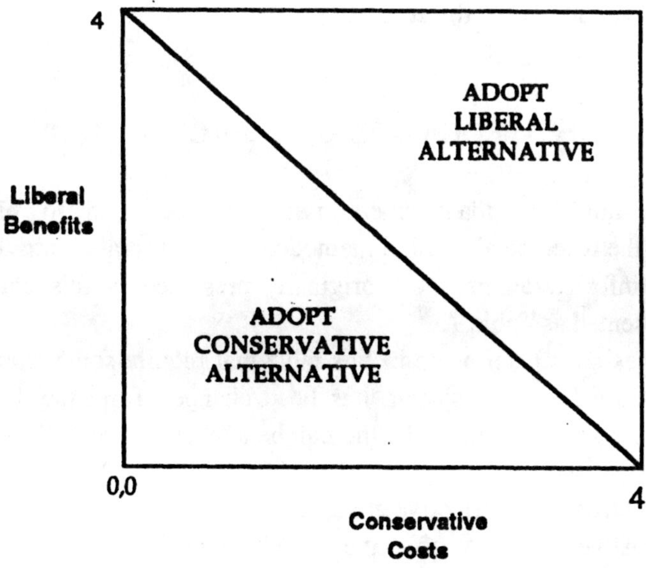

Figure 1 Graphical Analysis of the Threshold Value between the Conservative Costs (X_2) and the Liberal Benefits (X_3)

From this graph, we can see that if the scores for X_2 and X_3 were to fall below the threshold line, then the conservative alternative would be preferred. If they were above the line, then it would be the liberal alternative that would be preferred.

III. SIMPLICITY

Having all of this multiplicity regarding the goals could potential complicate the conclusions that can be drawn from the SOS analysis. By remaining cognizant of this point, and by taking a few simple steps at the beginning of the analysis, some of this complexity can be avoided.

The first consideration is to ensure that the goals and alternatives used in the analysis remain fairly simple and concise. Ensuring that these variables are structured in this way, helps prevent the likelihood of forcing inconsistencies between either the goals or alternatives. Unnecessary complexity increases the risk of not only confusing the analysis, but it may also introduce inconsistencies that neutralise the effectiveness of the SOS approach.

In a similar vein, undue complexity can be averted by using the simple 1-5 scale to express the relationships between the goals and alternatives. While this scale may seem relatively unsophisticated, its simplicity is really its strength. First off, scoring the relationships between goals and alternatives becomes a much easier task. Secondly, while the scale may not represent the true magnitude of difference between various scores, this is unlikely to matter because the relative relationships between scores is more important than the actual magnitude of the difference.

V. SOS Allocation of Scarce Resources

The tropical rainforest management issue can be used to highlight certain characteristics of the resource allocation methodology incorporated into the SOS analysis framework. The information that was originally presented in this example has been reworked and presented as Table 7.

Certain changes have been made in this table that require some elaboration. Firstly, note that the relational scoring system has been changed from the 1-5 scale used in question EII, to a 1-3 scale. In this scale, the numbers represent the following:

1 = Alternative is less effective at achieving goal
2 = Alternative is twice as effective at achieving goal
3 = Alternative is thrice as effective at achieving goal

Although this scale runs from 1 to 3, a score of zero is possible, and indicates that the alternative is either non- or negatively effective at achieving the desired goal.

Another point to note is that the totals are now expressed in dollar values, and represent the proportion of the total budget (which in this case is set at $200 million) that would be allocated to each alternative, on the basis of goal weights.

There are two means of arriving at SOS solutions in an allocation problem. Both of these are discussed.

A. Expanded Budget

One means of arriving at an SOS solution in this allocation problem is to expand the budget in order to more than satisfy the initial best expectations of both parties. From Table 7, we can see that in order to achieve this SOS solution, the allocation for the conservative alternative would have to be increased above the conservative total of $107 million, while the liberal alternative would simultaneously have to be more than the $164 million allocated to it under the liberal goal-weights.

Consequently, if the allocations are raised by, say, $1 million for each alternative, then the total budget would be expanded to $273 million. Therefore, in order to achieve an SOS solution simply by expanding the budget, a further $73 million would be required.

In the context of the tropical rainforest management issue, this budgetary increase could come about through several different means. Given that the bulk of the budget increase results primarily from the amount of money required to meet the liberal's expectations of the liberal alternative, then perhaps some effort ought to be expended on trying to raise the liberal expectations of the conservative alternative. If this relation score could be improved, then it would even out the allocated total. Having achieved this, the it should follow that the disparity between the total allocation of the conservative alternative and the total of the liberal alternative would be less, which would thus lessen the overall amount required to meet the expanded budget.

B. Increased Efficiency

It's quite possible however, that the budgetary requirements of this issue are fairly rigid, making an expanded budget SOS solution impossible. In this situation, achieving an SOS solution which betters the best initial expectations of both parties must rely on improving the perceptions that each party holds about the others alternative.

A casual glance at the relational scores expressed in Table 7 suggests immediately that the score for the conservative alternative under the liberal goal offers the most room for improving the overall status of this allocation problem. Similarly, if the score for the liberal alternative under the conservative goal could be increased, then this alternative may be more appealing to the conservatives.

Some of the things that could improved upon the conservative alternative in the eyes of the liberals would be to do away will clear-felling logging practices and use a less-destructive approach, such as selective logging, that leaves larger portions of the ecosystem in tact. Other improvements could include ensuring that riparian forests are not touched (in order to lessen the impact of logging on the aquatic ecosystem), and that timber is removed only from areas with gentle slopes, rather than from steep ridge-lines and the like (in order to lessen the effects of soil-erosion).

Their are various monetary incentives that are available which would help improve the perspective that conservative interests hold about the liberal alternative. If it is perceived that regulated forest uses diminish the returns available on investments in these areas, then tax or direct subsidies may help overcome this problem. Furthermore, incentives should be given to ensure that investors utilizing this resource get some sort of assistance to add value to their products (i.e. furniture production etc.), in order to increase the profits to be made. Such incentives (well-placed subsidies to manufacturers and the like) should induce a more efficient use of the forests, which should hopefully reduce the volumes of timber required.

Table 7. SOS Allocation Table: Tropical Rainforest Management

Criteria / Alternatives	CONSERV. GOAL * Maximise Return on Investments. Weights C=3 N=2 L=1	LIB. GOAL * Maximise Levels of Env. Protect. Weights C=1 N=2 L=3	TOTALS Budget=$200mil. C.	L.	N.	SOS ALLOCATION Expanded Budget
CONSERV. ALT. * Unreg. Resource Usage	2.5 *71%*	0 *0%*	107m *54%*	36m *18%*	71m *36%*	108m *40%*
LIB. ALT. * Reg. Resource Usage	1 *29%*	3 *100%*	93m *46%*	164m *82%*	129m *64%*	165m *60%*
TOTALS	3.5 *100%*	3 *100%*	200m *100%*	200m *100%*	200m *100%*	273 *100%*

Chapter 5

UNIVERSITY TO INDUSTRY TRANSFER

Dianne Rahm
Iowa State University
and
Veronica Hansen
University of South Florida

ABSTRACT

Utilizing the knowledge, know-how, technologies developed in universities to improve the competitiveness of U.S. industry is a super-optimum technology policy solution. Transferring technologies developed at universities to industry vastly expands the resource base by providing companies with no internal research and development effort with that capability and by augmenting the R&D of companies with some level of internal effort already in place. By taking advantage of university technology transfer, all companies and policy-makers can emphasize innovation as a goal to be included in a competitive business strategy. Having universities as participants in technology transfer activities maximizes the benefits and minimizes the costs to all by providing for shared equipment, personnel, and laboratory facilities. This last fact is particularly clear when pre-competitive research is undertaken at university-based centers or consortiums which draw their members from wide groups of industry participants. Drawing on data gathered as part study of university-industry research and development (R&D) interactions, this paper examines the factors that lead to successful collaborations.

INTRODUCTION

Super-optimum policy solutions are those through which liberals, conservatives, and people holding other major viewpoints all believe themselves to be winners in policy outcomes. Distinct from compromises, where each side is forced to accept less than the desired outcome, super-optimum policy solutions are consensual. They have the characteristics of fairness, efficiency, stability, and wisdom. Various methods can be utilized to achieve these outcomes including expanding the resource base, setting higher goals, and maximizing the benefits to all while minimizing the costs. (Nagel, 1994; Susskind and Cruikshank, 1987).

Utilizing the knowledge, know-how, technologies developed in universities to improve the competitiveness of U.S. industry is a super-optimum technology policy solution. Transferring technologies developed at universities to industry vastly expands the resource base by providing companies with no internal research and development (R&D) effort with that capability and by augmenting the R&D of companies with some level of internal effort already in place. By taking advantage of university technology transfer, all companies and policy-makers can emphasize innovation as a goal to be included in a competitive business strategy. Having universities as participants in technology transfer activities maximizes the benefits and minimizes the costs to all by providing for shared equipment, personnel, and laboratory facilities. This last fact is particularly clear when pre-competitive research is undertaken at university-based centers or consortiums which draw their members from wide groups of industry participants.

Since the early 1980s, U.S. public policy has sought to cultivate this super-optimum technology policy by providing economic incentives for closer ties between institutions of higher education and business enterprises. Much of this competitiveness policy has been formulated in legislation[1]. The Bayh-Dole Act of 1980 began the new policy direction by supplying financial impetus to universities. Since its passage, U.S. research universities have been increasing their technology transfer activities. Bayh-Dole was a watershed because its provisions allowed universities to collect royalties on patentable inventions developed by researchers funded with federal money. Prior to Bayh-Dole, the federal government maintained rights to any invention resulting from research paid for with taxpayer dollars. Since federal grants comprise the bulk of research money at the top U.S. institutions, this change in public policy has had a large impact (Nelson, 1989).

While revenues generated from patents and licenses are still a relatively small portion of total university research expenditure (about 1.5%), their contribution to the university budget is of increasing importance (Grassmuck, 1991). In 1992, the nation's top research universities earned in total $172 million from royalties and licenses. That amount was up 30% from the prior year (Blumenstyk, 1994). Because of these rapid increases in royalty income, most research universities encourage the pursuit of patents and dedicate scarce resources to technology transfer and licensing activities.

These efforts on the part of universities raise important questions. What defines a "successful" university-firm technology transfer relationship? What do university personnel perceive as the costs and benefits of engaging in technology transfer activities?

What hinders the transfer of knowledge, know-how, and technology from the university to industry? What facilitates such interaction? This paper addresses these questions by drawing upon data collected as part of a national study of university-firm linkages for industrial innovation[2]. The results of a survey sent to administrators and researchers at the top 100 U.S. research universities are discussed.

LITERATURE REVIEW

DEFINING "SUCCESSFUL" TECHNOLOGY TRANSFER

"Successful" technology transfer is a concept not well defined in the literature. What is usually meant by "success" stems from the narrow notion of a linear passage of a device from one organization to another. There is an under emphasis on the need for R&D knowledge and know-how to accompany the technology in the transfer, if the transfer is to be of use.

Much of the literature implicitly defines successful transfer in terms of the diffusion of technologies into the economy and adoption of technologies by transfer recipients (Allen, 1977; Feller, 1988; Florida and Kenney, 1990; Frye, 1988; Mahajan and Peterson, 1985; Mansfield et al, 1977; Nelson and Winter, 1977; Rogers, 1983; Sahal, 1981; Sahal, 1982). Indeed, the mathematical models used to describe the process of innovation have been compared to infectious disease models. Presumably, the more infection, the greater the innovation's penetration into the economy and the greater the "success."

While this notion of "success" is not without its merits, another litmus test has been suggested in the literature. This one centers around the notion of novelty or originality as distinguished by the possession of patents (Cockburn and Griliches, 1988; Griliches, 1988; Griliches and Berndt, 1988; Pakes, 1985; Pavitt, 1982). "Success" of a technology transfer interaction between university and firm could perhaps simply be defined by whether or not the collaborative effort resulted in a patentable product which then the university might license to produce royalty revenue.

COSTS AND BENEFITS

For a university to undertake technology transfer as part of its mission, it must expect to pay some costs. At the same time, universities would not undertake technology transfer efforts unless there were the potential of benefits. What does the literature suggest some of these costs and benefits might be?

Geisler and Rubenstein (1989) discuss the benefits of cooperation between universities and firms. They suggest firms cooperate with universities because they benefit from access to students and professors, state-of-the-art technology as well as scientific knowledge. Other benefits are prestige, efficient use of resources, and access to university facilities. They suggest that universities cooperate with industry to gain other benefits including access to scientific and technical areas in which industry has great expertise, exposing students to practical "real world" problems, the use of ear-marked government funds, and potential employment for graduates. Some of the costs to the university are entailed because of the organizational mechanisms set up to encourage and manage technology transfer. These include industrial extension services, offering professional symposia and seminars, establishing joint research projects with firms for which the university assumes some of the cost, developing and running formal research consortia, research parks, business incubators, and spin-off enterprises.

Organizational units have costs other than their start-up and maintenance costs. Ruscio (1984) suggests that the development of formal, standardized, elaborate, and innovative structural arrangements reveals the university's successful attempt to deal with increasing numbers of entrepreneurial scientist. By creating the institutions and becoming a "broker" in facilitating what were informal researcher-firm arrangements, the university maintains control. According to Ruscio, bureaucratic arrangements with industry can be interpreted as the university's attempt to maintain itself as central negotiator as opposed to acting as a "holding company" for entrepreneurial scientists. The presence of new organizational structures are a real cost to the university. They indicate an expanded infrastructure which needs to be maintained but they also show what some might consider a hidden cost -- the willingness of the university to invest in maintaining a permanent link with industry. Fassin (1991) outlines some of the more pervasive pressures on universities to shift from what he calls a 'public model' to a 'commercial model'. The adoption of the commercial model imposes certain costs on the university and creates a tension by demanding attention to the increased value of knowledge and patentable technologies to the universities, scientification of technology, increased costs for scientific equipment, insufficient government funding, pressures to shift from fundamental to applied research, and requests for greater monetary incentives from entrepreneurial researchers.

Barriers and Facilitators

While universities may endure environmental pressures to cooperate with firms, there are many barriers to such involvement. These included differences in mission, objectives, organization structure or policies, research orientation, and research interests. Crow and Emmert (1984) argue that the inability of professors to reach beyond their academic discipline lines for communication with firm personnel is a barrier to technology transfer. Perhaps one of the greatest organizational culture barrier to technology transfer interaction between researchers and firms rests with firm demands for secrecy and insistence on delaying or denying publications coming for the cooperative research. The consequence of this demand can be a substantial barrier to a researcher facing an annual evaluation based largely on published research.

Face to face interactions are generally noted in the literature and trade press as essential to technology transfer activities. The phrase usually used is that technology transfer is a "contact sport." That being the case, the more opportunities for one-to-one contacts a university can establish, the greater the transfer potential. Stewart and Gibson (1990) discuss the importance of classroom interactions. Classroom linkages come because industry requires that its personnel take refresher courses to keep current given the fast pace of knowledge growth. Classroom face-to-face interactions result in interpersonal "networking", not only between student and teacher, but among students (industry professionals) as well. Universities offering firm-friendly course schedules and times will have an advantage in technology transfer.

There are other factors mentioned in the literature as possible facilitators of technology transfer interaction such as faculty consulting for industry, on-going co-op or internship programs, graduate students doing field work on industry projects, presence of a clear university patent policy, technology transfer advisory councils, cross-disciplinary research, team research, meetings on both campus centers and member company facilities so that the cultures of each environment may be learned, and a sensitivity to the recent direction of public policy (Owen and Entorf, 1989; Marazita , 1991).

SURVEY METHODS

The study population was defined as researchers and technology transfer administrative personnel within the top 100 U.S. research universities. The initial population list of the top 100 universities was drawn from National Science Foundation data where universities were ranked based upon annual R&D expenditure. Two specially tailored surveys were developed. One emphasized issues of potential concern to professors and was sent to researchers. The other stressed university-wide administrative issues and was sent to technology administrators.

For each university, administrative surveys were sent to two individually identified[3] administrative offices most likely to be the focal point of university technology transfer or licensing efforts (such as: offices of Patents and Technology Licensing, Sponsored Research, or Technology Transfer). Additionally, three researcher surveys were sent to the Chairs of the departments of Biology, Chemistry, Computer Science, Electrical Engineering, and Physics. These disciplines are each ranked highly as recipients of R&D funds and research results coming from these areas are likely to be directly related to industry. Each department Chair was asked to fill out 1 survey and to select 2 other researchers within the department to complete the others. A sub-sample of centers affiliated with targeted departments was also taken. Directors of these centers likewise received a researcher survey. In this way, each university received a minimum of 17 survey forms (2 administrative surveys and at least 15 researcher questionnaires). The number of centers varied by department and university. The total identified sample frame, including technology managers and academic researchers, was 2,049. The total researcher sample frame consisted of 1,849 (1,500 department researchers and 349 center researchers). The administrative sample frame was 200.

In August of 1993, the questionnaire was pre-tested and an alert letter requesting assistance with the study was sent to the selected administrators, department Chairs, and center Directors. The survey was mailed in September and a second wave mailing to non-respondents occurred in October of 1993. Each questionnaire included a return postage-paid envelope with a pre-printed address. Personally addressed cover letters were sent to administrators, center Directors, and department Chairs. The cover letter included an office phone number and electronic mail address so that respondents could make contact should they have any questions. Eighty-eight identified respondents declined to be included in the study, thus reducing the sample size to 1,961 (1,774 researchers and 187 administrative officials). Of those, 1,134 completed surveys were returned yielding an overall response rate of 58%. Returns included 1,013 researcher and 121 administrator questionnaires, producing within group response rates of 57% and 65%, respectively.

SURVEY RESULTS AND DISCUSSION

From the university perspective, there are three actors that should be viewed separately: technology transfer administrative personnel, Ph.D. level researchers with no industrial experience (hereafter referred to as *university-bound researchers*), and Ph.D. level researchers who have interacted with businesses in an effort to transfer knowledge, know-how, or a technology (hereafter referred to as *industry-linked researchers*). The sample data contains questionnaire responses from 121 technology transfer administrators, 254 university-bound researchers, and 759 industry-linked researchers. This discussion explores how the viewpoints of these actors differ regarding the definition of "successful" technology transfer interactions with firms, perceptions of the costs and benefits associated with transfer activities, and the factors which may inhibit or promote university linkages to firms.

SUCCESS

What constitutes "successful" technology transfer from a university to a firm? To examine this issue, industry-linked researchers were asked to respond freely to the open-ended survey question: "Not all researcher-firm interactions are 'successful.' From your point of view, what constitutes a 'successful' interaction with a firm?"

The text responses to this open-ended question were content analyzed in the following manner. First, a random sample of responses for the question was drawn. Each individual response from this sample was carefully read to identify systematic categories or typical responses. A list of categories was thus developed. Using these categories as a general guideline (adding or deleting categories as seemed appropriate), the rest of the responses were read and frequencies for categories were coded[4]. Inter-coder reliability for research assistants participating in the coding of the open-ended questions was maintained at 90% to assure accuracy of translation from text to systematic categories of responses.

The responses of the industry-linked researchers to the question of what constitutes a successful interaction with a firm were compiled into 12 independent (although perhaps related) categories.

Table 1
What Constitutes a "Successful" Interaction with a Firm?

Percent of Industry-Linked Researchers Responding by Category

N=726

Category	**Percent**
Benefit to the firm	30%
Benefit to the researcher	28%
Mutual benefit to the firm and the researcher	27%
A new product is developed	16%
A trusting and strong collaborative relationship is built	14%
Long-term or repeated interaction with the firm results	13%
Benefit to the university	11%
Expectations are met (the project is completed)	11%
There is a transfer of information, people, technology, money, facilities, or the sharing of ideas	10%
A mutual understanding between the researcher and firm develops	10%
Frequent site visits occur (researcher to firm and firm personnel to university)	3%
Benefit to society	2%

As Table 1 shows, industry-linked researchers tend primarily to define successful technology transfer in terms of its benefit to the firm, the researcher, or both. Benefits to either the university or society play a clearly smaller role to industry-linked researchers, at least in terms of defining a successful interaction.

COSTS AND BENEFITS

What are the costs and benefits to the university of engaging in technology transfer interactions? Administrators were asked to describe from their vantage point the affect of industry linkages and these responses were content analyzed. Table 2 details the results of this analysis.

Table 2
Costs and Benefits of Technology Transfer Activities to Universities

Percent of Administrators Responding by Category

N=95

Category	Percent
Benefits	
Money for research	68%
Employment and support for students	39%
"Real World" experience and training for students	39%
Potential licensing revenue and extra income for faculty	37%
Benefit society by enhancing the economic position of the nation through technology transfers	23%
Advance the progress on research problems and programs	14%
Good public relations for the university	12%
Access to industrial equipment	6%
Enhance applied research	3%
Costs	
Distortion of academic principles and the university's mission	34%
Creation of conflicts of interest	23%
Time consumption	21%
Administrative and legal costs	19%
Intellectual property disputes	14%
Threat to basic research	10%
Firm support is extremely short lived	7%
Lack of control over work	3%
Need for increased accountability measures	3%

As Table 2 shows, revenue enhancement in one form or another seems to be noted by many administrators as a primary benefit of interaction with firms although the benefit of exposing students to industrial problems is not overlooked. Interestingly, a significant number of administrators cite the overall benefit to society as important. This position is of note especially given industry-linked researchers low emphasis on social payoff. Costs, are apparently seen across two dimensions. The first is in the loftier realm of university purpose. Clearly there are some concerns being expressed regarding the affect of technology transfer activities on the traditional role of the university (the marketplace of ideas with the emphasis on basic research and educating the next generation of basic researchers). On the second dimension, costs are denoted on a practical level. Here administrators refer to the very real details of implementation where conflicts of interest, intellectual property disputes, and legal costs loom large.

INHIBITING AND PROMOTING FACTORS

From a policy implementation perspective, understanding the factors which retard or promote university-firm technology transfer interaction is paramount. Removing barriers and providing enticements will result in more universal adoption of the desired policy. From the perspective of university personnel, what are these factors?

Administrators and researchers were all asked to respond to the open-ended question: "In your judgment, what are the most important factors inhibiting or promoting the involvement of university researchers in technology transfer and industrial innovation efforts?" Tables 3 and 4 report these findings.

As Table 3 shows, university administrators tend to see conflict of interest concerns, intellectual property disputes, and the different organizational cultures of universities and firms as inhibiting factors. Administrators highlight financial motives as promoting factors.

Table 3
Factors Inhibiting and Promoting University-Firm Technology Transfer

Percent of Administrators Responding by Category

N=93

Category	Percent
Inhibiting	
Different organizational cultures	36%
Conflict of interest	34%
Focus on basic research	24%
Intellectual property disputes	23%
Ambiguous university policies	14%
Time consumption	11%
Publication disputes	10%
Lack of incentives	8%
Lack of knowledge of technology transfer process	7%
Promoting	
University and faculty need for research funding	30%
Development of commercial application for profit through royalty	12%
Frequent contact between university and firm personnel	11%
University service mission (to industry, to government)	9%
Technology transfer experienced scientists with prior good experiences with firms	8%
Provides "real world" experience for students	5%

Table 4
Factors Inhibiting and Promoting University-Firm Technology Transfer

Percent of Researchers Responding by Category

N=772

Category	Percent
Inhibiting	
Different organizational cultures	21%
Conflict of interest	14%
Limited interaction with firm personnel	13%
Lack of incentives and poor university reward structure	13%
Time consumption	12%
Short-sightedness of firms	12%
Firm failure to fund research projects	10%
Intellectual property disputes	9%
Focus on basic research	7%
University bureaucracy	7%
Lack of knowledge of technology transfer process	5%
Ambiguous university policies	5%
Publication disputes	5%
Promoting	
University and faculty need for research funding	9%
Mutual needs and interests of university and firm personnel	8%
Frequent contact between university and firm personnel	7%
Provides "real world" experience for students	3%
University service mission (to industry, to government)	2%

Researchers, as Table 4 shows, provide more variety in their responses. While agreeing with administrators that conflict of interest and differing organizational cultures inhibit technology transfer activities, researchers also cite factors such as extensive time demand of technology transfer activities, lack of exposure to firms, and the short-sightedness of firms as obstacles. Researchers agree with administration that financial incentives promote technology transfer interactions but researchers also point to factors such as finding mutual interests among participants and having frequent contacts with firm personnel as helpful.

CONCLUSION

Technology transfer from universities to industry can be seen as a super-optimum policy solution to the problem of U.S. competitiveness in several ways. First, university-industry technology transfer establishes the higher policy goal of improving competitiveness by increasing and speeding the diffusion of innovations. Second, technology transfer maximizes the shared benefits of increased R&D to all firms while minimizing the costs to all by taking advantage of shared personnel, equipment, and facilities. Finally, university transfers of knowledge, know-how, and technology to industry enlarge the R&D resource base of the entire nation.

Given the possibility of revenue enhancement since the passage of the Bayh-Dole Act, technology transfer activities are of increasing concern to research universities. Universities can perform better in this arena if their knowledge of the technology transfer process is improved. One way to improve that understanding is to examine how university technology transfer administrators and researchers conceptualize and evaluate certain aspects of technology transfer. This paper has examined how actors within the university answer three key questions: What constitutes "successful" technology transfer? What are the costs and benefits? What are the most important factors which inhibit or promote technology transfer?

The researchers responding to the survey results presented here do not generally define technology transfer in the typical linear approach presented in the literature. University researchers tend to see success far more in the wider terms of researcher-firm mutual benefit than in the narrow terms of merely passing a device to a firm. There is little social perspective, however, in the researchers' construct for benefit to society through innovation diffusion and adoption are not considered.

University administrators see the benefits of technology transfer activities in financial terms while the costs are defined in terms of the stresses placed on the university. Particularly highlighted are the stresses associated with the movement to a commercial model and its impact on the traditional university mission of basic research performed by a researcher with no other self-interest than the advancement of science.

What clearly emerges from the analysis of the question of promoting factors is that direct economic pressures serve to drive both administrators and researchers to undertake technology transfer efforts. On the other hand, the major obstacle to university-firm technology transfer is the differing organizational culture of the universities and businesses.

ACKNOWLEDGMENT

The material presented here includes research funded by the National Science Foundation under grant SBR-9305591.

REFERENCES

Allen, T. J. *Managing the Flow of Technology*. Cambridge: MIT Press, 1977.

Bayh-Dole Act of 1980, 35 U.S.C. secs. 200-211 (1988).

Blumenstyk, Holdie. "Universities' Income From Commercial Licensing of Inventions Rises 30%, to $172-Million." *The Chronicle of Higher Education* January 26, (1994): A22.

Cockburn, Iain and Zvi Griliches. "Industry Effects and Appropriability Measures in the Stock Market's Valuation of R&D Patents." *American Economic Review* Vol. 78, No. 2 (May, 1988): 419-424.

Crow, Michael M. and Mark Emmert. "Interorganizational Management of R&D: University-Industry Relations and Innovation" in *Strategic Management of Industrial R&D* edited by Barry Bozeman, Michael Crow, and Albert Link. Lexington, MA: D.C. Heath and Company, 1984.

Fassin, Yves. "Academic Ethos Versus Business Ethics." *International Journal of Technology Management* Vol. 6, No. 5/6 (1991): 533-546.

Federal Technology Transfer Act of 1986, 15 U.S.C. secs. 3701-3714 (1988).

Feller, Irwin. "Evaluating State Advanced Technology Programs." *Evaluation Review* Vol. 12, No. 3 (June 1988): 232-252.

Florida, Richard and Martin Kenney. *The Breakthrough Illusion: Corporate America's Failure to Move from Innovation to Mass Production.* New York: Basic Books, 1990.

Frye, Alva L. *From Source to Use: Bringing University Technology to the Marketplace.* New York: American Management Association, 1985.

Geisler, Eliezer and Albert H. Rubenstein. "University-Industry Relations: A Review of Major Issues," in *Cooperative Research and Development: The Industry-University-Government Relationship* edited by Albert N. Link and Gregory Tassey. Boston, Dordrecht, London: Kluwer Academic Publishers, 1989.

Grassmuck, Karen. "Major Research Universities Report Big Increases in Royalty Revenues From Patented Discoveries." *The Chronicle of Higher Education* March 6, (1991): A23-24.

Griliches, Zvi. "Research Costs and Social Returns: Hybrid Corn and Related Innovations." *Journal of Political Economy* Vol. 66, No. 5 (1958): 419-431.

Griliches, Zvi and Ernst R. Berndt. "Productivity and Technical Change." *NBER Reporter* (Winter 1988): 1-4.

Mahajan, Vijay and Robert A. Peterson. *Models for Innovation Diffusion.* Beverly Hills, London, New Delhi: Sage, 1985.

Mansfield, Edwin, John Rapoport, Anthony Romeo, Samuel Wagner, and George Beardsley. "Social and Private Rates of Return from Industrial Innovation." *Quarterly Journal of Economics* Vol. 91 (May, 1977): 221-240.

Marazita, Carlo F. "Technology Transfer in the United States: Industrial Research at Engineering Research Centers Versus the Technological Needs of U.S. Industry." *Technological Forecasting and Social Change* Vol. 39 (1991): 397-410.

Nagel, Stuart S., *The Policy Process and Super-Optimum Solutions.* Commack, New York: Nova Science Publishers, 1994.

National Competitiveness Technology Transfer Act of 1989, 15 U.S.C. secs. 3710 et seq. (1988).

National Cooperative Research Act of 1984, 15 U.S.C. secs. 4301-4305 (1988).

Nelsen, L.L. "Intellectual Property and the University" *in Proceedings of the Albany Law School Annual Conference on Intellectual Property.* New York: Mathew Bender & Co, 1989.

Nelson, Richard. and S. Winter. "In Search of a Useful Theory of Innovation." *Research Policy* Vol. 6 (1977): 36-76.

Owen, Jean V. and John F. Entorf. "Where Factory Meets Faculty." *Manufacturing Engineering* Vol. 102, No. 2 (February, 1989): 48-71.

Omnibus Trade and Competitiveness Act of 1988, 19 U.S.C. secs. 2901-2902 (1988).

Pakes, Ariel. "On Patents, R&D, and the Stock Market Rate of Returns." *Journal of Political Economy* Vol. 93, No. 2 (1985): 390-409.

Pavitt, Keith. "R&D Patenting and Innovative Activities: A Statistical Exploration." *Research Policy* Vol. 11, No. 1 (1982): 33-51.

Rogers, W.M. *The Diffusion of Innovations.* New York: Free Press, 1983.

Ruscio, Kenneth. "University-Industry Cooperation as a Problem in Interorganizational Relations," in *Strategic Management of Industrial R&D* edited by Barry Bozeman, Michael Crow, and Albert Link. Lexington, MA: D.C. Heath and Company, 1984.

Sahal, Devendra. *The Transfer and Utilization of Technical Knowledge.* Lexington, MA: Lexington Books, 1982.

Sahal, Devendra. *Patterns of Technological Innovation.* London: Addison-Wesley Publishing Company, 1981.

Susskind, Lawrence and Jeffrey Cruikshank, *Breaking the Impasse: Consensual Approaches to Resolving Public Disputes*, New York: Basic Books, 1987.

Stevenson-Wydler Technology Innovation Act of 1980, 15 U.S.C. secs. 3701 et seq. (1988).

Stewart, G. Hutchinson and David V. Gibson. "University and Industry Linkages: The Austin, Texas Study," in *Technology Transfer: A Communication Perspective* edited by Frederick Williams and David V. Gibson. Newbury Park, London, New Delhi: Sage Publications, 1990.

Technology Competitiveness Act of 1988, 19 U.S.C. secs. 2906 et seq. (1988). Also see House Report 100-266 (August 4, 1987) and Senate Report 100-80 (June 22, 1987).

Trademark Clarification Act of 1984, 15 U.S.C. secs. 1064-1127 (1988).

ENDNOTES

[1] This legislation includes the Stevenson-Wydler Technology Innovation Act of 1980, the Bayh-Dole Act of 1980, the Trademark Clarification Act of 1984, the Federal Technology Transfer Act of 1986, the Omnibus Trade and Competitiveness Act of 1988, and the National Competitiveness Technology Transfer Act of 1989. Federal policy has also been set by presidential action such as by Ronald Reagan's executive order 12428 which on June 28, 1983 established a federal advisory committee on industrial competitiveness.

[2] The material presented here includes research funded by the National Science Foundation under grant SBR-9305591.

[3] The identification of these units, centers, and the names of technology managers, department chairs, and center directors came from university graduate catalogues and campus directories. Catalogues and directories were requested by letter from the Graduate School at each targeted university.

[4] There were six open-ended questions included in the study (3 on the researcher survey and 3 on the administrator survey). Responses to each question were content analyzed in the same fashion as described for this question.

Chapter 6

BRAIN BIOCHEMISTRY AND THE VIOLENCE EPIDEMIC: TOWARD A "WIN-WIN" STRATEGY FOR REDUCING CRIME

Roger D. Masters
Dartmouth College and Gruter Institute for Law and Behavioral Research*
Myron Coplan
Intellequity
with the assistance of
Brian T. Hone, David J. Grelotti, David Gonzalez, and David Jones

ABSTRACT

Paradoxically enough, there may be a win-win strategy for reducing violent crime. As with many public policies, the first step involves a reconceptualization of the problem -- in this case in terms of evolutionary medicine. Because what has been called the American "epidemic" of violence shows largely unexplained variation from place to place, geographical differences in rates of violence can be used to explore the causes of crime. Among the many "risk factors" for violence is the consumption of alcohol and drugs, suggesting that disturbances of brain biochemistry may be implicated in violent behavior. This hypothesis is reinforced by evidence of an additional and unsuspected risk factor for violence: neurotoxic metals, absorbed due to poor diet or vitamin and mineral deficiencies, that disturb normal brain development and neurotransmitter function, thereby contributing to loss of impulse control and increased likelihood of violent behavior. Lead and manganese, two known neurotoxins, have been found in higher concentrations in head hair of violent criminals than nonviolent offenders; several prospective studies show that lead absorption at age seven predicts violent behavior later in life. Data from the Environmental Protection Agency's Toxic Release Inventory were used to test the neurotoxicity hypothesis for environmental emissions of these two metals and their interaction with rates of alcoholism. In a sample of 1165 counties from sixteen states with a total population of 130 million, releases of lead and manganese as well as rates of alcoholism are significant predictors of violent crime rates. Interactions between measures of the toxic metals and alcoholism are significant, as predicted by the neurotoxicity hypothesis, and these factors influence rates of violence controlling for conventional explanatory variables. The combination of dietary deficiencies in calcium or other vitamins and minerals, environmental pollution, and alcoholism may thus help account for both geographic and ethnic variations in crime rates. A strategy of biochemical normalization, including dietary supplementation, combined with pollution control holds out the promise of reduced rates of crime, lower costs of incarceration, and improved cognitive performance -- all at a fraction of the cost of current corrections policies.

INTRODUCTION

Criminal behavior has many costs to society, as does the expanding system of prisons and correctional institutions. Despite recent declines in rates of violent crime in many American cities, its overall incidence remains extremely high in the United States. "Tough" enforcement strategies entail costs not only for an expanding system of prisons and correctional bureaucracies, but -- if punishment becomes an end in itself -- concerns for civil liberties. Social rehabilitation programs are also costly, and their failures -- with the resulting outrage at the recidivism symbolized by "Willie Horton" -- undermine public confidence and the legitimate need for a sense of security. An alternative win-win strategy may, however, be possible. To this end, it is first necessary to reconceptualize violent crime in terms of evolutionary medicine, neurobiology, and epidemiology.

Violence has many causes, including such risk factors as poverty, cultural expectations, availability of guns, social and ethnic stress, and individual personality (for a recent survey, Wilson and Petersilia, eds., 1995). Increasingly, however, attention has been directed to biological factors that interact with conventional socio-economic variables (Raine, 1993; Masters and McGuire, 1993: ch. 6, 11, 12, 14; Denno, 1994). Because loss of impulse control and increased frequency of aggressive behavior has been linked to deregulation of neurotransmitter function, the possibility of a relationship between neurotoxicity and criminal violence is of particular interest (Gibbs, 1995).

Behavioral and cognitive deficits caused by lead, noted in antiquity by Hippocrates, have been the subject of widespread scientific analysis (Hunter, 1972; Jones and Rutter, 1983; Rice, 1984; Rabin, 1989). Although legislation prohibiting lead in gasoline additives and paint reduced lead levels in blood by 78% between 1976-1978 and 1988-1991 (Pirkle, 1984), toxic release of lead and lead compounds remains a serious problem due to aging water systems and industrial pollution. In Massachusetts, controlling for other variables, lead uptake in children has been correlated with such environmental factors as age of housing stock and presence of old industrial factories (Bailey, et al., 1994). And while leaded gasoline is no longer sold in the U.S., its prolonged use left lasting lead residues in soil, particularly around the foundations of houses; lead-contaminated soils have been demonstrated to cluster in urban neighborhoods where children have abnormally high lead levels in Baltimore (Mielke, et al., 1983), Minneapolis (Mielke, et al., 1984, 1989), and New Orleans (Mielke, 1992, 1994; Viverette, et al., 1996). Despite the belief that direct exposure leaded gas and house-paint are the primary vectors for lead absorption, other sources now seem equally if not more important (Mielke, 1992).[1]

Exposure to subclinical doses of this neurotoxic metal can be a major hazard for four principal reasons: 1) children absorb up to 50% of lead they ingest, compared to 8% for adults (Hammond, 1982); 2) prolonged exposure to even very low doses of lead can cause neuronal damage during early development, resulting in lasting cognitive and behavioral deficits (Bryce-Smith, 1983; Needleman, 1989); 3) current lead exposures have direct effects on neurotransmitter function, thus influencing cognition and impulse control (Bryce-Smith, 1983; Needleman, 1989; Needleman and Gatsonis, 1990; Cory-Sletcha, 1995; Aschner and Kimelberg, 1996: ch. 9; Needleman et al., 1996); and 4) highest levels of lead uptake are reported for males and minorities -- i.e., those who are most likely to commit violent crimes (Mielke, 1992; Brody, 1994; Viverette, et al. 1996).[2]

Behavioral traits frequently associated with juvenile delinquency, including attention deficit disorder (ADD) or attention deficit hyperactivity disorder (ADHD) as well as learning deficits and dyslexia, have been traced to prolonged exposure to lead (Hunter, 1972; Jones and Rutter, 1983; Rice, 1984; Rabin, 1989; Bryce-Smith, 1983; Needleman, 1989; Needleman; Needleman and Gatsonis, 1990; Cory-Sletcha, 1995; Aschner and Kimelberg, 1996: ch. 9). In two prospective studies, each using different methods, lead absorption has been associated with violence (Denno, 1994; Needleman, et al., 1996), and analyses of the head hair of violent offenders (Cromwell, 1989; Pihl and Ervin, 1990) often show abnormally high levels of lead (Table 1). That subclinical plumbism has behavioral effects is, moreover, consistent with reports of the successful use of detoxification to reduce behavior problems of hyperactive children (Bryce-Smith, 1983; Needleman, 1989).

Manganese has also been associated with subclinical behavioral disturbances due to its effects on catecholamine function (Donaldson, LaBella and McGregor, 1982; Donaldson, 1987; Gibbs, 1995; Aschner and Kimelberg, 1996: Ch. 8). Although industrial manganism can be traced to direct exposure to large quantities of manganese dioxide or manganese nitrate (Fairhall and Neal, 1943; Kilburn, 1987; Cawte and Florence, 1989). chronic exposure to low levels of manganese is probably more relevant to outbursts of violent behavior.

It is hypothesized that manganese uptake in the brain lowers levels of dopamine and serotonin, perhaps through its effects on monoamine oxidase (Aschner and Kimelberg, 1996: ch. 8; Crinella and Hodges, 1994). It is now well known that low levels of serotonin are associated with mood disturbances, poor impulse control, and increases in aggressive behavior (Higley et al, in press) -- effects that have increasingly been treated with Prozac and other psychotropic medications which enhance serotonin function (Masters and McGuire, 1993; Kramer, 1993). The combination of calcium insufficiency and manganese toxicity could therefore be described as "reverse Prozac."

In several studies of prison inmates, analysis of head hair revealed levels of manganese as much as five times higher in violent criminals than in non-violent offenders and controls (Table 1). This relationship was statistically significant for white, Hispanic, and black subsamples (Gottschalk, 1991; Flores-Arce, Schrauzer and Shrestha, 1992; Marlowe, in preparation). Abnormally high manganese levels have also been found in several studies of children with learning disabilities (Bryce-Smith, 1983; Collipp, Chen and Maitinsky, 1983).[3]

Vitamin and mineral deficiencies play a central role in lead and manganese uptake (Bryce-Smith, 1983, 1986). In laboratory studies of environmental exposure to manganese, for example, only animals with deficits in calcium intake show significant manganese retention (Murphy, 1991) . Other dietary factors also play a role. Of particular importance is the finding that rats raised on infant formula or cow's milk have cellular retention of manganese that is four to five times greater than controls raised on human mother's milk (Keen, Bell and Lönnerdal, 1986).

Conversely lithium -- an element which lowers the levels of manganese and other toxic metals in the brain -- is lower in hair samples of violent offenders than controls (Gottschalk, 1991; Marlowe, in preparation). At the population level, homicide rates in Texas were inversely related to levels of lithium in the water supply (Schrauzer and Shrestha, 1990). Other studies of violent or violence-prone individuals have shown abnormally high levels of cadmium and other toxic metals (Bryce-Smith, 1983; Marlowe, Schneider and Bliss, 1991).

Alcohol, known as a major "risk factor" in crime (Wilson and Petersilia, eds., 1995: ch. 13), also needs to be understood as a neurotoxin. Ethanol has both a direct influence on neuronal function and enhances the uptake and functional effects of other neurotoxins (Aschner and Kimelberg, 1996: ch. 3, 6). Although many people obviously do not become violent after drinking, combinations of alcoholism with other neurochemical factors have been found to play an important role in criminal violence (e.g., Masters and McGuire, 1993: ch. 6). At the populational level, therefore, rates of alcoholism -- as measured, for example, by statistical measures of deaths from alcohol related causes -- should not only be correlated with rates of violent crime but should enhance the correlations of violence and indices of other sources of neurotoxicity.

Materials and Methods

The hypothesis that neurotoxicity is among the factors related to violent crime can be explored by correlating ecological data on the distribution of environmental pollutants with reported rates of criminal violence, which vary widely from one county to another for reasons that are not well explained in conventional studies of crime (cf. Wilson and Petersilia, 1995). Amounts of lead and manganese recorded in the Environmental Protection Agency's Toxic Release Inventory (TRI) were correlated with FBI crime

Table 1. Element Levels in Hair of Violent Offenders
Ratio of Violent / Control

Element	Pihl & Ervin[a]	Marlow et al.[b]	Gottschalk et al.,#1[c]	Gottschalk et al.,#2[d]	Gottschalk et al.,#3[e]	Schauss et al.[f]	Schrauzer et al.[g]
Lead	2.31***	2.38*	1.66		Sig.**		
Cadmium	1.50***	2.06*	.68			Sig.**	
Manganese	1.04	1.50	7.33***	3.39***	2.15**	.78	2.28***
Chromium		1.14					
Sodium	1.33	1.41					
Mercury		1.41*					
Silicon		1.26*					
Copper	.95	2.07*			Sig.**		
Cobalt	.91	1.39					
Lithium		0.58*					.28***
Calcium	.87						1.14
Magnesium	.73						.64
Potassium	1.33						
Iron	.95						
Zinc	.97						

*p < .05 ** p = .01 *** p < .0005

Sources:

[a]Pihl RO, Ervin F. Lead and Cadmium Levels in Violent Criminals, *Psych. Reports*; 1990;66:839-844.

[b]Marlowe M, Schneider HG, Bliss LB. Hair: A Mineral Analysis in Emotionally Disturbed and Violence Prone Children. *Biosocial Med. Research*,1 1991;13:169-179.

[c]Gottschalk L, Rebello T, Buchsbaum MS, Tucker HG, Hodges EL. Abnormalities in Trace Elements as Indicators of Aberrant Behavior. *Comprehensive Psychiatry*. 1991;32: 229-237 (Study #1)

[d]Gottschalk L, Rebello T, Buchsbaum MS, Tucker HG, Hodges EL. Abnormalities in Trace Elements as Indicators of Aberrant Behavior. *Comprehensive Psychiatry*. 1991;32: 229-237 (Study #2)

[e]Gottschalk L, Rebello T, Buchsbaum MS, Tucker HG, Hodges EL. Abnormalities in Trace Elements as Indicators of Aberrant Behavior. *Comprehensive Psychiatry*. 1991;32: 229-237 (Study #3).

[f]Schauss AG. Comparative hair-mineral analysis results in a random selected behaviorally "normal" 15-59 year old population and violent criminal offenders. *Int. J. Biosocial Research*. 1981;1:21-41.

[g]Schrauzer GN, Shrestha KP, Flores-Arce MF. Lithium in Scalp Hair of Adults, Students, and Violent Criminals. *Biological Trace Element Research*. 1992;34:161-176.

NOTE: Comparable data on learning disabled children reveals significantly higher levels of lead (ratio 5.75*), cadmium (ratio 1.59*), manganese (ratio 1.43*), chromium (ratio 2.78*) and sodium (ratio 1.78*), and lower levels of cobalt (ratio .70*) and lithium (ratio .55*). Source: Bryce-Smith D. Lead Induced Disorder of Mentation in Children. *Nutrition and Health*.. 1983;1:179-194.

reports from 1165 counties in sixteen states (New York, Pennsylvania, Massachusetts, New Hampshire, Vermont, Georgia, Florida, Alabama, Mississippi, Texas, Illinois, Wisconsin, Minnesota, Arizona, California, and Washington -- states with a total population of over 130 million). These data are, of course, only ecological indices of risk factors that have previously been established in biochemical studies at the individual level.

Analysis of variance (ANOVA) results were computed for the EPA's index of lead and manganese pollution as well as for rates of death from alcoholism (dichotomized at the sample mean). Two-way and three-way ANOVAs, which allow tests of predicted interactions as well as of main effects of each source of neurotoxicity, were also checked with multiple and stepwise regression models using traditional demographic and socio-economic variables.

The data are, of course, imperfect (for a detailed description of all sources, see Masters, Hone and Doshi, 1998). Errors due to inaccurate reporting can be minimized, however, by using the EPA's toxic release inventory only as a simple dichotomous variable (recording the presence or absence of lead or manganese pollution in a county). There are three reasons for this approach. First, prior research has shown that, controlling for demographic and socio-economic factors, the presence of industrial factories likely to use -- or have used -- toxic metals is a significant correlate of individual uptake of lead (Bailey, et al., 1994). Because recorded releases of lead or manganese are correlated with the types of industrial or mining facilities that have left toxic residues in water, buildings, or ground-soil, the TRI may serve to identify counties likely to include long-lasting sites of toxicity. Second, insofar as the TRI provides a measure of current exposure to lead or manganese, there is no reason to assume a linear relationship between recorded toxic releases (measured in thousands of pounds per year) and an individual's toxic uptake (measured by micrograms per deciliter of blood). Because industries responsible for extensive toxic releases are more likely to understate amounts than to attempt to hide them altogether, a dichotomized measure is therefore likely to indicate whether important sources of pollution with lead and manganese are present in a county. And finally, absorption of toxic metals from residues left in soil has now been shown to be a major source of elevated lead in children (Bailey, et al., 1994; Mielke, 1992, 1993, 1994; Mielke and Adams, 1989; Mielke, et al., 1983, 1984a, 1989; Viverette et al., 1996).

It is also the case that FBI crime data are sometimes unreliable. For example, a few counties report no acts of either violent crime or property crime for an entire year -- an outcome that is exceedingly unlikely in most of the locations at issue; such counties need to be dropped from analysis. Remaining reporting errors need not, however, invalidate the statistical analysis: there is no reason to believe that inaccuracies in three different sets of data, which were collected by three different organizations (EPA for toxic releases, FBI for crime, and HHS for alcoholism), can explain highly significant statistical effects including two-way interactions.

Although the EPA's Toxic Release Inventory provides a plausible index of current exposure to toxic metals and the presence of historically important industrial sources of pollution, it does not directly measure exposures in childhood environments that might have caused developmental deficits. Barriers to upward social mobility (particularly among the poor and minorities) suggest, however, that the county of current residence has a reasonable probability of being ecologically similar to environments during infancy. As a result, for much of the population at risk, present exposure to toxic metals may also be a rough index of environments during development.

Results

The Effects of Lead and Manganese. The distribution of manganese and lead pollution is highly skewed: over 75% of counties have no release of either manganese and its compounds, or lead and its compounds recorded in the Environmental Protection Agency's Toxic Release Inventory. Although correlations between pollution from these two metals and several behavioral outcomes are highly significant, the relationship is non-linear. Since toxicity occurs at levels of micrograms per gram, even an "average" level of toxic release (2,540.9 pounds of manganese and 4,101.5 pounds of lead per year) could adversely effect a substantial population.

When counties are dichotomized for the presence or absence of lead and manganese toxic releases, the two way ANOVA (Figure 1) shows that pollution from each of these neurotoxic metals is significantly associated with increased rates of violent crime: in the 166 counties with pollution from both sources, rates of violent offenses were 520 per 100,000 (as compared to the sample average of 350 per 100,000). The effects are highly significant for both manganese toxic releases ($p = .0039$, $F_{1,1139} = 8.36$), and lead toxic releases ($p = .0001$, $F_{1,1139} = 31.22$), with no statistically significant interaction between them.[4]

These effects are confirmed by focusing on counties whose rates of violence are either well above average or unusually low. Among the 310 counties with relatively high rates of the FBI's four categories of violent crime (more than 400/100,000 per year), releases of both manganese and lead are significantly higher than in the 255 low crime counties with rates under 100/100,000 per year (Figure 2). Other statistical measures, such as analysis of the those counties in the top decile of toxic releases of either lead or manganese and the independent effects of toxic releases of the element of each metal and its compounds, are consistent with the hypothesis.

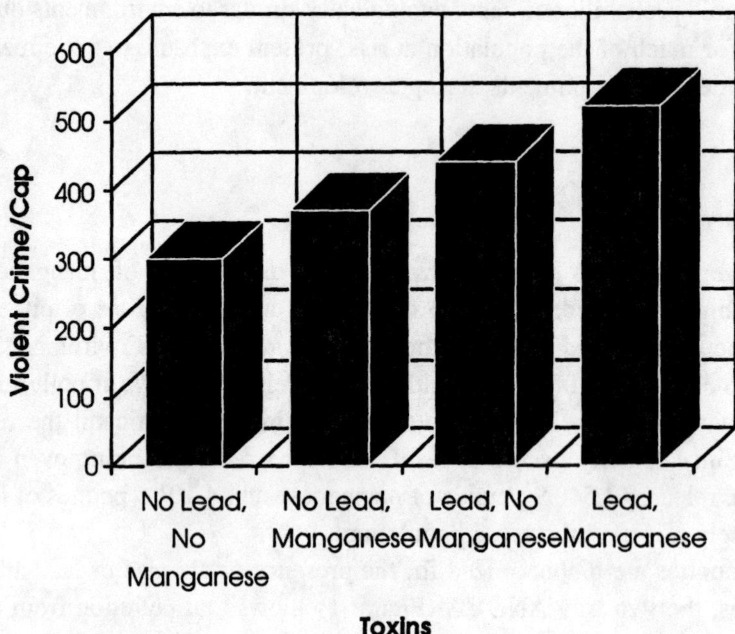

Figure 1. Toxic Release of Lead and Manganese as a Predictor of Rates of Violent Crime, by County (16 State Sample, 1165 Counties)

Source: FBI Crime statistics, 1991 (total rate of homicide, aggravated assault, sexual assault, and robbery). Total releases of toxic metals: Environmental Protection Agency, Toxic Release Inventory, 1991. Parentheses: number of counties. Data from 1141 counties (24 counties deleted from sample for missing data). Significance: total manganese release: p = .0039, $F_{1,1137}$ = 8.36; total lead release: p = .0001, $F_{1,1137}$ = 31.22; interaction between manganese and lead, n.s.
(16 State Sample, 1165 counties)

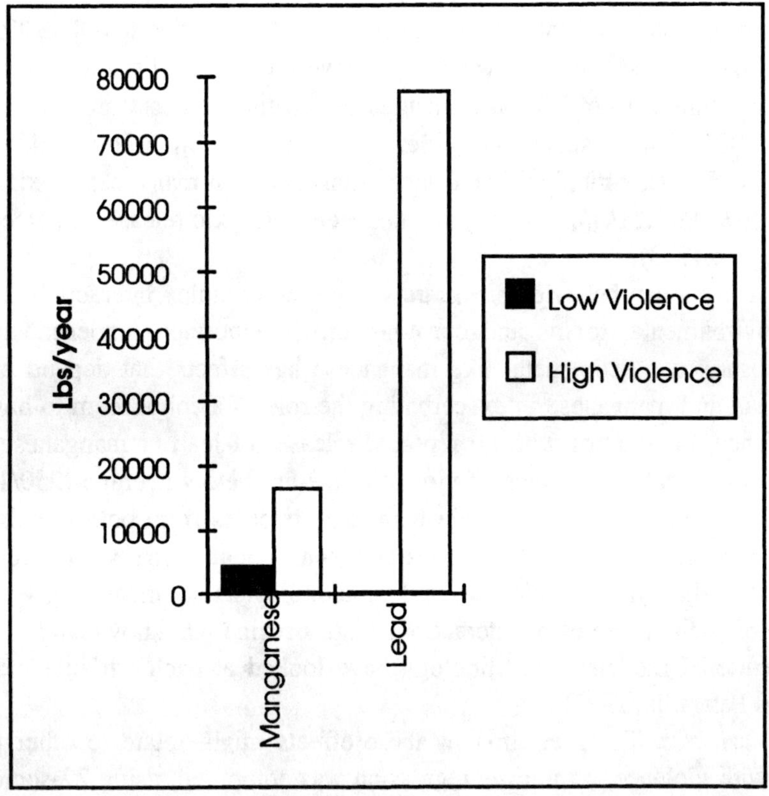

Figure 2. Annual Toxic Release Inventory of Manganese and Lead in Counties with Low and High Crime Rates (16 State Sample, 1165 Counties)

Low violence counties (n = 255): < 100/100,000 per year
High violence counties (n = 310): > 400/100,000 per year
Statistical significance: Manganese, p = .0094; Lead, p =.0027
(1 tailed Chi-square)

These correlations between environmental pollution and crime do not seem to be statistical artifacts. Multiple regression models, predicting the level of pollution in each county on the basis of socioeconomic and ethnic variables (population composition, per capital income, unemployment rates, etc.), explain less than 5% of the variance for either lead or manganese releases. Although few rural counties (with population densities below 20 per square mile) have reports of either lead or manganese releases, the geographic distribution of pollution from these sources seems to be a distinct variable which criminologists have not adequately studied.

Alcoholism. Because consumption of alcohol is frequently associated with violence, the neurotoxicity hypothesis predicts rates of alcoholism at the population level will interact with measures of environmental pollution. This prediction, which provides a more rigorous test of the neurotoxicity hypothesis, was explored by dichotomizing deaths from all forms of alcoholism at the average for the 1156 counties sampled. The three way ANOVA (Figure 3) shows that when high levels of alcoholism are combined with exposure to pollution from lead and manganese, all three factors are highly significant (lead: $p = .0001$, $F_{1,1111} = 48.11$; manganese, $p = .0001$, $F_{1,1111} = 16.84$; alcoholism, $p = .0001$, $F_{1,1111} = 70.22$), with significant interactions between manganese toxic release and alcoholism ($p = .0001$, $F_{1,1111} = 15.51$) and between lead toxic release and alcoholism ($p = .0347$, $F_{1,1111} = 4.4733$).

Students of human behavior have rarely explored complex interactions or synergies between environmental toxins and consumption. In laboratory experiments, as noted above, exposure to a toxic metal like manganese has effects that depend on diet. The effects of lead and manganese in exacerbating the role of alcohol seem to have a similar synergy. Hence, in counties with no reported releases of lead or manganese and below average rates of alcoholism, rates of violent crime are below average (250/100,000). In contrast, the 57 counties of our sample with toxic releases from both metals and above average alcoholism rates have three times as much violent crime, with a county rate of 790/100,000. Although neuroscientists and epidemiologists are increasingly aware of the importance of such synergies or interactions (e.g., Brezina, Orekhova, and Weiss, 1996), most conventional models in criminology have looked at each variable independently (Wilson and Petersilia, 1995).

Other Variables. To ascertain how these effects might relate to other risk factors associated with violence, a multiple regression was computed, using 22 socio-economic and demographic variables to predict rates of violent crime. Consistent with a multi-causal model, nine of these variables had significant effects, predicting over a third of the variance (adjusted $r^2 = .351$). Although such multiple regression equations are notoriously sensitive to the variables included and the linearity of effects, the results are consistent with the hypothesis that both alcoholism and dietary insufficiencies in calcium and other essential elements are risk factors that interact with environmental pollution. Two of the variables with the highest standardized coefficients are alcoholism (which is associated with higher crime rates) and per capita expenditure on welfare (which predicts *lower* rates of violent crime, perhaps because of the contribution of food stamps to improved diet among the poor). Independent contributions of white, black, and hispanic poverty, controlling for rates of unemployment, urbanism, and the overall wealth of a county, also suggest that violent behavior is more likely for those with dietary insufficiencies in calcium and other essential elements which lead to increased uptake of toxic substances in the environment.

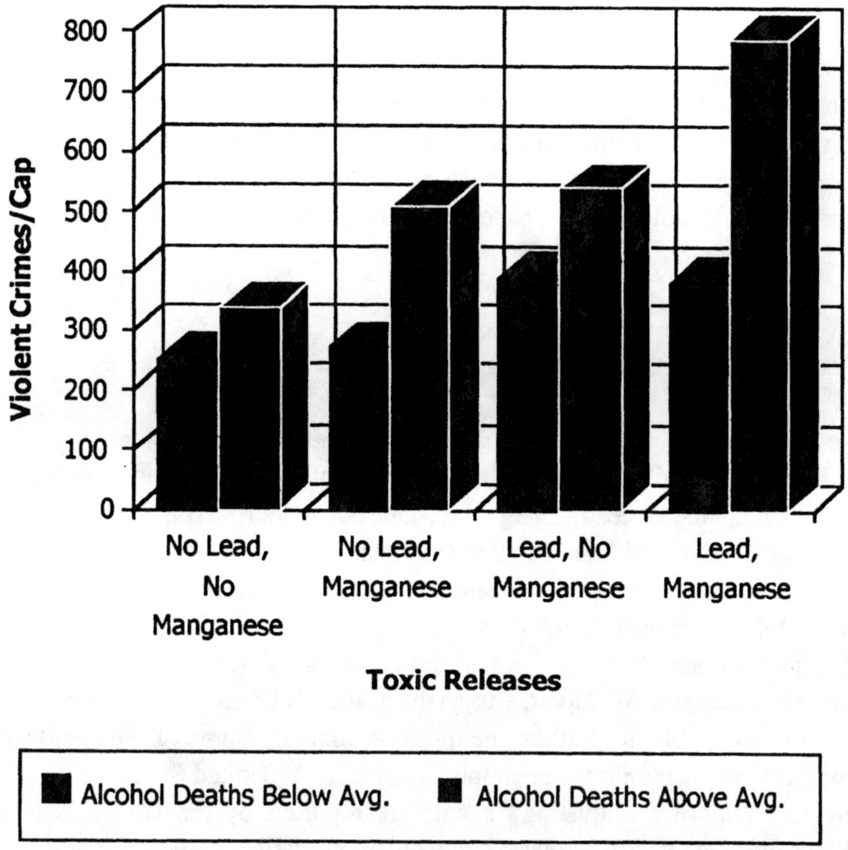

Figure 3. Association of Manganese and Lead Pollution and Rates of Alcoholism with Violent Crime (16 State Sample, 1165 Counties)

NOTES: Three-way ANOVA, data from 1119 counties (22 counties from Table 3 deleted for missing data on alcoholism). Rates of Death from Alcoholism dichotomized at average (42.4/100,000 per year). Significance of main effects: Presence or Absence of Manganese Pollution (TRI): p = .0001, $F_{1,1111}$ = 16.836; Lead Pollution (TRI): p = .0001, $F_{1,1111}$ = 48.114; Alcoholism: p. .0001, $F_{1,1111}$ = 70.217. Significance of interactions: Manganese and alcoholism: p = .0001, $F_{1,1111}$ = 15.512; Lead and Alcoholism: p = .0347, $F_{1,1111}$ = 4.473.

Because leaded paint, accumulated lead in soils along high density traffic corridors, and aging water systems, especially in decaying urban areas, can be an important source of lead and manganese, the data presented here could well underestimate the effects of toxic metals. Because calcium, zinc or other vitamin and mineral insufficiencies are associated with uptake of lead and manganese, moreover, differential vulnerability to toxic chemicals must be considered in explaining high rates of violent crime, particularly among population groups with poor diets and low levels of breast feeding (Fairhall and Neal, 1943; Kilburn, 1987; Cawte and Florence, 1989; Keen, Bell and Lönnerdal, 1986; Allen et al., 1989; Brody, 1994; DiIulio, 1994; Sahi, 1994, Mielke, 1992, 1993; Mielke et al., 1984; Viverette, et al., 1996).[5] The comparison of the regression equations predicting violent and property crime is consistent with this explanation: while white per capital income (overall wealth), unemployment, and poverty have similar effects on both types of criminal behavior, the relationship between violence and ethnicity differs for property crime. As would be predicted by the neurotoxicity hypothesis, moreover, the association between rates of alcoholism and property crime is only marginally significant, with a weaker coefficient than for violent offenses.

Water Fluoridation and Enhanced Toxic Uptake

While the data presented above point to industrial pollution as one source of toxic metals, it is hardly plausible to assume that it is the sole -- or even the principal -- vector causing cellular uptake of lead, manganese, and other neurotoxins. In addition to such sources as leaded paint in old housing and lead residues in soil, an additional factor seems to be involved: the unintended consequence of what has long been viewed as one of our most successful public health interventions since World War II: water fluoridation. Although a few scholars have questioned the consensus that fluoridated water supplies have been beneficial (e.g., Waldbott, Burgstahler, and McKinney, 1978), we here take no position on the general issue. Rather, the question concerns some of the chemical agents now in common use by public water supply systems in the United States.

Three water fluoride "adjusting" agents are reported by the United States Public Health Service's Center for Disease Control "Fluoridation Census" census of water treatment facilities.[6] (1) A 30% solution of fluosilicic acid (H_2SiF_6), which is bought as such and injected via a metering pump into a main at the water plant; this treatment requires addition of a metered amount of neutralizing agent. (2) Granular sodium fluosilicate or sodium silicofluoride (Na_2SiF_6), which is dissolved at the water plant to make up a saturated solution which is metered into the water plant discharge mains -- often without an attempt to deal with the acidity it may induce. (3) Powdered sodium fluoride (NaF), which is made into a saturated solution at the water plant, where it is metered into a main, requiring no pH adjustment. In addition, naturally occurring fluoride may be present in some local water supplies at a level sufficient to meet the so-called "optimum" fluoride level of 1 ppm. Such water may be used without further adjustment exception that any concentration over 4 ppm must be reduced.

Of these agents, the silicofluorides (fluosilicic acid and sodium fluosilicate) are unusual for several reasons. Contrary to statement in a CDC manual for fluoridation plant operators, they are not neutralizable as readily as other acids or salts of strong acids. Silicofluoride anion must first undergo a fairly slow dissociation to release all the available fluoride and silica by-products. Ultimately, this reaction has the concomitant effect of lowering pH -- that is, increasing acidity. In fact, chemical research demonstrated as far back as the 1920s that -- depending on precise conditions of acidity and temperature -- it can take up to twenty minutes to reach a final state of dissociation. Recent laboratory tests confirm these results (Burgstahler, personal communication).

The specifics of silicofluoride chemistry have important consequences for water at the user's faucet. Despite the expectation that fluoride dissociation is complete, it is possible that some partially dissociated residues of silicofluoride remain in water. Silicofluorides and the precursor silicon tetrafluoride (SiF_4) are corrosive acids and known toxins. Even if dissociation is complete, the chemical reactions involved in silicofluoride dissociation lower pH, resulting in increased acidity (Burgstahler, personal communication). There is reason to believe that either or both of these effects may facilitate lead transport across the gut membrane into the blood.[7].

We have conducted extensive analysis to assess the possibility that silicofluoride usage is associated with enhanced uptake of lead and increased rates of crime (and other social dysfunction). To test this hypothesis, data from Massachusetts communities in 1990-1991 were analyzed to correlate blood lead levels of children aged 0-4 with lead levels and fluoridation agents in public water supplies. Multiple regression analysis combined these variables with socio-economic and demographic factors for each community to predict local rates of behaviors previously associated with neurotoxicity, including poor school performance and rates of violent crime.

Blood level data are taken from a previously reported comprehensive screening program analyzing capillary blood from approximately 280,000 children from 350 Massachusetts communities, along with venous blood from a smaller sample of approximately 100,000 children (Bailey, et al., 1994; Sargent, et al., 1995). Because the focus is on environmental variables, individual measures are aggregated for the 227 communities with data on lead levels, fluoridation agents, age of housing, and other socio-economic, demographic, and behavioral measures. Due to missing data, a few of these communities had to be dropped from statistical analysis.

For each community, lead uptake was assessed by average blood levels of lead (μg/dL) as well as by percent of children tested with lead levels greater than the CDC maximum tolerable level of 10 μg/dL. Data for capillary blood were used in statewide multivariate assessments since they provide the best population-level sample, especially for small towns. Because venous lead measures rely on smaller samples and may represent follow-up examination of children already found to have elevated capillary blood, this measure was only used to ascertain incidence rates of children exceeding the CDC maximum tolerable lead level. Lead in public water supplies was measured as the community's reported average of 90th percentile first draw in parts per million (ppm). Behavioral measures included community rates of all violent and property crimes (FBI), percent adults failing to complete high school and percent welfare households (US Census), and average scores on standardized educational tests (MEAP).

Although reported lead levels in public water supplies are significantly correlated with lead uptake in children, the specific chemical agents used in fluoridation are an important intervening variable. In 51 towns using fluorosilicic acid (H_2SiF_6) and 7 towns using sodium silicofluoride (Na_2SiF_6), average levels of capillary blood in children 0 to 4 were respectively 2.78 μg/dL and 2.66 μg/dL. In contrast, children's blood levels were 2.02 μg/dL in the 116 towns that did not fluoridate and 2.07 μg/dL in the 39 towns using sodium fluoride (NaF). (One way ANOVA, $p = .0006$; DA 3, 209, F 6.073). Using either capillary or venous blood measures for each community, similar differences were found in the percent of children screened whose blood lead levels were above 10 μg/dL. In a sample of 30 non fluoridated towns (total population 837,000), only 0.76% of children had venous blood lead in excess of 10 μg/dL, whereas in 30 comparable towns using silicofluoride water treatment (population 845,100), the rate was 1.94% (a risk ratio of 2.55; $p < .0001$ by chi-square).

Levels of lead in water supplies were also substantially above the 15ppb action level set by the EPA in many -- but not all – of the towns using silicofluorides. In Massachusetts communities that introduced the use of fluorosilicic acid after 1975, average 90th percentile first draw lead levels were 40.3 ppb, compared to those that started using fluorosilicic acid earlier (average = 31.1 ppb), indicating that fluoridation procedures are probably a key factor. Among sampled communities using either fluorosilicic acid or sodium silicofluoride, moreover, significantly higher levels of blood lead are only found in the subset of systems which also have above average levels of lead in water (which suggests that the silicofluorides may act indirectly by enhancing solubility or organic uptake of lead). Multivariate analysis reveals that the resulting differences in children's blood lead levels were significant predictors of communities with higher rates of behaviors previously associated with chronic lead neurotoxicity, including not only violent crime but learning deficits, high school drop out, and increased numbers on welfare (Table 2).

Table 2. Children's Capillary Lead Blood and Rates of Welfare Households, High School Dropout and Crime in Massachusetts Communities

	Population Density	Income per Capita	% Black	% Hispanic	% Houses pre 1950	Silicofluoride Agent	Lead in Water	Capillary Blood Lead	r-square	F
% Welfare Households	(.105)*	(.420)****	n.s.	.502****	.238****	n.s.	n.s	.124*	0.752	80.97
% High School Dropouts	n.s.	(.607)****	n.s.	.226****	.281****	n.s	n.s	.088*	0.669	51.45
Violent Crimes/Capita	n.s	(.215)*	.391****	.170*	n.s.	n.s.	n.s.	.228***	0.634	33.73
Property Crimes/Capita	n.s.	(.201)*	n.s.	.241*	(.150)?	0.159?	n.s	.205*	0.303	9.9

Entries are standardized coefficients (parentheses = negative sign)
p values:**** $p < .0001$, *** $p < .0005$, ** $p < .001$, * $p < .01$. Marginally significant variables (?) $p < .10$

These findings reveal an unexpected environmental factor -- itself generated by a public policy designed to enhance health -- that increases rates of violent crime. Moreover, silicofluoride usage may be an important contributor to the racial differences in criminal behavior which have been so widely debated and so poorly understood (DeIulio, 1994). Blacks are unusually susceptible to lead uptake and its effects on behavior (Masters, et al., 1997). When Massachusetts communities are divided into those that have first draw lead levels below and above the 15ppb action level set by the EPA, into those that do and do not use silicofluorides, and into those with low, intermediate, and high percentages of blacks, an analysis of variance of rates of violent crime reveals a highly significant three-way interaction (p = .0003) as well as significant effects of all three independent variables (Table 3). Preliminary analysis of comparable data from two additional states -- West Virginia and Georgia -- confirms that communities using silicofluorides in water treatment average crime rates that are twice those found where these compounds are not added to the water -- and, in Georgia, that these effects are highest in communities with larger than average percentages of blacks in the population .

Table 3: Percent Black Population, Silicofluoride Usage, and Lead in Water as Predictors of Rates of Violent Crime (per 100,000 population)

	Less than .02% Black		Between .02 and .05 Black		Over .05 Black	
	No Silico-fluoride	Silico-fluoride	No Silico-fluoride	Silico-fluoride	No Silico-fluoride	Silico-fluoride
Less than 15pbb	210	276	357	581	232	1300
	71	17	11	3	5	3
Over 15pbb	237	238	300	477	2174	1508
	27	31	3	8	1	2

Significance:
Dichotomized level of lead: p = .0001 (DF 1,153; F 16.73)
Percentage blacks: p = .0001, DF 2, 153, F55.515)
Interaction of lead and # black: p = .0001
Silicofluoride agent: p. 074; DF2,153; F 3.25)
Interaction of lead and agent: p = .09992
Interaction of % Black and agent: p. n.s
Three way interaction of level of lead, % black and fluoridating agent: p. .0003; DF 2, 153;

To establish a full understanding of the bioinorganic and neurochemical processes underlying the enhanced lead uptake here associated with solicofluorides, animal testing will be required. While low "hardness" and low pH (high acidity) may be possible explanations for our findings, the various methods of water fluoridation have never been exhaustively studied for effects on health and behavior, and other practices in public water systems may also be implicated. Further research is urgently needed to explore the potential risks of water treatment procedures that apparently have the unintended effect of enhancing lead neurotoxicity, particularly in large communities using fluorosilicic acid or sodium silicofluoride to fluoridate water supplies.

Discussion

Describing violence in the United States as "a public health emergency," two leading physicians have asserted: "Regarding violence in our society as purely a sociologic matter, or one of law enforcement, has led to unmitigated failure. It is time to test further whether violence can be amenable to medical/public health interventions" (Koop and Lundberg, 1992). The hypothesized relationships between brain biochemistry, diet, alcohol and drug usage, water treatment practices, neurotoxic metals and violent behavior, while not definitive, support this view. This approach may also explain geographical and historical differences in rates of violence that often seem puzzling.[8]

From an evolutionary perspective, moreover, the existence of a correlation between dietary deficiencies, toxic uptake, and aggressive behavior is not difficult to explain. There is no reason to suppose that if the mechanisms described above emerged in hominid evolution, they would have been subjected to negative selection pressures. Well-nourished individuals normally excrete metal ions beyond the levels naturally needed; glia detoxify the brain from neurotoxics that cross the blood-brain barrier. While lead is not likely to have been a major toxin in ancestral hominid environments, manganese is the twelfth most abundant metal in the earth's soil, and is often found today in such foods as blueberries, wheat bran, dried legumes, nuts, lettuce, beet tops, and pineapple -- but not in meat or fish (USDA, 1989: 177). Throughout hominid evolution, therefore, the neurotoxic effects of manganese might have been associated with increased aggressiveness in times of poor food availability, especially among marginal males. As the behavioral strategies of Hanuman langurs indicate, such aggressive behavior during food shortages would probably be adaptive.

If confirmed, the neurotoxicity hypothesis will have obvious implications for public policy. Crime prevention and improved educational performance may be greatly enhanced by parent-training in proper diet. Breast feeding and vitamin supplementation, which some studies suggest can increase IQ (Bryce-Smith, 1983; Needleman, 1989; Lucas et al., 1992; Rogan and Gladen, 1993; Benton and Buts, 1990; Benton and Cook, 1991). could also be useful in improving school performance and cognitive development. Pre-school programs, which have been found to reduce rates of crime (Schweinhart, et al., 1993; Zervignon-Hakes and Graham, 1994), may need to be evaluated in terms of their effects on diet rather than by conventional educational assessments. If releases of neurotoxic metals are associated with rates of crime, as this study suggests, reducing environmental pollution would take on higher priority; even where removal can be questioned -- as is the case with leaded house paint -- dust control methods can reduce exposure and uptake of lead (Mielke, et al., 1992). In our criminal justice system, because existing means of predicting recidivism are little better than chance, it has been proposed that the assay of toxic metals in head hair might provide an inexpensive marker for potential violence in probation decisions (Gibbs, 1995). With adequate identification of the precise biochemical imbalances associated with violent crime, vitamin and mineral normalization could contribute to improved rehabilitation.

This is a classic illustration of a "win-win" approach. It is "soft" or sensitive to the needs of children for healthy development in a decent environment. Moreover, while this perspective identifies environmental factors that increase criminal behavior, it also emphasizes the role of life-style choices that mediate toxic uptake. As a result, the neurotoxicity hypothesis rejects such disclaimers of responsibility as the infamous "Twinkie Defense," insisting instead that the adult be held responsible for his or her actions (including especially the individual's diet and alcohol consumption). Once a criminal act has been committed, therefore, this approach is "tough" in two senses: first, it holds the offender responsible for actions on the grounds that many of the relevant risk factors are under individual control; and second, it provides resources and options that could be called "kind but unusual punishment" -- such as a choice among probationary conditions, one of which might include mineral supplementation or dietary management (Masters and McGuire, 1993).

Given the extraordinary level of violence in urban America and the failure of traditional policies to meet it, further confirmation of the hypothesized relationships between dietary deficiencies, neurotoxic uptake, and violence is therefore urgently needed. Of particular importance will be direct studies correlating environmental exposure, diet, neurotoxic uptake, and behavior. Equally important will be experimental studies of the effects of vitamin and mineral normalization for violent offenders. Although changes in public policy should not be implemented without further evidence, the neurotoxicity hypothesis may require important changes in the way Americans think about crime.

REFERENCES

Allen, P.K., L.G. Borrud, R.S. McPherson, G.R. Newell, M.Z. Nichaman, and P.C. Pillow. (1989). "Food Group Contributions to Nutrient Intake in Whites, Blacks, and Mexican Americans in Texas." *J. Am. Diet Assn.* 89:1061-1069.

Aschner, M. and H.K. Kimelberg, eds. (1996). *Role of Glia in Neurotoxicity*. Boca Raton, FL, CRC Press.

Bailey, A.J., J.D. Sargent, D.C. Goodman, J. Freeman, and M.J. Brown. (1994). "Poisoned Landscapes: The Epidemiology of Environmental Lead Exposure in Massachusetts Children 1990-1991." *Social Science Medicine* 39: 757-766.

Benton, D. and J.P. Buts (1990). "Vitamin/mineral Supplementation and Intelligence. *Lancet.* 12:1158-1160.

Benton, D. and R. Cook (1991). "Vitamin and Mineral Supplements Improve the Intelligence Scores and Concentration of Six-year-old Children " *Pers. Ind. Diff*, 12: 1151-1158.

Brezina, V., I.V. Orekhova, and K.R. Weiss. (1996). "Functional Uncoupling of Linked Neurotransmitter Effects by Combinatorial Convergence," *Science*: 273:806-810.

Brody, D. (1994). "Blood Lead Levels in the U. S. Population".*JAMA* 1994; 242: 277-283.

Bryce-Smith, D. (1983). "Lead Induced Disorder of Mentation in Children." *Nutrition and Health*, 1: 179-194.

Bryce-Smith, D. (1986). "Environmental Chemical Influences on Behaviour and Mentation," *Chem. Soc. Rev.*, 15:93-123.

Cawte, J. and M.T. Florence. (1989). "A Manganic Milieu in North Australia." *Int. J. Biosocial Med Res* 11: 43-56.

Collipp, P.J., S.Y. Chen, and S. Maitinsky. (1983). "Manganese in Infant Formulas and Learning Disability." *Ann. Nutr. Metabl.* 27: 488-494.

Cory-Sletcha, D.A. (1995). "Relationships between Lead Induced Learning Impairments and Changes in Dopaminergic, Cholinergic, and Glutamatergic Neurotransmitter System Functioning." *Ann. Rev. Phmacol. and Toxicol.*, 35: 391-45.

Crinella, F. and E.H. Hodges (1994). "Effects of Nutritional Supplementation on Violent Behavior of Incarcerated Youthful Offenders." Dept. Pediatrics, Univ. Cal. Irvine, 1994, unpublished.

Cromwell, P.E., et al. (1989). "Hair Mineral Analysis: Biochemical Imbalances and Violent Criminal Behavior." *Psych. Rep,* 1989; 64: 259-266

Denno, D.W. (1994). "Gender, Crime, and the Criminal Law Defenses," *J. Criminal Law and Criminology*, 85:80-180.

DiIulio, J.J. (1994). "The Question of Black Crime," *Public Interest*, 1994; 117: 3-32.

Donaldson, J., F.S. LaBella, and D. McGregor. (1982). "Manganese Neurotoxicity: A Model for Free Radical Mediated Neurodegeneration?" *Can. J. Physiol. Pharmacol* 60: 1398-1405.

Donaldson, J. (1987) "The Physiopathologic Significance of Manganese in Brain: Its Relation to Schizophrenia and Neurodegenerative Disorders." *Neurotoxicol.* 1987; 8: 451-462.

Ervin, B. and D. Reed, eds. (1993). *Nutrition Monitoring in the U.S., Chartbook I: Selected Findings from the National Nutrition Monitoring and Related Research Program.* Hyattsville, MD, Public Health Service.

Fairhall, L.T. and P.A. Neal. (1943). *Industrial Manganese Poisoning*; National Institute of Health Bulletin, No. 182. Washington, DC: U. S. Government Printing Office.

Gibbs, W. (1995). "Seeking the Criminal Element." *Sci.Am.* 1995; 272: 100-107.

Gottschalk, L, T. Rebello, M.S. Buchsbaum, H.G. Tucker, and E.L. Hodges. (1991). "Abnormalities in Trace Elements as Indicators of Aberrant Behavior." *Comp. Psych* 32:229-237.

Hammond, P.B..(1982). In: *Lead Absorption in Children*, J. J. Chisholm and D.M. O'Hara, eds. Baltimore, Urban and Schwartzenberg, pp 11-20.

Highley, J.D., P.T. Mehlman, D.M. Taub, S.B. Highle,B. Fernald, J.L. Vickers, S.G. Lindell, S.J. Suomi, M. Linnoila. In Press "Excessive Mortality in Young Free-Ranging Nonhuman Primates with Low CSF 3-HIAA Concentrations.

Hunter, D. (1972). *Diseases of Occupation.* Boston, Little Brown.

Johnson, L. (199). *Sources of Residential Lead in Rural New England.* (Thesis, Dept Chem., Dartmouth College)

Jones, R.R. and M. Rutter, eds. (1983). *Lead versus Health* New York, John Wiley.

Keen, C.L., J.G. Bell, and B. Lönnerdal. (1986). "The Effect of Age on Manganese Uptake and Retention from Milk and Infant Formulas in Rats."*J. Nutrition.* 116:395-402

Kilburn, C. (1987). "Manganese, Malformation and Motor Disorders: Findings in a Manganese exposed population." *Neurotoxicol.* 1987; 30: 421-430.

Koop, C.E. and G.D. Lundberg G.D. (1992). "Violence in America: A Public Health Emergency." *JAMA*, 267: 3075-3076.

Kramer, P. (1993). *Listening to Prozac* . New York, Viking Press, 1993.

Lovewell, M. (1995).*Vineyard Gazette*, 11 July, p. 6.

Lucas, A. et al. (1992). "Breast-milk and subsequent intelligence quotient in children born preterm." *Lancet* 1992 339: 261-284.

Marlowe, M. (In prep.) "Hair Mineral Analysis in Emotionally Disturbed and Violence Prone Youth. Manuscript, Appalachian State University, Boone, NC. In Preparation.

Marlowe, M., H.G. Schneider, and L.B.Bliss (1991).. "Hair: A Mineral Analysis in Emotionally Disturbed and Violence Prone Children." *Biosocial Med Res.* 1991; 13: 1044-81.

Masters, R., D.J. Grelotti, B.T. Hone, D. Gonzalez, and D. Jones Jr. (1997) "Brain Biochemistry and Social Status: the Neurotoxicity Hypothesis." In E. White. ed.,.*Intelligence, Political Inequality and Public Policy.* Westport, CT: Praeger. pp. 141-87.

Roger D. Masters, R. D., Hone, B. and Doshi, A. (1998) "Environmental Pollution, Neurotoxicity, and Criminal Violence,"in J. Rose, ed., *Aspects of Environmental Toxicity.* London: Gordon & Breach, pp. 13-48.

Masters, R. and M.T. McGuire, eds. (1993).*The Neurotransmitter Revolution*,Carbondale, S. Ill. Univ. Press.

Mielke, H.W. (1992). "Lead Dust-Contaminated Communities and Minority Health: A New Paradigm," in B.L. Johnson, R.C. Williams, and C.M. Harris, eds., *The National Minority Health Conference*, Princeton: Princeton Scientific Publishing Co.

Mielke, H.W. (1993). "Lead Dust Contaminated U.S.A. Communities: Comparison of Louisiana and Minnesota," *Applied Geochemistry,* Sup. 2: 257-261.

Mielke, H.W. (1994). "Lead in New Orleans Soils: New Images of an Urban Environment," *Environmental Geochemistry and Health,* 16: 123-128.

Mielke, H.W., J.E. Adams, B. Huff, J. Pepersack, P.L. Reagan, D. Stoppel and P.W. Mielke, Jr. (1992). "Dust Control as a Means of Reducing Inner-City Childhood Pb Exposure, *Trace Substances in Environmental Health* 15: 121-128.

Mielke, H.W. and J.L. Adams. (1989). *Environmental Lead Risk in the Twin Cities*, Minneapolis, Minn.: University of Minnesota, Center for Urban and Regional Affairs.

Mielke, H.W., J.L. Adams, P. L. Reagan, and P. W. Mielke, Jr. (1989). "Soil-dust Lead and Childhood Lead Exposure as a Function of City Size and Community Traffic Flow: the Case for Lead Abatement in Minnesota," in B.E. Davies and B.G. Wixson, eds., *Lead in Soil: Issues and Guidelines, Supplement to* Environmental Geochemistry and Health, 9: 253-271.

Mielke, H.W., J.C. Anderson, K.J. Berry, P.W. Mielke, R.L.Chaney, and M. Leech. (1983). "Lead Concentrations in Innner-City Soils As a Factor in the Child Lead Problem," *American Journal of Public Health* 73: 1366-1369.

Mielke, H.W., B. Blake, S. Burroughs, and N. Hassinger. (1984a). "Urban Lead Levels in Minneapolis: The Case of the Hmong Children," *Environmental Research*, 34: 64-76.

Mielke, H.W., S.Burroughs, R.Wade, T. Yarrow, P.W. Mielke (1984b), "Urban Lead in Minnesota: Soil Transect Results of Four Cities," *Jounral of the Minnesota Academy of Science,* 50: 19-24.

Murphy, V.A., et al. (1991). "Elevation of Brain Manganese in Calcium-Deficient Rats." *NeuroToxicology,* 12: 255-264.

National Center for Health Statistics. (1994).*Advance Data Number 258*; Hyattsville, MD, Public Health Service.

Needleman, H. ed. (1992). *Human Lead Exposure* . Boca Raton, FL: CRC Press.

Needleman, H., J.A. Riess, M.J. Tobin, G.E. Blesecker and J.B. Greenhouse (1996). "Bone Lead Levels and Delinquent Behavior". *Journal of the American Medical Assn,* 275: 363-369.

Needleman, H. (1990). "The Long-term Effects of Exposure to Low Doses of Lead in Childhood,"*NE Journ. Medicine*; 1990; 322: 83-88.

Needleman, H. and C. A. Gatsonis, (1990). "Low-level Lead Exposure and the IQ of Children: a Meta-analysis of Modern Studies.*JAMA* 263: 673-678.

New York Times, 23 July 1995, Sect. 4, pp. 1,4.

Pihl, R.O. and F. Ervin (1990). "Lead and Cadmium Levels in Violent Criminals." *Psych. Rep.* 66: 839-844.

Pirkle J. et al. (1994). "The Decline in Blood Lead Levels in the United States." *JAMA* 272:284-291.

Rabin, R. (1989)."Warnings Unheeded: A History of Child Lead Poisoning." *Am. J. Publ. Health*, 79: 668-674.

Raine, A. (1993).*The Psychopathology of Crime*. San Diego, Academic Press.

Rice, D.C. (1984). "Behavioral Deficit (Delayed Matching Sample) in Monkeys Exposed from Birth to Low Levels of Lead."*Toxicol. Applied Pharm*, 75: 337-345.

Rogan, W.J. and B.C. Gladen (1993). "Breast-feeding and cognitive development." *Early Human Development* ; 31: 181-193.

Sahi, T. (1994). "Genetics and epidemiology of adult-type hypolactasia." *Scand. J. Gastroenterol.*; 29Suppl 202: 7-20.

Sargent J. D., Brown M. J., Freeman J. L., Bailey, A., Goodman, D.C. and Freeman D. H. (1995). "Childhood Lead Poisoning in Massachusetts: Its Association with Sociodemographic and Housing Characteristics,"*Am J Public Health* 85: 528-534

Sampson, J. B.; Crow, J. P., Strong, M. and Beckman, J. S. (1997). "Copper/Zinc Superoxide Dismutase in Familial Amyotropic Lateral Sclerosis," in M. Yasui, M. M. Stropng, K. Ota, and M. A. Verity, *Mineral and Metal Neruotoxicology* (Boca Raton, CRC Press.

Schrauzer, G.N. and K.P. Shrestha (1990). "Lithium in Drinking Water and the Incidences of Crimes, Suicides, and Arrests Related to Drug Addictions." *Biol. Trace Elem. Res.*; 25: 105-113.

Schrauzer, G.N., K.P. Shresta, and M.F. Flores-Arce. (1992). "Lithium in Scalp Hair of Adults, Students, and Violent Criminals. *Biological Trace Element Research*, 34: 161-76.

Schweinhart, L., H. Barnes, and D. Weikart. (1993) *Significant Benefits*. Ypsilanti, MI: High Scope Press, 1993.

U.S. Census Bureau. (1994). *USA Counties on CD-Rom*, based on *State and Metropolitan Area Data Book*, 1982, 1986 and 1991, Washington, D.C.: Government Printing Office

U. S. Department of Agriculture. (1899). *Nutrients in Food--Their Digestion, Absorption and Metabolism*. Washington, D.C.: Government Printing Office.

U.S. Department of Health and Human Services. (1994). NIH Publ No. 94-3747. County Alcohol Problem Indicators, 1986-1990, U.S. Alcohol Epidemiological Data Reference Manual, Vol. 3, Fourth edition.

Viverette, L., H.W. Mielke, M. Brisco, A. Dixon, J. Schaefer, and K. Pierre. (1996). "Environmental Health in Minority and Other Underserved Populations: Benign Methods for Identifying Lead Hazards at Day Care Centres of New Orleans," *Environmental Geochemistry and Health*, 18: 41-45.

Waldbott, G. L., Burgstahler, A.W., and McKinney, H. L. (1978). *Fluoridation: the Great Dilemma* Lawrence, KS: Coronado Press.

Walsh, W. J., Isaacson, H. R., Rehman, F and Hall, A. (1997). "Elevated blood copper/zinc ratios in assaultive young males," *Physiology and Behavior* 62: 327-29.

Wilson, J.Q. and J. Petersilia, eds. (1995). *Crime*. San Francisco: Institute for Contemporary Studies

Zervigon-Hakes, A. and M. Graham. (1994). *Florida's Children: Their Future is In Our Hands*. Tallahassee, Florida: Florida State University Center for Prevention and Early Intervention Policy

ENDNOTES

1 In addition to industrial pollution, aging public water supplies may also be dangerous sources of neurotoxic metals. For example, the superintendent of the Edgartown, Massachusetts water department recently described renovations in the town's water system: "When we dismantled the standpipe, we found two and a half feet (sic) of a substance with the consistency of pudding." Mark Lovewell, *Vineyard Gazette*, 11 July 1995, p. 6. In multi-story buildings, water supplies in the upper floors may be particularly high in lead: even in a new science building at Dartmouth College, where the first three floors had lead levels around the EPA water standard of 15• g/dL, the fourth floor faucet had levels between 100 and 200 • g/dL (Johnson, 1993).

2 Analysis of lead in head hair of large samples over the last decades reveals lead levels between 30% and 100% higher among blacks than whites (Robert Smith, Doctor's Data Lab., W. Chicago, IL, pers. com.)

3 Specialists in one treatment center report, however, that some violent offenders have abnormally *low* levels of manganese, and respond favorably to treatments that include supplements of this metal. (R. Isaacson, Pfeiffer Treatment Center, Napierville, IL, pers. comm.) This need not contradict the neurotoxicity hypothesis since it is well established that "acute symptoms of Mn *deficiency or excess* (poisoning) are primarily related to malfunctioning of the peripheral and central nervous systems" (Wedler, in Aschner and Kimelberg, eds., 1996: 156, italics added). In contrast to the precise effects of excessive levels of manganese, however, mechanisms linking manganese deficiency to violent behavior have not been clearly proposed.

4 These results are not a result of the convention used: significant effects were also found when dichotomizing TRI statistics at the 90th percentile (ANOVA results: manganese, p = .0001, F 15.82; lead, p = .0009, F 11.11, lead x manganese interaction, p - .0716, F 3.25). In the 48 counties in the highest decile of both lead pollution (> 8594 lbs/yr) and manganese pollution (>5879 lbs/yr), the frequency of violent crimes averaged 600/100,000 -- or twice the rate of the 917 counties in the lowest 90% of toxic releases for both elements. Similar results had been obtained from the first state analyzed (NY), the first four state subsample (NY, IL, FL, CA), and an eight-state subsample (NY,IL, FL, CA, AL, MS, WI, MN), as well as from TRI reports of elemental releases of lead and manganese as well as their compounds, analyzed separately. (Masters et al., in press).

5 National Center for Health Statistics, *Advance Data Number 258*; Hyattsville, MD, Public Health Service, 1994. Table 1. Data are based on two national probability samples (National Health and Nutrition Surveys I and III, 1976-1980 and 1988-91). Although intake of calcium has risen somewhat more among blacks than whites over this period, in 1988-91, black males 16-19 years old still had only 78% the calcium intake (1076 mg/day) of comparable white males (1373 mg/day). RDA for adolescents is 1200 mg/day.

6 *Fluoridation Census 1992* (Atlanta, GA: USPHS Centers for Disease Control, 1993).

7 Although it is well known that "overall nutritional status and eating behavior appears to influence the absorption and toxicity potential of lead in several ways" (Daland R. Juberg, *Lead and Human Health* [New York: American Council on Science and Health, 1997], p. 9), a recent update on lead toxicity notes that "the exact mechanisms of absorption are unknown" (Henry Abadin and Fernando Llados, *Draft Toxicological Profile on Lead,* [Atlanta, GA: Agency for Toxic Substances and Disease Registry, Department of Health and Human Services, August 1997], pp. 202-3). This survey does not refer to studies relevant to silicofluorides, but it does indicate that smaller lead particles are more easily dissolved in gastric acid than larger ones (ibid., p. 167). Anything that dissolves lead into smaller particles or increases gastric acidity might therefore increase lead uptake to the blood. An additional mechanism of behavioral dysfunction may be triggered by silicofluoride usage, since lowering pH has the effect of increasing the binding of copper relative to zinc (Sampson, et al, 1997) -- and higher copper/zinc ratios have been associated with high rates of aggressive and violent behavior (William Walsh, et al., 1997).

8 Recent reports of a decline in violent crimes in New York and other major cities have been described as "mysterious," especially since prevailing explanations do not account for all of the variation observed (*N. Y. Times*, 23 July 1995, Sect. 4, pp. 1, 4). Given the 15-20 year time-lag between the effects of lead on neonatal and infant development and the onset of criminal violence, reductions in lead and increases in calcium intake (note 4) begun in the late 1970's may only now have begun to lower crime rates. Further research will be needed to test this aspect of the neurotoxicity hypothesis.

Chapter 7

OVERCOMING PROCESS HURDLES IN SOS ANALYSIS: LAND RIGHTS FOR INDIGENOUS PEOPLES

Simon Montagu
Australia

In Australia, and in many other countries around the world, the question of right to land for the displaced, indigenous peoples of these countries has produced much public interest and discussion. In this SOS analysis, this question will be investigated, and used to highlight some of the different ways of generating SOS solutions.

Table 1 sets out this issue, as it directly applies to Australia, in an SOS table. This table presents four goals and proposes two alternatives. The four goals are described below:

Conservative: This conservative goal seeks to ensure that no matter what alternative is eventually adopted, that the costs to the taxpayer, involved in adopting this alternative, do not increase;

Liberal: This liberal goal seeks to offer Australian Aborigines the right to self-determination and control, by ensuring them land rights;

Liberal: The second liberal goal seeks to grant land rights as a moralistic attempt to provide some measure of remuneration for the colonization and alienation of land that once belonged to these people;

Neutral: The neutral goal, supported by both of the other parties, seeks to ensure that whatever alternative is adopted, that it helps ensure self-support for the aboriginal community, lessening their dependence on welfare assistance.

The two alternatives proposed for this issue represent a liberal and conservative perspective of this problem. The liberal alternative calls upon the government to either purchase, or use its eminent domain powers to reacquire (on behalf of the aboriginal community) the traditional lands of these people. The conservative alternative on the other hand, stresses the use of private funds (of the communities, supporters etc.) to acquire only that land which private owners are prepared to sell.

TABLE 1
Aboriginal Land Rights in Australia

Goals / Alternatives	C * No New Taxes Weights C=3 N=2 L=1	L * Remuneration Weights C=1 N=2 L=3	L * Self-Determ. Weights C=1 N=2 L=3	N * Decreased Welfare Depend Weights C=2 N=2 L=2	TOTALS		
					Conserv.	Lib.	Neutral
CONSERV. ALT. * Private Buy-ups of available land.	4	2	2	3			
LIB. ALT. * Govern. buy-ups/ 'takings' of trad. Aboriginal land	2	4	4	3			
NEUT. ALT. * Bit of Both	3	3	3	3			
S.O.S. ALT.							

I. GENERATING AN SOS ALTERNATIVE

There are perhaps fifteen potential ways of arriving at super-optimum solutions. These are: Expanding the resources, Setting higher goals, Big benefits to one side, but small costs to other, Use a third-party benefactor, Decrease the source of conflict, Develop multi-faceted package, Redefine the problem, Raise the benefits and lower costs, Technological fix, Sequential SOS, Combining the alternatives, Remove cause of problem, Contracting out, Use international communities, and Socialization.

Of these, there are three that are particularly relevant to the aboriginal land rights issue. These are discussed in turn.

A. Redefining the Problem:

The idea behind the notion of redefining the problem is the try and clarify the goals of each party. This may bring to light commonality between the parties, which could result in the bettering of the best expectations of both sides.

Redefining the problem in the case of aboriginal land rights from one of an eminent domain taking, to an issue of efficient land usage could reveal some commonality between goals. The conservatives do not want to increase the costs to taxpayer, while the liberals seek more moralistic objectives. In either case, if the problem could be perceived as one in which aboriginal ownership would stimulate some form of economic activity (such as extensive grazing, 'outback' tourism, indigenous handicrafts and the like), then it is conceivable that such enterprises would not only add to the tax-base, but would also grant aboriginal communities a degree of economic and social independence and self-determination.

B. Multi-faceted Package of Alternatives:

Developing a package of alternatives that would satisfy both liberal and conservative expectations would also result in an SOS solution. In the case of aboriginal land rights, such a package could include aboriginal control over certain national parks within Australia. Many of these national parks were gazetted for both their scenic amenity, and because they contain many outstanding aboriginal artifacts. It is also the case that many of the scenic features that comprise these parks also hold special significance in aboriginal folklore.

Consequently, an alternative in which state-owned parks were under the control and management of aboriginal communities would not only allow them exclusive access to their sacred areas, but would also allow them to draw revenue from tourists wishing to visit these sites. Such a solution meets the liberal's goals, in that it offers aboriginal communities some means of self-determination as well as returning to them their traditional lands. It also meets the key conservative goal, in that it grants land rights to aborigines over land that is already under government control, and thus does not increase the costs to taxpayers.

C. Contracting Out:

One final way of arriving at a super-optimum solution in the case of aboriginal land rights is a variation on the theme of 'contracting out'. In this case, private owners of land that traditionally belonged to an aboriginal community could enter into a lease, in which the community is granted the use-rights to land, in return for some lease fee. This solution satisfies a key liberal goal, in that these communities gain access to their former lands, while it also satisfies the key conservative goal, in that it shouldn't raise taxes.

II. Facilitating SOS Solutions

This question again addresses the issue of aboriginal land rights in Australia, but this time focuses on the factors that need to be considered in facilitating the adoption and implementation of an SOS alternative. This matter is addressed in three parts.

A. Adopting an SOS Alternative

Having expended the effort to arrive at a possible SOS alternative, it is all important that this policy recommendation be adopted. It is recognised that there are five factors that can hinder the adoption of an SOS alternative. These are:

1. 'Upping the ante'
2. Satisfying the mediator
3. The revenge factor
4. Suspicion of a trap
5. Vested jobs or property at stake

Of these, the notion that jobs and or property are at stake is probably the most applicable to the land rights issue. Private property ownership (that has resulted from a number of different decisions made in the past) presents itself as a significant barrier to the adoption of an SOS alternative seeking to solve the dilemma over aboriginal land rights. Eminent domain takings, the most common approach of gaining land for land rights issues, represent a form on inequality to the owners of this land, irrespective of whether they are prepared to accept fair market value for their properties. These inequalities occur as a result of the fact that owners is forced to sell their land!

The end result of this situation is that governments are usually loathed to instigate eminent domain takings. Consequently, any SOS alternative that is likely to require such actions needs to be very carefully re-considered, in order to evaluate its chances of being adopted.

B. Implementing an SOS Alternative

Following the successful generation and adoption of an SOS alternative, this solution may still fail to achieve its results, because it fails to be effectively implemented. There are at least five reasons why this may be so:

1. There were no strings attached to the solution;
2. Insufficient funding was supplied for its implementation;
3. Bureaucratic conflicts over, or indifference to, the solution;
4. Improper timing and sequencing of the events stipulated in the solution;
5. Unimaginative personnel hindering its successful implementation.

In the specific case of aboriginal land rights in Australia, the lack of sufficient funding for the implementation of the government's programme of granting land to aboriginal communities has definitely been a problem, and hence is likely to also hinder any SOS alternative to the issue.

It is also conceivable that a situation in which land is granted without any stipulations as to is use and maintenance may cause the SOS solution to fail. If productive land turned over to aboriginal communities is allowed to become unproductive, then the resulting decline in GNP adversely affects all Australians. Consequently, it is in the best interests of all involved to ensure that the SOS alternative does not proceed without proper checks and balances for all of the vested interests.

C. Facilitators of Super-Optimum Solutions

Amongst the essential prerequisites of generating, adopting and implementing an SOS alternative, there is also certain other factors that help facilitate super-optimum solutions. These include such concepts as:

Ensuring that politics is open and competitive;
Ensuring that business also remains competitive and that the economy is healthy so that national productivity remains high;
Aiding the solution with well-placed subsidies and tax breaks;
Helping resolve the issue over the long-run, by increasing public education/ socialization toward the problem;
Improving the institutions and methods for evaluating different policy alternatives;
Foster innovative initiatives that may lead to technological fixes to the problem;
Increase public sensitivity to the opportunity costs of failing to innovative, or of continued intransigence toward a problem;

Ensure that SOS alternative is precise in terms of its estimations of the state of things: make sure its 100% right in its pessimistic estimations about where were are, and where we are likely to be if the problem continues;
Constantly seek higher goals, and higher goal-achievement should follow.

Obviously, land buy-ups for land grants is never going to occur unless the Australian economy moves out of its current recession, and that it continues to grow. Consequently, fostering these aspects will be beneficial in facilitating any proposed SOS alternative. Moreover, public education and socialization to the consequences of the loss of aboriginal culture may help overcome some of the public intransigence to the problem. If people are socialized into seeing aboriginal culture as a key component of Australian culture, then perhaps this will help facilitate super-optimum solutions to the issue of land rights.

Chapter 8

PREVENTING SEXUAL HARASSMENT WHILE PRESERVING ACADEMIC FREEDOM: A WIN-WIN ANALYSIS

Thomas R. Dye
Florida State University

Sexual harassment cannot be tolerated, especially in academic life. Sexual harassment corrupts the very purpose of a university--the advancement of learning. It is professionally unethical and morally wrong.

The prevention of sexual harassment on the campus requires a clear and precise definition of the specific behavior that violates the rights of others--a definition that everyone can understand. To be effective, sexual harassment prohibitions must conform to the rule of law; they must not depend on personal perceptions, subjective interpretations, or individual thoughts or feelings. Sexual harassment must be dealt with promptly and firmly, with due process of law and respect for the dignity and rights of all. And most importantly, sexual harassment prohibitions must not be subverted or misused to undermine academic freedom.

I. CONCERNS ABOUT ACADEMIC FREEDOM

The National Association of Scholars has expressed its concern that many universities have failed to adequately protect students, faculty, and staff from sexual harassment by enacting vague, ambiguous, and imprecise policies and regulations, and using language that engenders confusion, resentment and injustice. The NAS is fearful that vague definitions of sexual harassment are undermining academic freedom, suppressing the free expression of opinions and attitudes, and inhibiting teaching and research on sensitive but important topics. And NAS worries that the failure to provide due process in sexual harassment cases encourages frivolous, self-serving, and vindictive charges. The result is to needlessly bring anti-harassment policy into conflict with academic freedom--a result that will eventually "diminish the opprobrium that rightly attaches to sexual harassment."

In a statement of the National Association of Scholars on *Sexual Harassment and Academic Freedom* the following concerns are expressed:

Sexual harassment is always contemptible. Because it also subverts education, it is particularly damaging in an academic setting . . . . Such behavior constitutes a serious violation of an educator's responsibilities and is morally wrong. It cannot be tolerated.

Editor's Note: Much of the analysis which follows may also be applicable to the concept of ethnic harassment or to its alleged occurrence. Such an allegation was made of a professor at the University of Illinois saying that some people advocate equalizing law school admissions by asking questions about soul food. The University of Illinois is currently under a federal injunction prohibiting continued punitive action under such circumstances.

However, academic freedom and the rights of individuals can be--and have been-violated by misguided efforts to combat sexual harassment. Too many institutions have adopted vague definitions of harassment that may all too easily be applied to attitudes or even to a scholar's professional views.

Specifically:

1. The criteria for identifying "harassment" are often nebulous, allowing for expansive interpretations of its meaning . . .
2. When definitions of sexual harassment are expanded to include opinions and attitudes, academic freedom is violated. Such definitions have already significantly inhibited discussion inside and outside the classroom. Ambiguous phrases like "callous insensitivity to the experience of women" have inspired complaints against professors accused of slighting gender-based literary analysis, or who have discussed theories and findings, such as Freud's, that run counter to the prevailing consensus about sexual differences.
3. Some definitions of sexual harassment embrace a wholly subjective test of its occurrence--for example, the complaint having been made to "feel uncomfortable." Proof relies not on the objective behavior of the alleged harasser but on how one perceived that behavior.
4. Charges of sexual harassment are sometimes entertained long after the alleged offense, when the memories of the parties have faded, their motives have altered, and evidence has been lost.

5 Mid-level administrators with meager academic experience but a strong commitment to fashionable causes are frequently accorded a major role in drawing up harassment regulations, interpreting them, counseling complainants, investigating charges, administering hearings, and determining guilt and penalties. Sometimes one and the same person performs all of these functions

and, in addition encourages students and others to make harassment charges. This leads to violations of academic due process.

6. Investigation of alleged sexual harassment can provide a pretext for engaging in the ideological persecution of persons whose views are out of favor. (These six points come from a statement by National Association of Scholars, 575 Ewing Street, Princeton, NJ 08540, tel. 609-683-7878.)

II. SEXUAL HARASSMENT DEFINITIONS AT FLORIDA UNIVERSITIES

A review of the sexual harassment policy statements of Florida's public universities reveal that the concerns of the National Association of Scholars are well-founded. Some universities have published statements largely in conformity with clear, lawful definitions of sexual harassment, derived from federal civil rights statutes and court interpretations thereof, other universities have published statements that serious jeopardize academic freedom.

Consider, for example, the dangers to students and faculty inherent in a sexual harassment definition offered in a policy statement by a state university in Florida:

"Any gesture or remark of a sexual nature that makes you feel uncomfortable, threatened, intimidated or pressured may be a sign that you are experiencing sexual harassment. Trust your instincts."

"Your classmates or colleagues may make your work, study or living environment uncomfortable through continued sexual comments, suggestions, or pressures. It may include . . . leering at a person's body, whistling, catcalls or sexual remarks or jokes . . ."

Another university policy statement provides examples of "what constitutes sexual harassment" including:

"Unsolicited familiarity . . . personal or intimate remarks that may fall short of sexual inquiries"

"remarks that degrade another person or group on the basis of gender"

"sexist remarks regarding a person's . . . clothing or intellectual capacity"

"sexual visuals such as pin-up calendars, cartoons, posters, etc."

"Explicit body language, leering, looking the person up and down, ogling."

At another university "examples of sexual harassment" includes:

"inappropriate communications, notes, letters, or other written materials"

"remarks about a person's clothing"

"suggestive or insulting sounds"

Yet another university asserts in its *Faculty Handbook* that sexual harassment includes:

"leering at or ogling of a person's body"
"innuendo . . . attempts to embarrass . . .
"nonsexual slurs about one's gender, contrived work or study assignments"
gestures and other symbolic conduct"

Statements such as these place everyone on campus--faculty, students, and staff--at risk of official disciplinary action based upon idle comments, friendly banter, and overheard conversations on the campus, as well as classroom lectures, discussions, readings, and assignments. Real protection against sexual harassment requires a clear understanding by everyone in the university community about what really constitutes sexual harassment. These are quotations from published statements of universities in the State University System of Florida. Attribution to specific universities has been deleted to avoid institutional embarrassment.

III. Guidance in Defining Sexual Harassment

Federal civil rights law, as well as U.S. Supreme Court interpretations of it, provide guidance to universities in the development of sexual harassment definitions and prohibitions. Title VII of the Civil Rights Act of 1964 makes it "an unlawful employment practice . . . to discriminate against any individual with respect to his [sic] compensation, terms, conditions or privileges of employment because of such individual's race color religion sex or national origin" (42 U.S.C. 2000e). In the employment context, the U.S. Supreme Court has approved the following definition of sexual harassment in *Meritor Savings Bank v Vinson* 477 U.S. 57 (1986).

"Unwelcome sexual advances, requests for sexual favors, and other verbal or physical conduct of a sexual nature constitute sexual harassment when (1) submission to such conduct is made either explicitly or implicitly a term or condition of an individual's employment, (2) submission to or rejection of such conduct by an individual, or (3) such conduct has the purpose or effect of unreasonably interfering with an individual's work performance or creating an intimidating, hostile, or offensive working environment.

The Court determined that the language of this statute "is not limited to 'economic' or 'tangible' discrimination. The phrase 'term conditions or privileges or employment' . . . includes requiring people to work in a discriminatory hostile or abusive environment." Moreover, when the workplace is "permeated with discriminatory intimidation ridicule and insult" that is "sufficiently severe and pervasive to alter the condition of the victim's employment and create an abusive working environment," then Title VII is violated, as quoted in *Los Angeles Department of Water and Power v. Manhart* 435 U.S. 702 (1978).

But the Supreme Court was careful to note that "a mere utterance of an epithet that engenders offensive feelings is not sexual harassment. Sexual harassment must be "conduct sever and pervasive enough" to convince a "reasonable person" that the environment is "objectively" hostile and abusive. The Court has specifically rejected definitions of sexual harassment that depend exclusively upon the subjective feelings of the complainant. Moreover, a "reasonable person" must "objectively" find the environment hostile and abusive (*Harris v. Forklift System* (1993). Writing for the opinion of the Court, Justice Sandra Day O'Conner held that sexual harassment "can be determined only by looking at all of the circumstances," including "the frequency of the discriminatory conduct; its severity; whether it is physically threatening or humiliating, or a mere offensive utterance."

Although these Court guidelines were developed for the workplace, they are useful in thinking about sexual harassment in an academic setting.

IV. PROTECTING ACADEMIC FREEDOM

The faculty-student relationship is the center-piece of the academic function; if it is compromised or corrupted, the very purposed of the university is undermined. The explicit or implicit conditioning of grades, evaluations, recommendations, or academic standing on romantic attachment or sexual submission is morally contemptible, professionally unethical, and legally indefensible. Faculty members must exercise great care in their personal relationships with students enrolled in their classes, or working as their graduate or undergraduate assistants, or dependent upon their evaluations and recommendations.

Yet is vitally important that sexual harassment prohibitions not infringe upon the freedom of faculty and students to express themselves in the classroom, the campus, and the community on sensitive topics, including human sexuality, race and gender differences, sexual roles, racial and gender history and politics, including human sexuality, race and gender differences, sexual roles, racial and gender history and politics, and related important and legitimate subjects. Teachings and research on such topics must not be constrained by the threat that the views expressed will be labeled "insensitive," "uncomfortable" or "incorrect." Faculty must feel free to provide their best academic and professional advice to students, collectively and individually, without fear that their comments will be officially labeled as "offensive" or "unwelcome." Students must feel free to express themselves on matters of race and gender, whether or not their ideas are biased or ill-formed, or immature or crudely expressed.

It must be recognized that the creation of a hostile, intimidating or abusive academic environment--an environment that interferes with a reasonable person's ability to learn--is also unprofessional and illegal. But universities have a special responsibility to define sexual harassment in this context in a way that does not infringe upon academic freedom, that does not constrain research or teaching.

The test for sexual harassment that creates a "hostile environment for learning" must be (1) whether it is *severe and pervasive* enough, (2) to convince a *reasonable* member of the academic community, that (3) the environment is *objectively* hostile. *Severe and pervasive* means that the university must examine the context, that is, the "totally of circumstances," surrounding the alleged harassing conduct; the university must consider the frequency as well as the severity of the conduct. A single offensive epithet, off-color remark, or ill-chosen example, *does not* constitute a hostile environment. Moreover, the conduct must be such that *reasonable* members the academic community--faculty and students--must be convinced that it creates a hostile environment. That definition must not rest upon the complainant alone or even an unrepresentative, interested group of faculty or students. Finally, the conduct must be *objectively* defined; it cannot rest upon anyone's subjective feelings of offense or discomfort.

Admittedly these tests themselves lack specificity and they encompass speech (verbal conduct) as well as action. But they provide considerably more guidance than the published standards at most of Florida's public universities.

V. Providing Due Process

Because of the potential clash between academic freedom and the prevention of sexual harassment, it is particularly important that complaints be dealt with promptly and fairly. That is to say, because the "hostile environment" definition of sexual harassment encompasses expression, we must insure that due process be followed in the handling of complaints that focus on speech, writings, lectures, readings or assignments. Complaints must be brought within a reasonable period of time following the alleged harassing conduct. University officials charged with the investigation of complaints must provide prompt written notice to alleged offenders providing a full account of the conduct giving rise to the charges permitting them to inspect and copy all documents relating to the charges, and providing them with a fair opportunity to demonstrate that there is no probable cause to believe that harassment occurred.

In this preliminary investigation, university officials should undertake consultations with the complainants, the alleged offenders, and other relevant parties, to determine whether there is reasonable cause to believe that harassment occurred, or alternatively whether the charges stem from mis-communication or misunderstanding of the definition of sexual harassment, or whether the charges can be resolved by agreement among the parties. This investigative and consultative phase of the process should be carried out with due regard for the dignity of all individuals involved.

If after investigation and consultation, university officials are convinced that probable cause exists to believe that harassment occurred and a specific defendant is identified, then they should promptly provide written notification of a hearing before disinterested members of the university community. Such a hearing must *not* be conducted by the same officials who counseled complainants, or investigated the charges, or called for the hearing. The hearing must be conducted with full administrative due process; the burden of providing by weight of evidence that sexual harassment occurred rests on the university; the defendant must have the right to have counsel present, to confront complainants, and to present testimony and evidence on his or her own behalf.

VI. Preserving Academic Freedom and Preventing Sexual Harassment

University communities should act now to insure that the prevention of sexual harassment does not become the enemy of academic freedom. Both values will be diminished or lost altogether if sexual harassment prohibitions are allowed to infringe upon free and open discussion, scholarship, and research on our campuses. The potential for unnecessary conflict, and the resulting diminution of both values, is clearly evident in the published policy statements of our universities. Now is the time to review definitions and procedures in sexual harassment prevention at all of our universities, in order to prevent such a conflict from arising.

Editor's Note: The preceding analysis emphasizes verbal activities which allegedly create a sexually hostile environment. An example is the questionable hostile sexual environment charges against a financial whistle blower at the University of Illinois. The analysis is not meant to apply to the substance of charges of assault or rape, as allegedly occurred between a psychology professor and a student at the University of Illinois. The analysis is also not meant to apply to the substance of the charges of intimidation or threats of job retention for sexual favors, as allegedly occurred at the University of Illinois in its fund-raising Foundation.

Chapter 9

RESEARCH EVIDENCE ON RACIAL/ETHNIC DISCRIMINATION AND AFFIRMATIVE ACTION IN EMPLOYMENT

Marc Bendick, Jr.
Bendick & Egan Economic Consultants, Inc.

ABSTRACT

Empirical research, summarized here, clearly establishes that racial and ethnic minorities continue to experience substantial discrimination in employment. However, this discrimination is often subtle and unconscious. Because discriminatory practices are so intertwined with apparently-neutral employment practices, affirmative action remains an important means of combating them. Properly designed, affirmative action can benefit employers and non-protected employees as well as the minorities directly covered.

ACKNOWLEDGMENT

An earlier version of this paper was presented as testimony before the Committee on the Judiciary, California State Assembly, on May 4, 1995. It is based on research supported by the Rockefeller Ford, John D. and Catherine D. MacArthur, Norman, Russell Sage, and Public Welfare foundations. However, all findings and conclusions are those of the author.

Dr. Marc Bendick, Jr., a labor economist, has spent 25 years as a researcher and policy analyst examining employment discrimination and other issues of access to mainstream economic opportunity. He is a principal in Bendick & Egan Economic Consultants, Inc., 4411 Westover Place, N.W., Washington, D.C. 20016, (202) 686-0245, egan@gwis2.circ.gwu./edu.

This paper reviews research on racial/ethnic discrimination in employment conducted by my colleagues and myself at the Fair Employment Council of Greater Washington in

Washington, D.C. and other non-profit, non-partisan research organizations. It makes five key points relevant to debate on the controversial issue of affirmative action:

- A substantial amount of racial/ethnic discrimination still operates in the American labor market today;
- "Reverse" discrimination against non-minorities occurs relatively rarely;
- Much of today's discrimination involves subtle cognitive and interpersonal processes;
- When properly implemented, affirmative action remains an important tool for addressing these problems; and
- Affirmative action can represent a "win-win" development which benefits employers and white males as well as women and minorities.

This paper discusses each of these points in turn.

DESPITE GREAT PROGRESS, EMPLOYMENT DISCRIMINATION HAS NOT BEEN ELIMINATED

The first question our research has addressed is: To what extent does racial/ethnic discrimination still operate in the American labor market in the 1990s?

During the past decades, literally thousands of research studies have been conducted on this question by labor economists and other social scientists.(1) The clear consensus of this literature is that a tremendous amount of progress has been made since the days, prior to passage of the federal Civil Rights Act of 1964, when "Jim Crow" laws, personal prejudice, and social custom firmly maintained widespread segregation of employment by race and ethnicity.

These studies also reach consensus (although not unanimously) that the job of erasing the present impacts of these past patterns is not finished. Specifically, racial/ethnic minorities:

- remain under-represented in higher-level occupations and over-represented in lower-level occupations.(2)
- often do not command the same wages as non-minorities for performing the same work.(3)
- often do not receive the same payoffs for acquiring educational credentials.(4)
- on average experience greater unemployment than equally-qualified non-minorities;(5) and
- experience higher rates of job dismissal.(6)

In the statistical studies underlying such conclusions, researchers are careful to consider differences between minority and non-minority workers in education, experience, skills, and other job-relevant qualifications, which account for some of the observed differences between minorities and non-minorities in labor market success. However, technical and data problems often limit researchers' ability to control such factors, so that estimates of the extent of remaining discrimination remain controversial. To avoid such problems by examining discrimination directly, my colleagues and I employ a research method called "testing" or "auditing." We send out pairs of research assistants to apply for actual job openings listed in the "help wanted" section of newspapers or at a random sample of companies listed in the telephone "Yellow Pages." These research assistants are carefully matched in terms of age, appearance, and personality, and they carry resumes written by experts that credit them with equivalent education and experience. However, each pair of testers consists of persons who differ in their race or ethnicity -- an African American tester paired with a white or an Hispanic tester paired with an Anglo. Thus, we set up a *controlled experiment* in which, if the two testing partners are treated differently, it is reasonable to attribute that treatment to the one way the testers differ: their race or ethnicity.

Since 1990, the Fair Employment Council of Greater Washington and The Urban Institute have run this experiment more than 2,000 times in Washington, D.C., Chicago, and San Diego.[(7)] The job vacancies tested typically have been for entry-level positions ranging in qualifications from less-than-high-school-graduate to college graduate and drawn from a wide variety of industries. We have used both male and female testers and applied for jobs by mail and telephone as well as in-person.

Slightly less than 80 percent of the time that we have sent our testers to apply for jobs, employers did not appear to discriminate between our minority testers and their non-minority counterparts. That is, the equal credentials of the two testers met with equal success -- both testers are offered a job, both are rejected, or there is a random alternation in which receives the offer. This finding is consistent with previous research, referred to earlier in this paper, that documents the substantial progress in eliminating discrimination that has occurred since the 1960s.

In the remaining tests -- between 20 and 25 percent of our efforts -- the outcomes are quite different.[(8)] With *nearly one employer in four*, the minority applicant is treated significantly worse than the non-minority. For example:

- *Opportunities to Interview.* A vacancy for a receptionist in an optometrist's office in the Washington suburbs was advertised in a local newspaper. When an Hispanic tester called to apply for the job, she was put on hold, and then called by the wrong name (Carmen, when she had given her name as Juanita) and told that they were not taking any further applications. When her Anglo testing partner called thirteen minutes later, she was given an appointment for an interview the following morning.
- *Job Offers and Referrals.* An African-American female tester sought entry-level employment through a large employment agency in downtown Washington. After completing an application and being interviewed briefly, she was told that she would be called if a suitable vacancy became available. Shortly thereafter, her white testing partner arrived seeking similar

opportunities. After she completed an application and was interviewed, she was told about a receptionist/sales position at an upscale health and grooming firm. She was coached on interviewing techniques and scheduled for an interview later that day; in that interview, she was offered the position.

- *Compensation.* A major department store chain advertised in the *Washington Post* for sales assistants in the women's clothing department of a branch in an affluent neighborhood. When a pair of female testers applied for the position, both were interviewed by the store's personnel department, and both were offered permanent, full-time employment. However, the starting salary offered to the African-American tester was $6.50 per hour, while her white partner was offered $7.50 per hour.
- *Steering.* A major-brand auto dealer in the Washington suburbs advertised in the *Washington Post* for a car salesperson. An African-American tester who applied was told that to enter the business, he should accept a position as a porter/car washer. Arriving shortly thereafter with equivalent credentials, his white testing partner was immediately interviewed for the sales position that had been advertised.
- *Information About Unadvertised Opportunities.* A dating service in the Washington suburbs advertised in the *Washington Post* for a receptionist/typist. When an African-American tester applied for the position, she was interviewed but heard nothing further. When her white testing partner applied for the receptionist position and was interviewed, the employer offered her a position as a personal assistant to the manager. This new position would pay more than the receptionist job, would lead to rapid raises and promotions, and would provide tuition assistance. Followup calls by the African-American tester elicited no interest on the part of the firm, either for the receptionist position or the newly created opportunity, even after the white tester refused the offer.

In face-to-face tests by the Fair Employment Council in the Washington area, white testers obtained job interviews at a rate 22 percent higher than the rate for their equivalently-qualified African-American counterparts; whites who were interviewed received job offers at 415 percent the rate for African Americans who were interviewed; in tests in which both testers received job offers for the same position, whites received a higher wage offer than their African-American counterpart 17 percent of the time; and white testers were 37 percent less likely than their African-American partner to be diverted to a lesser-quality job than the one advertised and 48 percent more likely to be told about additional opportunities. Taken together, these effects make the labor market experiences of identically-qualified minority and non-minority job applicants profoundly different. And because in the course of finding one job a typical job seeker applies for dozens of positions, virtually no minority job seeker is likely to get through a job campaign without being touched by discrimination.

Our testers' encounters with discrimination have not been limited to any particular subsector of the economy. True, suburban areas appear nearly twice as discrimination-prone as central cities;[9] unadvertised vacancies are more subject to discrimination than widely advertised ones;[10] and discrimination was more likely to arise for jobs which offer higher pay and more opportunities for advancement.[11] And in employment agencies, our testers encountered discriminatory treatment an appalling 67 percent -- *two thirds* -- of the time they applied for job referrals. However, no industry, community, or type of employment is immune. We have observed discrimination in both large firms with professional personnel departments and in "mom-and-pop" owner-operated enterprises. We have discovered it in firms that are government contractors, in firms that advertise themselves as equal opportunity employers, and in firms bearing some of the most well-known business names in the nation.

Testing is most readily applied to job vacancies which are advertised in newspapers or listed with employment agencies. Such vacancies account for only about one-third of all employment opportunities, with the remaining two-thirds filled through more private means of recruitment such as word-of-mouth and personal referrals.[12] Employers may utilize the latter recruitment techniques -- those in which information about vacancies is not publicized -- to keep away minority and other "undesirable" applicants. Thus, the extent of discrimination in the overall labor market is almost certainly higher than the 20 to 25 percent rate found among vacancies that have been subject to testing.

In light of these findings, it is clearly appropriate to reach the first conclusion stated at the beginning of this paper: A substantial amount of racial/ethnic discrimination still operates in the American labor market today.

Reverse Discrimination Occurs Relatively Rarely

A second question our research addresses is the extent to which "reverse discrimination" operates in the labor market. Reverse discrimination refers to circumstances in which a white male experiences diminution of his success in the labor market for reasons attributable to race and gender.

Recent research on this subject has been conducted by Professor Alfred Blumrosen of the Rutgers University School of Law. His analysis of several thousand employment discrimination cases decided by United States District and Appeals Courts between 1990 and 1994 concluded that reverse discrimination claims constituted only between 1 and 3 percent of all employment discrimination cases during that period; and that within those cases, the Courts found the claims to be without merit a high proportion of the time.[13]

In testing, we measure reverse discrimination by counting the instances in which minority testers are favored over their equally-qualified white partners. Within our thousands of tests, we have observed that circumstance to arise in an average of 6 percent of tests for African Americans and 7 percent of tests for Hispanics.[14] However, these figures represent an upper limit for the rate of reverse discrimination -- an overestimate -- because many of the outcomes favorable to minorities represent random occurrences rather than systematic preferences for minority job seekers.

Such figures seem broadly consistent with those of Professor Blumrosen in suggesting that the number of instances of reverse discrimination is small, affecting at most a few percent of workers. Thus we reach the second conclusion stated at the beginning of this paper: Reverse discrimination against non-minorities occurs relatively rarely. The rate is only a small fraction of the rate at which discrimination against minorities arises.

THE INCREASINGLY SUBTLE NATURE OF EMPLOYMENT DISCRIMINATION IN THE 1990S

Public opinion polls report that the findings just described -- that discrimination against racial/ethnic minorities is still a substantial problem and that reverse discrimination is not -- are not widely believed by the non-minority public across the United States. For example, in a nationwide poll in 1989, only 37 percent of whites thought that an African-American applicant who is as qualified as a white is less likely to win a job that both want, and only 41 percent felt that the chances of African Americans to win a supervisory/managerial position were worse than those for whites.[(15)]

Such differences in perception reflect the nature of employment discrimination in the 1990s. When employment discrimination occurred in the 1960s, it was typically explicit and conscious, out in the open, and (in some circles) socially acceptable. It was often reflected in an "inexorable zero" -- instances where there had never been even one minority employee in certain jobs or certain companies. In the 1990s, in contrast, the complete absence of minorities has typically been replaced by their being present but under-represented, and discrimination is no longer generally seen as socially acceptable. Among our thousands of tests, racial epithets, obvious hostility to minorities, or similar explicit indications of bias were relatively rare. In the preponderance of cases, minority and non-minority testers were treated with at least approximately equal politeness.[(16)] Explicit, deliberate, conscious discrimination is not entirely gone from the American labor market, but it is more the exception than the rule.

This dramatic change is what the non-minority public is thinking of when they tell public opinion pollsters that discrimination is no longer a problem. But our testing studies reveal that they are only partially correct. Employment discrimination is still present, but it expresses itself less in the *treatment* of minorities during the hiring process than in *judgments* concerning their qualifications and abilities.

One indicator of employers' judgments of minority and non-minority job candidates is the stage of the application process to which minorities advance. In the Fair Employment Council's tests involving African Americans in the Washington, D.C. labor market, there was a modest (5 percent) racial difference in the probability of obtaining an interview, and a larger difference (54 percent) in the probability of being allowed to take skills tests. But such differences are dwarfed by differences in minority/non-minority hiring decisions. While 47 percent of white applicants who received a job interview obtained a job offer, only 11 percent of their African American counterparts did so, a rate of success for non-minorities *more than four times* that for minorities.

A second indicator of employers' judgments of applicants is the content of comments made to testers by the staff interviewing them. The average white tester who was interviewed but did not receive a job offer received 2.9 positive comments for every negative one,[17] while a counterpart African-American tester who got to the same stage of the job seeking process (interviewed, not offered a job) received only .5 positive comments for every negative one.

This juxtaposition of relatively even-handed treatment of job applicants with hiring judgments that are far from even-handed seems paradoxical. In some cases, it undoubtedly reflects the behavior of employers who, although they know that they would never hire a minority candidate, feel forced by social pressure or potential legal penalties to "go through the motions" of interviewing minority applicants. In other cases, however, the outcome reflects more complex cognitive processes.

In particular, it reflects the effect of traditional stereotyped beliefs held by employment decision-makers. Generalizations about a demographic group strongly influence how any individual from that group is perceived. This effect is particularly strong if exposure to that individual is brief and accompanied by only limited additional information. For example, in one social psychology experiment, two groups of university students were shown different videotapes concerning a fourth grade girl. Half the students observed the girl living in a depressed urban neighborhood, while the other half saw her living in an affluent suburb. Both groups were then shown the same videotape of her taking an oral achievement test. Students who had previously been exposed to the girl's "high class" background judged her to be of higher ability *and reported her obtaining a higher test score* than did students who had been exposed to her "low class" background.[18]

This experimental situation is closely analogous to that in applications for entry-level employment. Hiring decisions are generally made on limited information, typically, a one-page resume and an interview averaging in our sample about twenty minutes. It is therefore not surprising that interviewers' judgments of individuals are influenced by generalizations about the applicants' demographic group that the interviewer may have formed over a lifetime.

The process of interpreting new data in light of prior information is, of course, a common mechanism of human thought.[19] Nevertheless, it creates problems for minority job seekers because of the strongly unfavorable content of generalizations concerning African Americans and Hispanics held by the majority of Americans. According to public opinion research, widely-held "ethnic images" of both African Americans and Hispanics portray them, relative to non-minorities, as less intelligent, more lazy and welfare-dependent, and more prone to violence.[20] Correspondingly, managers and other personnel decision-makers readily generalize about ethnic groups, and the content of these generalizations is highly adverse to most minorities. In one study in Chicago, for example, common generalizations by employers concerning African-American and Hispanic workers emphasized their shortcomings in terms of work ethic, honesty, attitudes, communication skills, intelligence, educational preparation, and stability.[21]

When employers and their staffs bring such attitudes to a job selection process, virtually every minority candidate enters the process with a substantial handicap. However well a minority individual may perform in the interview and however impressive her/his resume, those qualifications are likely to be discounted or incorrectly perceived based on the prior generalizations. Indeed, stereotypical thinking can even turn applicants' positive attributes into their opposite. For example, a standard piece of advice to job seekers is to dress well for employment interviews.[(22)] But when one of our testing pairs wearing dress shirts and ties were interviewed by a Washington-area employment agency, the African-American tester was asked whether his ability to afford such clothes indicated that he participated in illegal activities.

The unconscious behavior of interviewers may also cause minority applicants to perform badly in interviews. In social settings such as the workplace, many persons feel more comfortable with persons who are "like themselves."[(23)] In one social psychology experiment, for example, white university students interviewed black and white job applicants. When the applicant was black, the interviewers sat further away, terminated the interview 25 percent sooner, and made 50 percent more speech errors than when the applicant was white. Then, in a second stage of the experiment, interviewers deliberately duplicated the behavior typical of interviews with either blacks and whites. The interview performance of white job applicants subjected to the "black" treatment was rated by neutral judges as more nervous and less effective than that of whites subjected to the "white" treatment.[(24)] Thus, what begins as a problem for the employer -- that she or he is socially uncomfortable with minority job applicants -- is transformed into a problem for the minority job-seeker -- not being selected for a job for which he or she may be qualified.

IS AFFIRMATIVE ACTION NEEDED IN ADDITION TO ANTI-DISCRIMINATION?

One possible reaction to the research findings just presented is that they make a strong case for *continued, vigorous enforcement of anti-discrimination laws*. That conclusion is further supported by research documenting positive impacts of such activities on the employment success of racial and ethnic minorities.[(25)] A more controversial question, however, is whether these findings also justify *affirmative action*, defined here as "...any measure, beyond simple termination of a discriminatory practice, adopted to correct or compensate for past discrimination or prevent discrimination from recurring in the future."[(26)]

Research findings imply an answer of yes, for four primary reasons:

- First, the problems of discrimination described here are so subtle and woven into apparently-neutral processes that they are difficult to isolate, document, and attack through conventional anti-discrimination enforcement alone.

- Second, the problems of discrimination described here reflect beliefs and attitudes held by non-minority employment decision-makers that can best be changed by the experience of working with racial and ethnic minorities.[27] But in the absence of affirmative action, these beliefs and attitudes continue to exclude minorities and thereby prevent that experience from accumulating. Affirmative action is thus a way to break the "chicken-and-egg" dilemma.
- Third, without continued pressure such as an obligation to take affirmative action, many employers are likely to neglect remaining problems of discrimination. For example, in 1990, the consulting firm of Towers Perrin conducted a confidential survey of 645 senior human resources managers at large corporations nationwide. Among respondents to this survey, 55 percent voiced concern about supervisors' ability to motivate diverse groups of employees, 29 percent reported that discrimination remained a problem within their organization, 25 percent stated that their corporate culture was not open to diversity, and 15 percent expressed concern about overt harassment of minorities. Yet fewer than half the firms acknowledging a problem indicated that the firm had current plans to do anything about it. [28]
- Fourth, when such reluctant employers are pressured by public requirements to address problems of inequality in employment opportunities, they do take action. For example, Professor Jonathan Leonard of the University of California examined the period 1974-1980, when the federal government first imposed substantial requirements for affirmative action on federal contractors. He concluded that, within firms subject to these new government requirement, affirmative action led to occupational advances for minority group members of both sexes -- for example, a relative increase in demand for black male employees of 8.5 percent. Another study of the same period estimated that minority employment in firms covered by these requirements grew 20.1 percent, compared to only 12.3 percent in uncovered firms.[29]

Thus, when appropriately designed and implemented, affirmative action can be an effective tool for creating work places in which, contrary to the circumstances in many workplaces today, individual merit can prevail.

Affirmative Action as a Win-Win Approach

When affirmative action enhances the prevalence of merit in the workplace, it benefits persons other than the minority group members who are its nominal beneficiaries.

Most discussions of affirmative action focus on a simple "win-lose" tradeoff: When a woman or minority is selected over a "more qualified" white male, then that white male loses an employment opportunity, and his employer loses efficiency and productivity. In reality, however, the situation is more complicated. This "win-lose" analysis implicitly assumes that, in the absence of affirmative action, employers select the most qualified candidates to be hired or promoted. At least five lines of evidence suggest that this key assumption is often not correct.[30]

First, employment decisions are sometimes based on considerations that have virtually nothing to do with qualifications. An extreme case is that of business owners' children who, whether or not they are competent to run a company, become bosses by inheriting a firm. A second example is the practice in many craft unions of favoring the sons or nephews of current union members in selecting apprentices.[31]

Second, as discussed earlier in this paper, employers often advertise job vacancies only in limited ways, such as by word-of-mouth among current employees. The result is that qualified job candidates often do not have their qualifications considered.

Third, for many jobs, differences in qualifications represent only modest disparities in work experience that would not have arisen had on-the-job assignments been distributed in a non-discriminatory manner. For example, in one manufacturing plant I studied, a key qualification for promotion to full-time fork-lift driver was eight hours of experience driving a fork lift. This experience was commonly acquired by substituting for drivers who were sick or on vacation. Because the warehouse foreman reserved these temporary driving assignments for white males, when vacancies arose for full-time fork-lift operators, no female or minority warehouse laborers were "qualified" for promotion.

Fourth, many employee selection procedures provide only weak predictions of employees' future performance. In particular, candidates' evaluations in job interviews typically predict only between 10 and 20 percent of employee-to-employee variation in actual subsequent job performance.[32] In those circumstances, it cannot be assumed that if a woman or minority is hired in place of a white male who obtained higher ratings from job interviewers, then future performance has been seriously compromised. Such an assumption is particularly suspect in light of the many ways, discussed earlier in this paper, in which social psychological processes lead job interviewers to under-estimate the qualifications of women and minorities.

Fifth, in the contemporary workplace, performance is often generated less by individuals working in isolation than by work groups. Recent research in organizational dynamics suggests that work groups that are demographically diverse are often more productive than those that are homogeneous.[33] One vivid example of this phenomenon involves a insurance company I have studied. For many years, this company typically hired only sales representatives who were white, male, and under age 45. When, as the result of employment discrimination litigation, the company began to broaden its hiring to encompass females, minorities, and older workers, its sales expanded dramatically; its newly-diverse workforce used their personal networks to penetrate markets not previously accessible to the company. Such results explain why many employers now report that they would retain affirmative action as part of their personnel practices even if laws requiring it were repealed.[34]

In these circumstances, affirmative action may not mean hiring or promotion of a woman or minority over a more qualified white male. Instead, it may mean employee selection with:

- increased emphasis on qualifications;
- consideration of a broader range of qualified candidates;
- opportunities for more employees to acquire qualifications;
- reduced reliance on selection procedures with little predictive validity; and
- increased productivity through employee diversity.

Such an environment would benefit employers and white males, not only their female and minority colleagues.

REFERENCES

Aigner, Dennis J. & Glen Cain, "Statistical Theories of Discrimination in Labor Markets," *Industrial and Labor Relations Review* 30 (2, 1977), pp. 175-87.

Arvey, R.D. & J.E. Campion, "The Employment Interview: A Summary and Review of Recent Literature," *Personnel Psychology* 35 (1982), pp. 281-322.

Bendick, Marc, Jr., *Employment Practices and Employment Discrimination, A Bibliography Combining Economic, Managerial, and Behavioral Science Research* (Washington: Fair Employment Council of Greater Washington, 1996).

Bendick, Marc, Jr., "Matching Workers and Job Opportunities: What Role for the Federal-State Employment Service?" in D. Lee Bawden and Felicity Skidmore, *Rethinking Employment Policy* (Washington, D.C.: Urban Institute Press, 1989), pp. 81-108.

Bendick, Marc, Jr., Charles W. Jackson & Victor A. Reinoso, "Measuring Employment Discrimination Through Controlled Experiments," *Review of Black Political Economy* 23 (Summer, 1994), pp. 25-48.

Bendick, Marc, Jr., Charles W. Jackson, Victor A. Reinoso, and Laura Hodges, "Discrimination Against Latino Job Applicants: A Controlled Experiment," *Human Resource Management* 30 (4, 1991), pp. 469-484.

Bergmann, Barbara, *In Defense of Affirmative Action* (New York: Basic Books, 1996).

Blumrosen, Alfred W. *How the Courts are Handling Reverse Discrimination Claims* (unpublished manuscript, Office of Contract Compliance Programs, U.S. Department of Labor, 1995).

Bowman, Philip J. "Work Life," in James S. Jackson (ed.), *Life in Black America* (Newberry Park, CA: Russell Sage, 1991), pp. 124-155.

Braddock, Jomills & James M. McPartland, "How Minorities Continue to be Excluded from Equal Employment Opportunities: Research on the Labor Market and Institutional Barriers," *Journal of Social Issues* 43 (1, 1987), pp. 5-39.

Brimmer, Andrew, *The Economic Position of Black Americans, 1976* (Washington, D.C.: National Commission for Employment Policy, 1976).

Brown, Charles, *The Federal Attack on Labor Market Discrimination: The Mouse that Roared?*(Cambridge, MA: National Bureau for Economic Research, 1981).

Cain, Glen, "The Economic Analysis of Labor Market Discrimination: A Survey," in Orley Aschenfelter and Richard Layard (eds.), *Handbook of Labor Economics* (New York: Elsevier, 1986), pp. 694-785.

Chiswick, Barry, "Differences in Education and Earnings Across Racial and Ethnic Groups: Taste, Discrimination, and Investments in Child Quality," *Quarterly Journal of Economics* 103 (August 1988), pp. 571-597.

Cook, S.W., "Motives in Conceptual Analysis of Attitude-Related Behavior," in W. J. Arnold and D. Levine, *Nebraska Symposium on Motivation* (1970), pp. 179-231.

Cox, T.H., *Cultural Diversity in Organizations: Theory, Research, and Practice* (San Francisco: Berrett-Koehler, 1992).

Culp, Jerome & Bruce Dunson, "Brothers of a Different Color: A Preliminary Look at Employer Treatment of Black and White Youth," in Richard Freeman and Harry Holzer, *The Black Youth Employment Crisis* (Chicago: University of Chicago Press, 1986), pp. 233-259.

Darley, J.M. & P.H. Gross, "A Hypothesis-Conforming Bias in Labeling Effects," *Journal of Personality and Social Psychology* 44 (1, 1983), pp. 20-33.

DeFreitas, G., "Ethnic Differentials in Unemployment among Hispanic Americans," in G. Borjas and M. Tienda (eds.), *Hispanics in the U.S. Economy* (New York: Academic Press, 1985).

DeFreitas, G., *Inequality at Work, Hispanics in the U.S. Labor Force* (New York: Oxford University Press, 1991).

Ehrenberg, R. & R. Smith, *Modern Labor Economics* (New York: Harper Collins Publishers, 1994).

Employment Patterns of Minorities and Women in Federal Contractor and Noncontractor Establishments, 1974-1980 (Washington, D.C.: Office of Federal Contract Compliance Programs, U.S. Department of Labor, 1984).

Employment Testing Manual (Washington: Fair Employment Council of Greater Washington, Inc., 1993).

Fix, Michael & Raymond Struyk (eds.), *Clear and Convincing Evidence: Measurement of Discrimination in America* (Washington: Urban Institute Press, 1993).

Freedman, J.L & S.C. Fraser, "Compliance Without Pressure, the Foot-in-the-Door Technique," *Journal of Personality and Social Psychology* 4 (1966), pp. 195-202.

Freeman, Richard, "Changes in the Labor Market for Black Americans, 1948-1974," *Brookings Papers on Economic Activity* 1 (1973).

Galster, George, et al., *Sandwich Hiring Audit Pilot Program* (Washington, D.C.: The Urban Institute, 1994).

Gill, Andrew, "The Role of Discrimination in Determining Occupational Structure, *Industrial and Labor Relations Review* 42 (4, 1989), pp. 610-623.

Good for Business: Making Full Use of the Nation's Human Capital (Washington: U.S. Department of Labor, 1995).

Hanson, Susan & Geraldine Pratt, "Dynamic Dependencies: A Geographic Investigation of Local Labor Markets," *Economic Geography* 68 (4, 1992), pp. 610-623.

Hill, Herbert, *Black Labor and the American Legal System: Race, Work, and the Law* (Madison: University of Wisconsin Press, 1985).

Holzer, Harry, *What Employers Want, Job Prospects for Less-Educated Workers* (New York: Russell Sage Foundation, 1996).

Jackson, Susan E. & Associates, *Diversity in the Workplace* (New York: Guilford Press, 1992).

Jaynes, Gerald & Robin M. Williams (eds.), *A Common Destiny, Blacks and American Society* (Washington: National Academy of Sciences Press, 1989).

Kluegel J.R. & E.R. Smith, *Beliefs about Equality: Americans' Views of What Is and What Ought to Be* (Hawthorne, N.Y.: Aldine de Gruyter, 1986).

Krueger, J. & M. Rothbart, "Use of Categorical and Individuating Information in Making Inferences About Personality," *Journal of Personality and Social Psychology* 55 (1, 1988), pp. 187-195.

Latane, B. & J.M. Darley, *The Unresponsive Bystander, Why Doesn't He Help?* (New York: Appleton-Century-Crofts, 1970).

Leonard, Jonathan, *The Impact of Affirmative Action* (Berkeley: School of Business Administration of the University of California, 1983).

Louis Harris, *The Unfinished Agenda on Race in America* (New York: NAACP Legal Defense Fund, 1989).

Molloy, John T., *Dress For Success* (New York: Warner Books, 1988).

Neckerman, Kathryn & Joleen Kirschenman, "Hiring Strategies, Racial Bias, and Inner-City Workers," *Social Problems* 38 (November 1991), pp. 433-447.

Neckerman, Joleen & Kathryn Kirschenman, "'We'd Love to Hire them, But...': The Meaning of Race for Employers," in Christopher Jencks and Paul E. Peterson (eds.), *The Urban Underclass* (Washington: Brookings Institution, 1991), pp. 203-234.

Oster, George & David Juba, *Assessing the Need for Affirmative Action: Race and Sex Inequality Among Federal Contractors* (Policy Analysis, Inc., 1984).

Portes, A. & R. Bach, *Latin Journey: Cuban and Mexican Immigrants in the United States* (Berkeley: University of California Press, 1985).

Raisin, John & Elaine Donovan, *Patterns of Real Wage Growth, 1967-1977: Who Has Prospered?* (Washington, D.C.: U.S. Bureau of Labor Statistics, 1980).

Reilly, R.R. & G.T. Chao, "Validity and Fairness of Some Alternative Employee Selections Procedures," *Personnel Psychology* 35 (1982), pp. 1-62.

Reimers, Carl, "A Comparative Analysis of the Wages of Hispanics, Blacks, and Non-Hispanic Whites," In G. Borjas and M. Tienda (eds.), *Hispanics in the U.S. Economy* (New York: Academic Press, 1985).

Silver, Hilary, *Firing Federal Employees: Does Race Make a Difference?*, unpublished manuscript, Brown University, 1995.

Smith, J. & F. Welch, "Black Economic Progress after Myrdal," *Journal of Economic Literature* 27 (1989), pp. 519-564.

Smith, James P. & Finis Welch, "Black-White Wage Ratios, 1960-1970," *American Economic Review* 67 (June 1977), pp. 323-338.

Smith, Tom W., *Ethnic Images* (Chicago: National Opinion Research Center, 1990).

A Study of Racial and Sexual Discrimination Related to Government Contracting in New York State (Albany: New York State Department of Economic Development, no date).

Thomas, R. Roosevelt, Jr., *Beyond Race and Gender* (New York: American Management Association, 1991).

Trimble, Joseph E., "Stereotypical Images, American Indians, and Prejudice," in Phyllis A. Katz and Dalmas A. Taylor (eds), *Eliminating Racism* (New York: Plenum Press, 1988).

U.S. Commission on Civil Rights, *Statement on Affirmative Action* (Washington: The Commission, 1977).

Wolpin, K.I., "The Determinants of Black-White Differences in Early Employment Careers: Search, Layoffs, Quits, and Endogenous Wage Growth," *Journal of Political Economy* 100 (3, 1992), pp. 535-6.

Word, C.O., M.P. Zanna & J. Cooper, "The Nonverbal Mediation of Self-Fulfilling Prophesies in Interracial Interaction," *Journal of Experimental Social Psychology* 10 (1, 1974), pp. 109-120.

Workforce 2000: Competing in a Seller's Market (Valhalla, N.Y.: Towers Perrin, 1990).

Yu, Corrine & William Taylor (eds.), *The Resource, An Affirmative Action Guide* (Washington: Citizens' Commission on Civil Rights, 1996).

Zahn-Waxler, C. & M. Radke-Yarrow, "The Origins of Empathic Concern," *Motivation and Emotion* 13 (2, 1990), pp. 107-130.

Zwerling, Craig & Hilary Silver, "Race and Job Dismissal in a Federal Bureaucracy," *American Sociological Review* 57 (5, 1992), pp. 651-660.

ENDNOTES

1. Overviews of this research can be found in Jaynes & Williams (1989), DeFreitas (1991); Cain (1986), Ehrenberg & Smith (1994, chapter 12), Bowman (1991, pp. 124-155), Portes & Bach (1985), and Smith & Welch (1989). For additional references, see Bendick (1996).
2. Gill (1989), Wolpin (1992). See also *Good for Business* (1995) (the "glass ceiling" report).
3. Reimers (1985).
4. Chiswick (1988).
5. DeFreitas (1985).
6. For example, Silver (1995) found that African-American white collar federal employees are 2.7 times as likely to be fired than white counterparts of similar age, education and work history. Native Americans also experienced a higher dismissal rate than comparable whites, but Hispanic and Asian employees did not. See also Zwerling & Silver (1992).
7. This work is summarized in Bendick, Jackson & Reinoso (1994). Additional information is provided in Bendick, Jackson, Reinoso & Hodges (1991), Fix & Struyk (1993), and *Employment Testing Manual* (1993). A small-scale, additional study in Los Angeles is described in Galster et al. (1994).

8. The precise proportions of tests in which discrimination has been encountered is: for Hispanics in San Diego and Chicago, 20 percent; for Hispanics in Washington, D.C., 22 percent; for African Americans in Washington, 24 percent; and for African Americans in Chicago and Washington in a study in which only limited types of discrimination were recorded, 13 percent. In all cases, these figures are "net" rates, representing the proportion of tests in which the minority tester was favored minus the proportion of tests in which the non-minority tester was favored; see Bendick, Jackson & Reinoso (1994), Table 2.
9. Extra problems in suburbs where minorities are discouraged from residing is consistent with the findings of other research. See Hanson & Pratt (1992) and Neckerman & Kirschenman (1991).
10. In Washington-area tests conducted by the Fair Employment Council, jobs advertised in the major metropolitan newspaper (the *Washington Post*) were associated with rates of discrimination between 14.7 and 19.7 percent, which were lower than the rate for jobs listed in suburban newspapers (22.3 percent) or "walk-in" applications where there was no newspaper advertising (34.3 percent).
11. For example, in the Fair Employment Council's tests with African Americans, where both applicants received a job offer, the average starting wage offered to whites was $5.45 per hour; in jobs where white applicants received an offer but their African American partner did not, the starting wage averaged $7.13 per hour.
While the effects of discrimination are serious for any worker, they are perhaps most destructive for job seekers just entering the world of work; being denied access to the bottom rung of "career ladders" can trap persons in a lifetime of dead end, low-paying, unstable employment. Unfortunately, our testing results demonstrate that discrimination is particularly common for such career-oriented opportunities.
12. Bendick (1989); see also Holzer (1996).
13. Blumrosen (1995).
14. Bendick, Jackson & Reinoso (1994, Table 2).
15. Harris (1989). In contrast, more than 80 percent of African Americans agreed with the first statement and 62 percent agreed with the second. See also Kluegel & Smith (1986).
16. For example, in tests conducted by the Fair Employment Council with African American testers in the Washington, D.C. area, there was only a modest difference in the proportion of interviews conducted by a line manager rather than by clerical or personnel staff (89 percent for whites, 83 percent for minorities), and only a one minute difference in the length of these interviews (23 minutes for whites, 22 minutes for minorities) (Bendick, Jackson & Reinoso, 1994, Table 4).
17. An example of a positive comment is: "You are just what we are looking for." An example of a negative ones is: "This really is a dead end job; you wouldn't want it anyway."
18. Darley & Gross (1983); see also Krueger & Rothbart (1988).
19. Aigner & Cain (1977).
20. Smith (1990). See also Trimble (1988).

21. Neckerman & Kirschenman (1991); see also Braddock & McPartland (1987) and Culp & Dunson (1986).

22. Molloy (1988).

23. Thomas (1991); Jackson (1992).

24. Word, Zanna & Cooper (1974).

25. Numerous studies have documented the rapid acceleration in African American economic status following promulgation of Title VII of the federal Civil Rights Act of 1964. Other studies have linked this progress directly to enforcement of the new law. For example, one study observed that African Americans' share in total employment rose much more rapidly in firms required to report the race-sex composition of their workforce to the Equal Employment Opportunity Commission than in firms not required to report. Another study identified a direct relationship between minority gains in employment and the amount of Title VII class action litigation pursued against an industry; for example, an average of one Title VII suit per corporation within an industry was associated with a doubling or tripling of the rate of increase in black employment in manufacturing. See Leonard (1983), Freeman (1973), Brown (1981), Brimmer (1976), Smith & Welch (1977), and Raisin & Donovan (1980).

26. U.S. Commission on Civil Rights (1977).

27. Cook (1970); Zahn-Waxler & Radke-Yarrow (1990); Latane & Darley (1970); Freedman & Fraser (1966).

28. *Workforce 2000* (1990), pp. 12-13.

29. Leonard (1983); *Employment Patterns* (1984); Oster & Juba (1984).

30. Bergmann (1996), especially pp. 100-118.

31. Hill (1985); *A Study of Racial and Sexual Discrimination* (no date), Appendix A, pp. 51-52.

32. Reilly & Chao (1982); Arvey & Campion (1982).

33. Cox (1992); Jackson (1992), Bendick (1996, Section 11).

34. Yu & Taylor (1996), pp. 1a-27a.

Chapter 10

SOS AIDING SOFTWARE: THE COMPOSITION OF THE GOVERNMENT IN FIJI

Simon Montagu
Australia

Several years ago, a Major in the Fijian army instituted a coup d'etat, ousting the newly, democratically elected government. The fundamental reason offered for the military takeover was that the composition of the new government gave too much power to the ethic Fijian-Indian minority of Fiji. The head of the coup used the parochial argument that Fiji should continue to be ruled by indigenous Fijians, and that the new Government, composed primarily of Fijian-Indians, would be unable to represent the interests of native Fijians.

This predicament is explored in the following SOS analysis. In this example, the SOS package P/G% is used to carry out the analysis. Attached is an SOS table (Table 2.1) setting out the goals, alternatives and relational scores for the issue, and also copies of screen dumps of each of the major steps of this process. Below is a description of the important elements of the analysis.

I. GOALS

The SOS analysis presented is relatively simple in terms of the goals and alternatives used in the analysis. The analysis investigates two major goals, one representing a liberal position, and one representing a conservative perspective.

The conservative goal is a fairly vague and very parochial. It calls for the continued control of Fiji, by native Fijians. The liberal goal is similarly vague, although it pursues a much more idealistic objective than the conservative goal does. It calls for the upholding of the fundamental principles of democracy and a truly representative government.

II. Alternatives

Excluding the SOS alternative for the moment, there are two alternatives proposed to this issue of political control in Fiji. The first alternative., proposed by the conservative interests, seeks a government in which the balance of power always remains with native Fijians. The liberal alternative, on the other hand, proposes a government that is representative in its makeup, of the ethnic mix of the population of Fiji.

The SOS alternative used in the threshold analysis part of this exercise (see Part 5) proposes a solution requiring some modifications to the current structure of the government. It suggests the a new Parliamentary system be formed consisting of two houses of Parliament. This proposal envisions that the lower house would comprise solely of members democratically elected from society at large, and that the upper house would comprise of members that proportionally represent the two main groups involved in the current conflict, namely the ethnic Fijian-Indians and the native Fijians.

III. Relations

The relational scores characterizing the relationships between the above mentioned goals and alternatives are presented in the cells of Table 2.1. These same scores are also shown in the attached screen-dump of the Alternative/ Criteria Scoring matrix, taken from the P/G% program. The scores listed for the SOS alternative were derived from a threshold analysis, undertaken after the calculation of the conservative and liberal totals for each alternative.

IV. Primary Analysis

The primary analysis undertaken by the P/G% program calculates the combined raw scores for each of the alternatives, based on weights set prior to each run of the analysis. The results of this analysis, for each of the liberal, conservative and neutral weights, are summarized below.

Combined Raw Scores

	Liberal Weight	Conservative Weight	Neutral Weight
Conserv. Goal	12.5	17.5	15.0
Liberal Goal	17.0	15.0	16.0

V. THRESHOLD ANALYSIS

The threshold analysis component of the P/G% program has used to evaluate the threshold relationship between the liberal alternative and the SOS alternative. The screen-dumps of this analysis is attached.

The results of this assessment indicate that in order of the liberal alternative to be raised up to the level of the SOS alternative, then the conservative goal must score at least a 4.1 on the 1-5 scale, while the liberal goal would need to score at least a 4.7, in order to cause a tie.

SIMPLIFIED SOS TABLE:
Political Control In Fiji

Criteria / Alternatives	CONSERV. GOAL • Native Fijian Sovereignty *Weights* C=3 N=2 L=1	LIB. GOAL • Uphold Principles of Democracy *Weights* C=1 N=2 L=3	TOTALS		
			Conserv.	Lib.	Neutral
CONSERV. ALT. • Govern. Controlled by Native Fijians	5	2.5	17.5	12.5	15
LIB. ALT. • Govern. Representative of the Entire Pop'n. of Fiji	3.5	4.5	15	17	16
S.O.S. ALT. • Two Houses of Parliament	≥4.375	≥4.375	≥17.5	≥17.5	≥17.5

Table 1. Conservative, Liberal, and Neutral Weights

Criterion	Meas, Unit	Weight
1) C-Fijian Sov.	1-5 Rel	3.00
2) L-Democracy	1-5 Rel	1.00
1) C-Fijian Sov.	1-5 Rel	1.00
2) L-Democracy	1-5 Rel	3.00
1) C-Fijian Sov.	1-5 Rel	2.00
2) L-Democracy	1-5 Rel	2.00

Table 2. Alternatives

Alternative	Budgets	
	Minimum	Actual
1) C-Native	0.00	0.00
2) L-Represent	0.00	0.00

Table 3. Relations

	Alternative/ Criteria Scoring	
	C-Fijian	L-Democr
C-Native	5.00	2.50
L-Represent	3.50	4.50
S-Two Houses	4.40	4.40

Table 4. Conservative, Liberal, and Neutral Primary Analysis

Alternative	Combined Raw Scores	X
1)C-Native	17.50	58.65
2)L-Represent	15.00	46.15
1)C-Native	12.50	42.87
2)L-Represent	17.00	57.63
1)C-Native	15.00	48.89
2)L-Represent	16.00	51.61

Table 5. Threshold Analysis

	L-Represen	S-Two Hous	Weight
C-Fijian Sov.	4.10	3.80	0.333
L-Democracy	4.70	4.20	9.000

Chapter 11

THREE SUPER-OPTIMUM SOLUTIONS IN A CUT-BACK MODE*

Robert T. Golembiewski
University of Georgia

ABSTRACT

This essay reviews three approaches toward achieving super-optimum solutions under the duress of organizational down-sizing. The first focus is on demotions as an alternative tool in adverse personnel actions. Several applications of the underlying demotion design have been made in the cases of employees who were satisfactory performers, and their goals include increasing individual mastery in community settings, recognizing past service, and retaining valuable human resources. The second focus has more macro-features, and describes a collective response of a field unit to a corporate demand for substantial emergency savings on an authorized budget. The third approach summarizes the major features of what might be called an 'operating philosophy' for seeking win-win features even in the most adverse personnel actions.

Various forms of the alternative resolution of problems have appeared in recent years, and Nagel (1989) adds to them the fertile notion of "super-optimum solutions." His focus is on public controversies or dilemmas, and he urges attention to that form of resolution whereby participants -- who are potential combatants -- all "come out ahead of their initial best expectations" (Nagel, 1989, p. 11). Generically, super-optimum solutions can involve:

1. Achieving some goal objectively beyond that considered the best attainable.

---

* An earlier version appeared in *Public Budgeting and Financial Management*, Vol. 4 (No. 1, 1991), pp. 231-254. Reprinted with permission of the publisher. Substantial changes and additions have been made.

2. Resolving policy disputes involving apparently-intractable positions in opposition, e.g., liberal and conservative goals and priorities.
3. Resolving adjudicative or rule-applying controversies.
4. Enabling all sides to a controversy to add substantially to the values received from a solution.

Terms like "super-optimum solutions" should be used sparingly, and always carefully. Here, the usage not only denotes a solution that is arguably "better" than a body of experience would lead one to expect. Moreover, this analysis adds the requirement that qualifying solutions must rest on a theoretic base of general applicability which helps solve relatively-targeted problems without creating other and less-tractable problems.

Expressed in another way, the purpose here is to expand a bit on the super-optimum solution genre. Policy disputes will not be at issue. The focus will be on alternative patterns of interaction and their products, in contrast to Nagel's basic emphasis on public policy. Three brief descriptions loosely labeled 'case studies' -- constitute the present vehicle for illustrating how one can usefully expand the sense of super-optimum solutions. All cases deal with the management of cutback situations -- adverse personnel actions required by obdurate economic conditions. Typically, cutback results in no-win or lose/lose resolutions, and the present purpose is to illustrate how an alternative model of interaction can help avoid such somber outcomes.

Dour Dynamics of Common Cutbacks

Cutback management is much with us nowadays, in all arenas, and hunkering-down seems the general order of the day. Native cunning encourages caution, closedness, avoidance, and more than a little whistling-in-the-dark. Few people can tolerate the experience, let alone grow from it or relish it, despite some brave talk about eliminating the deadwood or about becoming lean-and-mean. Bluntly, cutback sets a proverbial tiger loose in the streets, and neither theory nor experience suffice to manage those often-powerful forces. Even "adequate" solutions are rare.

Beta Plant illustrates the typical case of "resolution." An old facility in the so-called rust belt had seen its best days, and even the good ones. Management decided to close the plant, relocate whatever personnel possible, and deal with the others gently and as generously as possible. Employees resisted, however, and especially that substantial proportion of them approaching retirement. Many present employees had opened the plant over two decades ago. Just a bit more time would suit them just fine.

A reluctant management agreed to stretch-out the plant closing, in real appreciation for past good works under trying circumstances. Management also realized a demonstration of reasonableness might defang possible union resistance.

This strategy had some unexpected effects. For example, management predicted a substantial attrition of personnel as well as a leisurely end-of-game play by those remaining. Both would exacerbate the several and growing inefficiencies of Beta as a worksite for doing what a changing technology demanded, and some observers noted that such effects would serve management's purposes.

Many major expected effects did not occur, however. Overall, management was surprised, at times pleasantly: the stretch-out was put to good use for planning that paid dividends, and management even had the time to commission a study of the plant-closing. Curiously to management, however, only a few employees left. More curious still, the remaining employees began setting an almost-continuous succession of monthly production records.

These surprises to management imply they had an unreliable model of the human effects of the plant-closing, and strange events reinforced this conclusion. Despite constant and orchestrated announcements to the contrary, researchers found that a growing proportion of employees came to believe that "management can't close a going concern." In fact, the proportion of such true-believers actually peaked in the last survey before the closing, in the same month that Beta achieved its *highest production ever.* Employees paid little apparent attention to the schedule for closing, which was widely disseminated. Consistently, most workshop sessions for outplacement experiences had to be canceled because of insufficient attendance, despite the fact that they were on "company time."

Hence, Beta's closing came like a bolt out of the blue to many employees, and some suffered strong reactions. Indeed, over the next year so many ex-employees became suddenly unavailable for the study -- either because of illness or death, or due to a sudden unwillingness to have anything to do with Beta -- that research on the aftermath of the plant closing was canceled.

TOWARD A VALUE-GUIDED TECHNOLOGY FOR CUTBACK

These typical outcomes can be minimized by a standard technology-cum-values. The line of "action research" labeled Organization Development (or OD) has begun to accumulate theory and experience relevant to the cutback mode (Golembiewski, 1979, Vol. 2; Sutton, 1983), and some derivative applications can reasonably claim super-optimum status. In general, adverse personnel actions have strong lose/lose components for both employees and the employing organization. In specific cases, in contrast, OD provides a normatively-based technology for extracting some aspects of win/win gold from the lose/lose dross characteristic of cutback.

The purpose here is to illustrate three such cases of super-optimum solutions in cutback situations -- when individual needs were met to a greater degree than is usual under conditions of stringent organization demands. The associated contexts are not exotic and, if in distinct ways, commonly reflect how OD values and approaches can be helpful in cutback.

The three cases also differ in significant ways. The first case is labeled "unfolding" in that it relies on rudimentary structure and basically trusts the processes and values of OD and thus, in the OD vernacular, "let things happen" within the context of these processes and values.

The second case may be labeled "articulated." It relies on a detailed design, applied in several different contexts by different teams of facilitators, which seeks to encourage relatively-specific outcomes while also enlarging the normal range of choices for both individuals and organizations in cutback situations. In contrast to the first case, the second has an inclination to "make things happen."

The third 'case' is more a conflation of the major features of an 'operating philosophy' which one organization sought to apply to situations having major adverse personnel consequences. The total sense of it is a 'learning organization': a working memory of how to deal with people and adverse economic effects, as guided by a local set of values and ways to do business.

1. *Organizational Town Meeting as Unfolding Design*. The first case derives from the "oil patch," from the petroleum/gas exploration business which is infamous for its boom-and-bust cycles. The specific locus is the Canadian headquarters of a multinational firm, which will here be called 'Down Deep Oil,' had grown to several hundred employees in a short period of time under the stimulus of high oil prices. The case involves gently-guided participative responses to a budget crunch, and relevant description can be summarized by three emphases. In turn, following sections detail a start-up OD effort in the organization, describe a cutback response congruent with that OD effort, and review the super-optimum features of that response.

CRITICAL PRE-WORK TOWARD REGENERATIVE SYSTEMS

From start-up, the Down Deep management team sought to develop a model organization, and devoted considerable time and resources to building a high-involvement culture -- responsive *and* lean (Golembiewski & Kiepper, 1988). The creation of "regenerative interaction" constitutes *the* key feature of this culture. Figure 1 depicts how different combinations of four variables can generate contrasting models of interpersonal and group interaction. Two extreme combinations of those variables induce "regenerative" and "degenerative" interaction, respectively. Regenerative interaction facilitates dealing with adversity; and degenerative interaction makes it worse, often far worse.

The component variables can be briefly described, with details available elsewhere (Golembiewski, 1979, Vol. 1). One can be open without owning, as in this common statement: "They, but I can't tell you who, really dislike what you did on project X." Risk refers to the objective threat in some environment, and trust refers to the degree of confidence one has in colleagues that things will come out OK.

Figure 1 presents one other crucial piece of information. It depicts some common consequences safely attributed to the degenerative condition. These typical consequences motivate avoiding degenerative interaction, whenever possible and even where awkward.

More or less, an opposite set of consequences explains why the use of major resources can be justified for moving toward regenerative interaction, and for maintaining it.

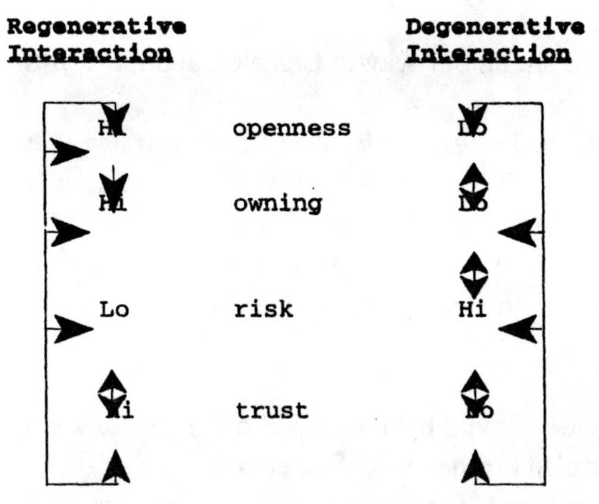

Some Probable Consequences of Degenerative Interaction

- Communication and decision-making processes become increasingly burdened
- Persons become less effective in isolating and resolving substantive issues
- The amount of unfinished business sharply increases
- Persons feel diminished interpersonal competence and psychological failure as they fail to solve problems that stay solved without creating other problems
- Persons become dependent and over-cautious, and respond by "tattling" activities, by preoccupation with being "safe," or by "don't rock the boat" attitudes
- Organization norms restricting owning and openness are re-inforced or developed by experiences like those of A and B
- Tendencies toward fragmenta-Ttion of organization units are enhanced, particularly as the basic organizing model uses functional or processual departmentalization, which is usually the case

Figure 1. Two Models for Interaction and Selected Consequences

An Unhappy and Unexpected Learning Opportunity

Progress in Down Deep toward a regenerative system got an early challenge -- an unexpected and unwelcome learning opportunity to test the strength and reaction-time of the organization. Progress toward the culture-building was advanced but still on-going when the price of oil experienced a double whammy -- both Canadian policies and those of the oil-rich Arabian states depressed prices, suddenly and sharply. The prime consequence for Down Deep? An organization in a sharply-growing mode was "tasked" by corporate to cut payroll by 20 percent. (This simplifies a bit: expenses also had to be cut. But the present description serves well enough.)

The General Manager put it directly. "We are on our way to Camelot, and the world intrudes on our plans."

During the morning the GM learned of the bad news, he also decided on a strategy, in collaboration with his management team and an OD consultant. "Decided" is too formal a description of the process, however: "We kind of reflexed into the decision," in the GM's words. After contacting corporate officials to assess degrees of local wriggle room, a rationale and associated design came to dominate the team's discussion. More or less, the words below expressed the emerging view:

> "Well, we could go into the common mode -- meet behind closed doors, try to keep the lid on things, and draw up the master plan for the fates of others.
>
> "But what the hell? That gets us tied in knots, encourages inevitable rumors, and risks losing precisely those people we want most to keep.
>
> "Above all, that's out-of-sync with the culture we've been building.
>
> "So, let's have a kind of organizational town meeting -- bring everybody together, beginning tomorrow morning, first thing. We'll lay out what we know, and decide our common fate."

The "town meeting" began the next morning, with little encumbering structure. The GM led a series of guided discussions in break-out temporary groups, relying heavily on many small "buzz groups" to permit simultaneous expressions of opinion, brain-storming, and so on, concerning individual issues. The town meeting spent the first 90 minutes or so in four basic kinds of activities:

- *ventilation*: how individuals felt about the "tasking"
- *corporate boundaries*: 20 percent payroll savings, any way, within certain time constraints
- *a needs assessment*: a discussion of priorities, given the "task"
- *general strategies*: a half-dozen were evaluated -- across-the-board cut, etc. -- but a participative strategy was the consensus choice
- *options available to individuals*: early retirement, educational leave, and so on.

In each activity, a brief input was followed by discussion or evaluation in buzz groups with shifting memberships, and then reports were made to the total assembly, where discussion continued until repetition set in. Then the process moved on.

An "aha!" experience came early. The motto became: "Let's do it our way, in our diverse ways." Special interest groups surfaced in a similar way. For example, a voice rang out: "All those interested in working 4 days a week meet over in the northwest corner." Pretty soon, 8 or 10 gaggles of special interests were clustered here and there in the large auditorium -- for early retirement, educational leave, a few persons considering voluntary separations, those interested in cutting-back their workweek for reduced compensation, and so on. To make a longer story very short, Down Deep soon had its 20 percent savings, basically before the day was over.

It did not all just occur, of course, as five points demonstrate. Paramountly, the prior successful work toward regenerative interaction fueled the effort, which required unusual openness and trust. Moreover, early on, a steering committee was established to coordinate the several personnel actions to assure that priorities could be met. In addition, a sophisticated Human Resources information system permitted quick turn-around on many details. Further, some decisions were left until the following week -- as persons checked with a relevant other, e.g., about planning to have a child; as part-time teaching opportunities at the local business schools were canvassed; and so on. Finally, some decisions applied for only 6 months, although most were for a year. So the associated details and risk would remain until much time had passed. Normal attrition was expected to provide sufficient flexibility for returning to the *status quo ante* after the contracted periods.

ASPECTS OF SUPER-OPTIMUM SOLUTION

No real-time data-gathering was attempted in this case, but many follow-up interviews and a master's project permit substantial confidence that the organizational town meeting generated major aspects of a super-optimum solution.

Four points illustrate the support for this conclusion. First, an unwelcome task was accomplished with a preponderance of win/win for both management and employees. In both cases, the design sought to empower, with a direct motivation. As Slaby notes (1989) succinctly: "A feeling of powerlessness goes hand in hand with a sense of unfairness."

Such empowering covered a substantial range, and especially for employees for whom choices appeared in many forms. Some employees had only a limited choice, to be sure -- as to decide on whether or not to reduce their workweek, usually with some costs either way. Other employees took fuller advantage of the unfortunate opportunity to do things that might ordinarily have been delayed, or even forfeited: begin a degree program, develop a business on a full- or part-time basis, or have a baby. In one case, an employee with marginal performance appraisals was empowered to seek greater clarity of his chances to succeed in the organization. The result? The individual began a program to remedy certain deficiencies in skills and knowledge, and negotiated a reduction in workhours.

Second, on very definite balance, awkward consequences were avoided. Paramountly, management avoided playing God, in general. This mode is energy-depleting, at best, and at worst often comes to be seen as arbitrary. Relatedly, little or no "survivor's mentality" developed, and this avoids variable but tricky potential for later mischief. Perhaps most of all, the town meeting largely avoided the several debilitations of a top, down effort: an intended secrecy, often compromised by rumors if not serious leaks; a dribbling-away of morale; the best people leaving in disgust as plans slowly get made; the often-observed but sad posturing, if not toadying, for favored treatment; and so on.

Win/win was not universal, of course. In a few cases, to choose a prime example, some employees were seen as "not doing what they could," and active efforts were made to put into reasonable proportion such flash-points as they occurred. An external consultant encouraged and facilitated such confrontations, with major multiple going-in presumptions: that individuals would differ in what they "could do"; that consequently any tendencies for a norm of "equal shares" should be resisted; but that in any case colleagues were better off if suspicions of "slacking" were raised, even if all could not be settled. Several employees also played similar facilitative roles, operating on similar assumptions.

Third, and obviously, the town meeting design both legitimated and drew strength from the culture of regenerative interaction. The style was applied in a tough case, and the shared risking was not only affirming but also heightened the probability of the persistence of a regenerative style. Reliance on regenerative interaction, and its persistence under adversity, perhaps best reflect a super-optimum solution in this case. Degenerative interaction is more common in organizational cutback, where avoiding law suits may seem the most desirable goal.

Fourth, some may propose that this approach "wasted time" and hence cannot be "adequate" let alone super-optimum. Perhaps. But contrast the town meeting with the typical cut-back scenario (for related summary details, see Golembiewski, 1999). There, often after poorly-hidden but top-secret discussions, those to be let go are informed close to a normal time-out boundary -- for example, noon on a Friday, or the afternoon before a holiday. People are given the afternoon to clear-out their desks, with the apparent expectation that the succeeding weekend or vacation provides sufficient emotional distance for both those remaining as well as the unbuckled.

The more likely short-run reality has very different features. Management's decision-making is likely to be extended, and even tumultuous; rumors will overstate the dimensions of the cutback, if anything; and an exodus is likely, with the most mobile people being the first to leave and the departures have been known to be so numerous or so strategic that an organization has at one and the same time been conducting a cutback as well as numerous personnel searches.

In the long run, moreover, the typical scenario does not promise benign effects. Let us be selective. For example, attempting to distance one's self and others from the immediate pain by quick shuffles very often will increase the long-run pain for all, as in later concerns about the justice of it all. Absent the information on which the original cutback was based, in addition, survivors may fear the other shoe will soon drop. Moreover, the fantasies underlying the typical cutback scenario probably will not mirror reality in important particulars, as Sutton (1983) and others have shown. For example, people's productivity does not necessarily deteriorate sharply if they are given substantial notice of an adverse personnel action, which represents the quintessential fear that typically rationalizes sudden personnel separations.

2. *Demotion Experience as Articulated Design*. This section describes a second example of a super-optimum solution via OD under cutback conditions, and the label "articulated" has multiple denotations. Basically, unlike the first case, the design is substantially programmed and comes closer to "making things happen" than to "allowing things to happen" (Golembiewski, Carrigan, Mead, Munzenrider, & Blumberg, 1972; Golembiewski, 1982-1983). Moreover, this second design of a super-optimum solution via OD under cutback conditions has been applied several times, beginning in 1971 when a national marketing organization had to sharply reduce its employment even as the national economy was booming. In addition, several teams of facilitators have applied the same or similar design, and in several decades. Various pre- vs. post-test measures also have estimated effects, and the overall results have been positive in all applications and often dramatically so. Finally, the demotion design was first used with organizational members who had substantial prior experience with OD values and approaches (Golembiewski, Carrigan, and Blumberg, 1973), but some subsequent applications involved no pre-work. The effects have been similar.

So the demotion design has a generic kinship with the town meeting just illustrated. Perhaps basically, it seeks to bring into awareness the joint responsibilities conditioned by prior good service. In the typical demotion, satisfactory performers are beset by troubles beyond their own making; it can make very good sense to safeguard a pool of experience, should things improve; and both designs reflect collaborative efforts to cope with the organizational winds and rains, as well as with the pleasant weather.

Nonetheless, the two designs differ in major ways. The town meeting was held only once, with one facilitator. Moreover, only post-intervention data are available for the town meeting, and those come largely from interviews. In addition, the town meeting design rested on substantial prior experience with OD values, while the demotion design seems to profit from such experiences but also has been applied successfully without them.

ELEMENTS OF OD DESIGN FOR DEMOTION

The initial demotion design was motivated by an unsuccessful effort to add to the product line of a pharmaceutical firm, which resulted in a major cutback that was long delayed by hopeful marketing executives. Among other actions, the original decision envisioned releasing 13 district managers of salespersons, all of whom had been satisfactory performers for periods of time -- often 5-10 years. Management found the decision unpalatable -- both in humanistic terms as well as in a loss of valuable experience that could be tapped later if sales permitted -- but executives saw no reasonable alternative. For example, demotion was seen by them as both unusual and beset with insurmountable difficulties for employer and employee. Demoted managers would suffer loss of income and important perks in "picking up the bag" of the salesperson again, and the required changes in attitude and behaviors were seen as beyond the reach of the ex-managers as well as of management.

However, a team of OD intervenors persisted in advocating a "demotion experience" for all willing ex-managers, and management relented. Most managers accepted the offer of demotion, and only 2 of 13 opted for a generous separation package. The willing ex-managers, along with two facilitators, met at a central location several days after the adverse personnel action.

The demotion design occurred over two days. Essentially, it was rooted conceptually in avoiding condition I and approaching condition II below:

I. Imaginings triggered by demotion + relative aloneness relative helplessness = increases in anxiety, hostility and depression, all associated with poor coping

II. Imaginings triggered by demotion + community + mastery = more effective coping, as reflected in reductions in initial anxiety, hostility, and depression

Details of the design are available elsewhere (Golembiewski, 1972; Golembiewski, Vol. 1, 1979, pp. 196-201) but several dominant themes economically suggest its character:

1. Choice was emphasized throughout the design, so as to maximize involvement, commitment, and ownership.
2. The first half of the design focused on building and utilizing a sense of community among the demotees: they shared reactions, feelings, hopes, and fears; they recounted how they dealt with news of the demotions, as in telling spouses; and they practiced ways of talking about their demotion to relevant others -- customers, peers, and so on.
3. The second half of the design dealt with establishing relationships between demotees and their new supervisors, who in cases were chosen by individual demotees. Pairs discussed sales philosophies, reviewed territories, and so on.

Effects were estimated via pre- and post-measures on the Multiple Affect Adjective Checklist (MAACL), as well as by the long-run performance of the demotees. For details from a specific application of the present design, see the selection above -- this editor's "Demotion Design." In this context, this selection is referred to as the "original application" of the design.

Four points summarize the overall results of several applications of the demotion design. First, the MAACL estimates three important affects -- hostility, anxiety, and aggression -- and the demotions not only seem to have sharply increased the levels of all three, but those elevated levels were maintained over the interval between the receipt of the news about the option and arrival at the training site. How high is high? Norms from other populations exposed to the MAACL imply that all populations of demotees of which I have specific knowledge scored "high" but not "unusually high," with the latter referring to decompensations implying the need for clinical intervention. Specifically, perhaps 10 percent of demotees' scores attain the top 2 percent of a standardization sample, with an additional 20 percent of the scores usually approaching that level. The demotees' pre-test scores usually average very much higher than their new managers, with all differences typically being statistically significant.

Second, the 2-day demotion experience typically has a major impact on the three MAACL measures for the demotees, and almost always in the expected direction. Specifically, in the original application, there were 33 total paired-comparisons of MAACL scores for individuals -- 11 demotees on 3 MAACL scales. Twenty-six of these comparisons showed reductions, and 3 indicated no change. One demotee did resent the "hand-holding," however. This is a typical set of effects of the demotion design.

Significantly, the participating managers seem to suffer no major adverse effects during the intervention, as far as the MAACL measures are concerned.

The MAACL reductions tend to persist. For the initial application, no major regressions in MAACL scores occurred throughout the long-post test, which followed the short post-test by about a month. Not only were all short post-test reductions maintained for demotees, but anxiety and depression also decreased significantly between the second and third administrations of the MAACL.

Fourth, interviews with participants typically reveal no broader adverse effects over time. Several (but not all) applications of the demotion design include a series of interviews -- shortly after the experience and extending over several years in one case. In the initial application, a third of the participants were re-promoted during a 3-4 year interval, and the population as a whole in the interval experienced no work difficulties beyond normal company experience. All but one of the original demotees continued employment, and he died of causes unrelated to work.

Aspects of a Super-Optimum Solution

The demotion design has numerous attractive features, on balance, and these qualify it as a super-optimum solution in a situation that is a usually a downer for all, and dire for some. Five perspectives suggest how the demotion design can improve this general state of affairs, although it cannot eliminate the sting of the personnel action felt by management as well as the demotees.

First, the demotion design increases the range of alternatives for both management and the demotees. Thus management can tangibly express its appreciation for a job satisfactorily performed in the past, and valuable experience may be husbanded for economic recovery. Moreover, the decisions by ex-managers relevant to separation/demotion give them real choices -- not only about staying-on or accepting generous separation settlements, but also about possibly moving closer to relatives or children and even in choosing their new supervisor.

In a critical sense, choice is at the heart of OD, and an enriched set of possibilities increases the chances that real psychological ownership of decisions will result. Hence one can expect greater commitment to make a success of the adaptations required from all by the decisions.

Second, of course, not just *any* choices will do: a choice that involves a probable failure has little to recommend it. The growing experience with the demotion design increases confidence that it presents reasonable, informed, and attainable choices. For both management and employees, in sum, experience indicates that the demotion design can help in the numerous adjustments that both supervisors and demotees must make in a workable demotion. A key factor may be that all applications of the demotion design of which I have knowledge involve people who were satisfactory performers, or better, in the role from which they were demoted.

Third, relatedly, the demotion design increases the mutual control by all participants in a difficult situation. Elements of risk and even coercion may exist for all actors, but such effects tend to abate. This generalization applies to the new supervisors of the demotees, for example, several of whom later reported they agreed to participate with faint heart. This may explain the significant decrease in anxiety over time for the new managers in Table 1. By hypothesis, the managers may have experienced sharply-elevated anxiety when they initially learned of the demotion experience, which the pre-test picks up. Evidence like that reviewed above may help managers in dealing with this up-front anxiety, ostensibly associated with facing the demotees and perhaps triggered by a conviction that demotions tend to be difficult or impossible for all.

Fourth, the design seems to have positive implications for the survivors of a cutback. In a significant sense, as interviews generally confirm, the demotion design seems to be viewed by many as a significant sign of a general organizational resolve to be "people-oriented," and this implies enhanced safety in commitment, and it probably removes a potential block to performance.

Fifth, the apparent palliative effects of the demotion design constitute a major reason for proposing super-optimum status. Of course, the MAACL scores suggest the stressful character of the adverse personnel action. What we know about their consequences motivates substantial efforts to moderate the stressful situations and their aftermath. Stress effects can be mundane, if troublesome (Golembiewski & Munzenrider, 1988); but those effects also can even unleash dangerous assaults on our immunological systems (Slaby, 1989).

However, the demotion design does not ease all problems associated with adverse personnel actions. Primarily, not all cutbacks permit demotion, although even close observers will be surprised at its incidence in today's human resources administration (Golder 1965; Hall & Isabella, 1985). Moreover, the initial application of the demotion design did attract some early unfavorable attention (Walton & Warwick, 1973, pp. 681-

699), essentially on ethical grounds. The major issue: Who is the client? Clearly, the management was the initiating client in the initial study, and some observers worried that this might leave the demotees unrepresented and thus potentially disadvantaged.

The issue and related ones are consequential, and the reader can consult the literature for efforts to address them (Golembiewski, 1978). Consider the answer of our consulting team to the question: Who is the client? We viewed our "client" in multiple and shifting terms, as moderated by our sense of an effective organization. Consequently, top management *was* our client. During the demotion experience, the demotees became the focal client and management understood the privileged status of off-site discussions.

3. *Working Philosophy for A Holistic Approach.* Finally, for present purposes, the view turns to what amounts to a 'working philosophy' under adversity. The brief synthesis below rests most on a single case (Golembiewski, 1990), but it also reflects a range of related experiences under economic duress.

Table 1. Summary of MAACL Scores, Days 1, 2, and 45, in One Application

	Mean scores, by *Administrations*			t-test for Differences *between Pairs of Means*		
	1	2	3	1 vs. 2	1 vs. 3	2 vs. 3
A. *Demotees*						
Anxiety	9.8	7.5	6.5	*	*	*
Depression	17.8	14.8	13.6	*	*	*
Hostility	9.5	7.2	7.2	*	*	NS
B. *Managers*						
Anxiety	6.3	5.3	4.6	*	*	NS
Depression	9.8	9.5	9.5	NS	NS	NS
Hostility	5.1	5.3	5.7	NS	NS	NS

* designates a statistically-significant difference at or beyond P = .05
NS designates a random difference

ECONOMIC REALITIES MEET OD IDEALS

In the specific case in question, a research and development operation of about 500 - part of a multinational firm - saw past success facing failure, and perhaps contributing to it. Directly, the mode in which R&D would be done in the near future - let us call it 'molecular biology' - was seen as very different from past approaches and training that had worked well enough, but would fall increasingly short as new initiatives came on-stream. Past experiences, training, and skills would have little direct influence on future successes.

What to do? The R&D unit had substantial experience with Organization Development or OD, and the values underlying it. As Figure 2 suggests, OD is explicitly value loaded. And what may be called macro-level values provide the broader contextual guides for the micro-level values/skills associated with regenerative interaction, which operate at micro-levels to induce desirable relationships between individuals and in group settings. It is a simplification, but a useful one, to begin the analysis of what is useful in R&D in terms of exploring ways to link micro- and macro-levels of values, on the order of Figure 2.

Figure 2. Linkage of Two Levels of Vales in OD

Macro-Level Values of OD		Associated Micro-Level Values/ Skills Regenerative Interaction
o an attitude of inquiry, including a hypothetical spirit and experiementation;		o high openness, or "telling it like it is"
o expanded consciousness and recognition of choice;		o high owning, or psychological acceptance of one's ideas/ feelings, and acceptance of responsibility for them and their consequences;
o a collaborative concept of authority including the open resolution of conflict and a problem-solving orientation;	⇒	o low risk, or objective threat in the environment; and
o an emphasis on authenticity in expressing feelings and dealing with their effects.		o high trust, or confidence in colleagues that "things will work out"

From Golembiewski, Vigoda, and Sun (1999).

We can only sketch the many ways in which such linkages were explored in R&D, but several illustrations are useful. Consider the nub of the new situation. A previously-successful organization will not be able to cope with the coming technology without major changes -- in skills, in missions, and relationships. Virtually all employees had high performance appraisals, but those relate mostly to then, less to today, and little to tomorrow. Employees are in the present pickle, basically, because they faithfully and competently provided what their employing organization mandated, and over the past 20 years. Quite suddenly - and, on average, at the middle stages of the employees productive lives - their organization world begins to shift beneath them.

Over time, a three-stage program of change evolves.

- the pace of worklife will have to be accelerated to make better use of hugely-expensive new methods, for dealing with heightened competition, and to facilitate coping with price and cost pressures;
- managerial styles and relationships at all levels will have to become more consistent with regenerative interaction, so as to maximize the most important resources in a knowledge industry which poses new challenges to people and capital;
- a major commitment would be made to 'reduce the barriers to creativity,' in whatever form necessary -- new training; better equipment; more collaborative relationships; new assignments for present employees outside of R&D; and voluntary changes in employees statuses;
- after some reasonable period to assimilate these reduced barriers, deliberate changes will be made in performance standards consistent with the fast-escalating requirements of the new focus on molecular biology.

Let us not gild the lily. These rough descriptions clearly imply the relevance of Figure 2: e.g., each of the stages is dominated by an expanded consciousness and a recognition of reasonable choices, given a general knowledge of what the future will bring.

An Early Initiative Via Force Field Analysis

Why choose to 'reduce the barriers to creativity?' A rationale underlays the simple words, as Figure 3 attempts to help show. Broadly, R&D was in a state of quasi-stationary equilibrium (A), with movement A - B being required by the impending changes. That point (A) is the resultant of two sets of forces - Driving and Restraining, contributors to which are sketched in Figure 3, with the length of the several vectors indicating the strength of the individual vectors.

How to induce that movement? Three possibilities exist:

- no doubt typically, new driving forces would be added, or the strength of old ones would be increased; typically, also, restraining forces would be increased;
- reduce old restraining forces; and
- convert old restraining forces into new driving forces, which is the premium strategy. For example, attitudes toward management initially constituted a moderate restraining force, as represented by C in Figure 3. Given major efforts by employees and managers, C in Figure 3 got converted into C -- i.e., a negative - positive shift in attitudes toward management.

'Reducing the barriers to creativity,' then, basically involves seeking to act on the second and third strategies above: to eliminate or reduce old restraining forces; and to convert old restraining forces into new driving forces. The last is a 'big bang' strategy. Visually, as Figure 3 suggests about this premium strategy, A is free to shift toward A-for two reasons: the old restrainer C is gone and, simultaneously, C- provides an additional push toward B.

Figure 3. Schema of Force Field Analysis

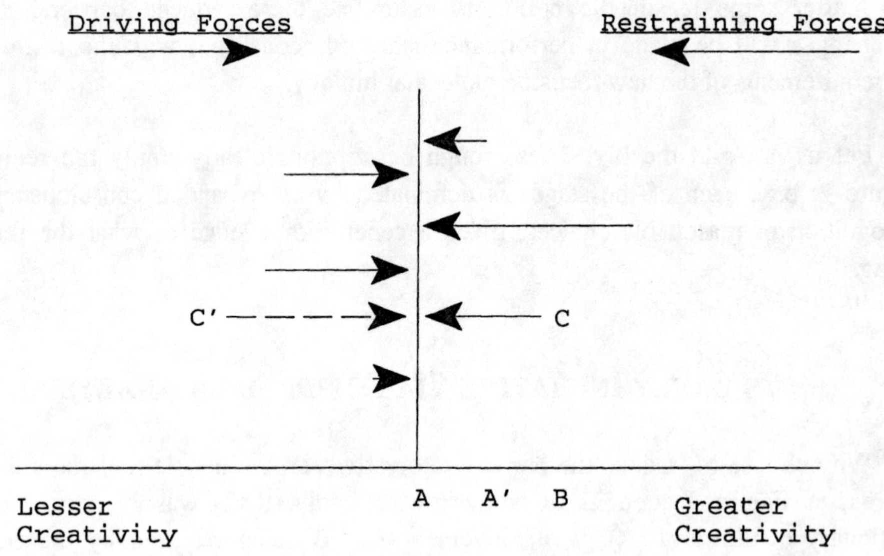

ASPECTS OF SUPER-OPTIMUM SOLUTION

These details could be elaborated in many ways, as has been done elsewhere (Golembiewski, 1990); but the general point should be clear enough. The employing organization faced escalating economic demands, but its key officials also had a strong sense of shared responsibility for what had been, and what was yet to come. In turn, employees were offered multiple opportunities for having a hand in how those looming pressures would be responded to in two basic ways – by helping induce more flexible and team-based worksite, as well as by initiating manifold ways of getting themselves and their skills in greater consonance with the demands of new R&D context taking on a molecular biology mission.

The characteristics of the organization-to-be were not clearly envisioned; but it was clear that major changes would be required, and many of these would involve new skills and knowledge suitable for molecular biology. Any brief description simplifies reality. In general, however, the 'new' system inclines toward (for example) the computer design of molecules for those target-specific human organs or tissues for which good models existed, and often to keep unwelcome things from happening in the first place. This research by design is contrasted with the 'old' R&D -- the discovery of a natural product that was shown to have some 'activity' when deposited on a 'screen' of organisms, which might in turn lead to tests of efficacy against some real-life disease entities, typically after-the-fact of unwelcome intrusion or infection.

Six features suggest the potential for a succession of super-optimum solutions in R&D. First, the focus was on developing a common ground concerning issues that could easily become conflictful, if not adversarial. Major changes and upgrades in skills would be required for most present employees retained in the new R&D. This would requires intense collaboration over time between the agents of the firm and its employees.

Second, it was widely recognized that changes in culture and relationships would be useful, if not necessary. These would require major changes in many values, attitudes, and skills. For example, from inception, substantial investments were made in training for regenerative interaction and its application intact work teams in the normal courses of their business.

Third, to maximize the burgeoning costs of research and development – both in general, and those specifically associated with molecular biology – extensive changes would have to be made in information sharing, collaboration, and even joint decision-making. The 'old' R&D was characterized by substantial balkanization of sub-units, and the 'new' pattern would require integrative changes in structure as well as attitudes and skills. Basically, the challenges here involved training and development of individuals and teams. In some cases, experienced employees might prove unable or unwilling to provide the appropriate behaviors, skills, and attitudes. Policies and procedures needed crafting for such contingencies.

Fourth, many 'old' policies and practices would require revision -- e.g., in the case of a more discriminative performance appraisal system, and various linkages to it such as career planning and career ladders. High degrees of involvement and commitment at all levels guided changes in policies and practices that were widely disparaged but in which many mangers and employees had vested interests.

Fifth, normative compacts were developed to work toward a value or cultural context for the 'new' R&D. Hence, the centrality of values like those in Figure 2. Specific learning experiences deal with the participative development of management credos, culture statements, mission statements, and so on, reflecting Figure 2 values (e.g., Golembiewski, 1990).

Sixth, since the anticipated changes were to a substantial degree a black box, trust levels had to be built, and their maintenance had to be justified in the minds of employees as well as their managers. In effect, each major phase at once challenged trust, and consequences could either reinforce that trust or weaken it. The ante kept being raised, in general.

Hence, some reasonable confidence was required about how highly-probable as well as unpredictable contingencies would be dealt with. For example, in the early program stages, the executive champion received one of those rare offers that 'no one can turn down,' and he joined another organization. As it turned out, this potential crisis of confidence became an affirming experience concerning values like those illustrated in Figure 2. Details are available elsewhere (Golembiewski, 1990).

DISCUSSION

These three candidates for super-optimum solution do double-duty. They illustrate a technology-cum-values, usually called Organization Development or OD, and they support the usefulness of Nagel's seminal metaphor. Three points add useful detail supporting these broad conclusions.

First, the three descriptions rest on a broadly-applicable approach to super-optimum solutions -- via inducing aspects of regenerative interaction between people and groups. This augments Nagel's (1989, pp, 12-15) original list of "procedures," which include: generating new or novel policy alternatives; proposing new goals; bringing in a third-party; and so on. The OD approach often involves a third-party -- a change-agent or intervenor -- but adds to Nagel's list a focus on useful interpersonal and intergroup processes and interaction that can enrich and enliven exchanges between people.

This focus on models of interaction is at once narrow, and yet ubiquitous in application. Thus regenerative interaction might well help facilitate policy development, whenever. For example, I hear -- but do not know for certain -- that the Camp David accords rested on the conscious effort to induce regenerative interaction by a skilled facilitator. And Nagel rightly highlights Camp David as illustrating a super-optimum solution.

Second, the three cameos also add a useful sense of reproducibility of approaches to super-optimum solutions. All the cases involve the induction of aspects of regenerative interaction, via techniques that typically "work" (Golembiewski, 1979, Vol. 1). Moreover, the demotion design has been replicated -- by different intervenors, in several settings, at various times. These two senses of reproducibility add to the appeal of super-optimum solutions, which can in part rest on foundations in addition to flashes of insight about (for example) new or novel policies.

Third, OD is a technology-cum-values that is broadly applicable, although not universally. Thus, a range of OD designs have substantial success rates in western worksettings -- a survey (Golembiewski, 1998) of 23 separate surveys of evaluations of such applications speaks to this point, and at impressive length. In addition, OD applications in 'developing' societies also reflect high success rates, but less formidable ones than in western worksettings (e.g., Golembiewski and Luo, 1994).

Fourth, the three serve to highlight the challenge inherent in the concept of super-optimum solutions. Their *basic* definition -- as referring to situations from which participants "come out ahead of their initial *best* expectations" constitutes a dynamic target. To illustrate, efforts to build regenerative systems are no longer rare, but neither are they ubiquitous. That situation may well change. Certainly, the trend-line of reliance on OD is sharply up over the last two decades. Today's super-optimum solution, in short, can become tomorrow's initial best expectation, or even a commonplace expectation. And so the continual search for super-optimum solutions will be motivated by its own successes.

In sum, S-O-S is a moving target, but one well worth pursuit.

REFERENCES

Goldner, F. H. (1965). Demotion in industrial management. *American Sociological Review, 30*, 714-724.

Golembiewski, R. T. (1978) *Public Administration as A Developing Discipline*. New York: Marcel Dekker.

Golembiewski, R. T. (1979). *Approaches to Planned Change*, Vol. 1. New York: Marcel Dekker.

Golembiewski, R. T. (1979). *Approaches to Planned Change*, Vol. 2. New York: Marcel Dekker.

Golembiewski, R. T. The demotion design. (1982-83). *National Productivity Review*, 2, (Winter), 63-70.

Golembiewski, R. T. (1990). American Research and Development. Pp. 490-479, in A. Glassman and T. Cummings, editors. *Cases in Organization Development*. Homewood, IL.: Irwin, 1990.

Golembiewski, R. T. (1998). Dealing with doubt and cynicism the old-fashioned way: Empirical data about success rates in OD and QWL. Pp. 17-35 in M. A. Rahim, R. T. Golembiewski, and C. Lundberg, editors, *Current Topics in Management*. Greenwich, CN.: JAI Press.

Golembiewski, R. T. (1999). Mission statement. In R. T. Golembiewski, editor, *Handbook of Organizational Consultation*. New York: Marcel Dekker, In press.

Golembiewski, R. T., Carrigan, S. B., & Blumberg, A. (1973). More on building new work relationships. *Journal of Applied Behavioral Science*, *9* (1), 26-28.

Golembiewski, R. T., Carrigan, S. B., Mead, W. R., Munzenrider, R. F., & Blumberg, A. (1972). Toward building new work relationships. *Journal of Applied Behavioral Sciences*, *8* (3), 135-148.

Golembiewski, R. T., & Kiepper, A. (1988). *High Performance and Human Costs*. New York: Praeger.

Golembiewski, R. T., & Luo, H. (1994). OD applications in developmental settings: An addendum about success rates. *International Journal of Organizational Analysis*, 2 (3), 229-235.

Golembiewski, R. T., & Munzenrider, R. F. (1988). *Phases of Burnout*. New York: Praeger.

Golembiewski, R. T., Vigoda, E., & Sun, B-C. (1999). Cacophonies in the contemporary chorus about change at public worksites, as contrasted with some straight-talk from a planned change perspective. Paper prepared for the Annual Conference, American Society for Public Administration, Orlando, Fl. April 11.

Hall, D. T., & Isabella, L. A. (19). Downward movement and career development. *Organizational Dynamics, 14* (Summer), 5-23.

Nagel, S. S. (1989). Super-optimum solutions in public controversies. *Futunes Research Quarterly*, 1989.

Slaby, A. E. (1989). *Aftershock.* New York, Villard Books.

Sutton, R. I. (1983). Managing organizational death. *Human Resource Management, 22* (Winter), 391-412.

Walton, R. E., & Warwick, D. P. (1973). The ethics of organization development. Journal of Applied Behavioral Science,9 (11), 681-699.

Chapter 12

The Dissolution of the Czechoslovak and Yugoslav Federations: A Lose-Lose Policy Outcome?

Jim Seroka
University of North Florida

Abstract

None of the three federations which had operated with Communist governments survived the transition from socialist rule. Some of the reasons for the collapse can be attributed to the close ties between the communist parties and the federal institutions, the symbiosis between nationalism, ethnicity and the sub-federal units, the ambivalence towards federalism by the new political elites, the failure of the new mass movements to accept or bond to the federal idea, the absence of a convincing military rationale for federation, and the resistance of the economic and commercial elites to the maintenance of the federal institutions. The continuance or reform of federalism was simply not acceptable as an option and objective rational calculi of the alternatives never entered into the picture. Thus, while the decision to disband had strong lose-lose overtones, the political context would not permit objective consideration of the federal option.

The Yugoslav federal collapse was accompanied by violence, war and conflict. The Czechoslovak dissolution was uneventful. Yugoslavia's violent dissolution, in comparison to the Czechoslovak case, can be explained by such factors as the presence of Serbia which was willing to defend the federation, the relatively large number of federal units in Yugoslavia and wide disparities among them, the divisions within the Yugoslav League of Communists, the role of the Yugoslav National Army as a protector of the socialist federal regime, and the non-constructive role of the world community.

I. Failure of the Federal Idea to Survive the Post Socialist Transformations in Czechoslovakia and Yugoslavia

The failure of the federal institutions and of the federal idea to survive the transition from state socialism in East central Europe is not the result of a single factor explanatory theory; nor can it be ascribed simply as an unexpected consequence of the collapse of Marxist-Leninist regimes. Also, we should not infer that the explanatory matrices of federal dissolution were identical for both the Socialist Federal Republic of Yugoslavia and the Socialist People's Republic of Czechoslovakia, or that the dissolutions of socialist federal republics are accidental artifacts of the emerging political leaders. In both the Yugoslav and Czechoslovak cases, timely and effective action by the new political leaders would have only served to affect the rapidity and violence associated with the federal dissolution, and even a determined opposition to dissolution by the federal political leaders would not have been able to alter the final outcome (i.e. the dissolution of the federal state).

Of greater concern to scholars is the need to explore why the federal idea in both Yugoslavia and Czechoslovakia had so few defenders; why its detractors were so passionate; and why both the elite and the masses cared so little about the federal framework. An objective cost-benefit analysis of the continuance or reform of the federal structures never occurred, and in both Czechoslovakia and Yugoslavia, the respective federations were perceived as anti nationalist, anti-reform and anti-democratic. Federal structures were also viewed as impediments to inclusion in the economic and military associations with the West, and most critically, they were perceived as part of the obsolete communist infrastructure that impeded the transformation process.

Significant parts of the answer to this puzzle can be found in the following circumstances: (A) the interaction between the Communist Parties and the federal institutions; (B) the symbiosis between nationalism, ethnicity and the sub-federal units; (C) the ambivalence towards federalism by the new political elites; (D) the failure of the new mass movements to accept or bond with the federal idea; (E) the lack of a military threat to encourage consociation; and (F) the resistance of the economic and commercial elites to continued association. Each of these factors made a significant contribution to the demise of the federal idea, and any attempt to reconstruct federalism in these states would be forced to overcome the resistance associated with these issues. Those new leaders who were in the position to decide the fate of the continuance of the federal system were not able to act upon the problem objectively and could not compare the relative objective costs and benefits of different structural approaches.

A. Co-option of Federal Institutions by the Communist Party

Defenders of federalism in both Czechoslovakia and Yugoslavia were constrained by the close bilateral association between the communist party and the federal institutions and structures. Many of those who were philosophically predisposed to favor the federal idea were constrained from articulating and working on behalf of these views by the practical difficulties in separating federalism from the socialist experience. President Vaclav Havel of Czechoslovakia, for example, vehemently disagreed with the break-up of the Federation, but he could not effectively defend it without relying on those institutions such as the civil service, army and police which had fought against the "Velvet Revolution. Havel's conundrum was intensified by the fact that federally oriented political forces such as Civic Forum had done poorly in the national elections, while Czech and Slovak "national parties had swept into power(Obrman, 1992. Even though only minorities in both republics backed dissolution, Havel and like-minded supporters would have risked political marginalization had they actively opposed the de-federalization of the state (Butorova, 1992; FBIS, June 30, 1992). As long as the focus was on the perfidies of the communist federal rulers, it was unacceptable to consider maintaining the old regime□s federal institutions.

In Yugoslavia, the association between communism and federalism was even stronger. Federal Yugoslavia was a creature of the Party, and Tito's imposition of a federal system after the war served as a vehicle to control political conflict and to assure Party dominance. The federal institutions, including the civil service and the army, were linked to the Party and became instruments of Party rule. In Socialist Yugoslavia, the army, Party, Tito and federalism were inseparable and highly interdependent upon one another (Rusinow, 1991). With the collapse of the communist monopoly, only the League of Communists -- Movement for Renewal, a party whose leaders were active members of the federal civil service and whose membership was dominated by the army officer corp, stood steadfastly by the federation. In these republics, the federation could not be judged separate from the activities and character of its communist proponents.

The close identification of the federal idea to the communist regimes was a clear consequence of Party policies. Since the Communists held a monopoly of power for more than forty years, all federal institutions had become dependent upon the Party. The legitimacy of the federal institutions, particularly in Yugoslavia, were derived from the legitimacy of the Party; and federal institutions, as transmission belts for the Party, enjoyed little autonomy and identification outside the umbrella of the Party. In these federal communist regimes, rotation between party and federal posts became routinized and party leaders would easily shift from one venue to another. Federal leadership posts in both Czechoslovakia and Yugoslavia were classrooms of instruction for future party leaders as well as sinecures for semi-retired Party functionaries. Thus, it is quite justified for the federal institutions and the cadre who staffed them to be perceived as puppets of the communist regime and untrustworthy confederates in the post-socialist transformation (Bernhard, 1993).

Politics associated with the transformation process from socialism also adversely affected the chances for the continuance of federal institutions in a post-socialist environment. In contrast to the situation in the unitary socialist states (e.g. Poland, Hungary) where resistance to communist rule had to be focussed on a single center of power, the political possibilities in the socialist federal systems permitted resistance to take different forms and intensity within different federal units. The multiplicity of centers of power in Czechoslovakia and Yugoslavia forestalled the emergence of a unified opposition and created, particularly in Yugoslavia, a situation where the political profiles in the federal units diverged dramatically from one another. Rather than engendering a single opposition movement, the multiple centers of power facilitated multiple opposition movements that hindered the possibility for a national consensus and a unified new elite.

Not surprisingly, the elites which emerged in the federal republics viewed the federal institutions and the cadre which served them as unnecessary remnants of the communist past and impediments to a multi-party democracy. Unlike the situation in such non federal socialist states as Poland and Bulgaria, the new elites did not need to control the national levels of government to seize and hold power. In contrast, the continuance of the federal levels of government could easily be perceived as an unnecessary risk for the survival of the leaders in these embryonic liberal states (Franck, 1968).

Within Yugoslavia, the danger of the return of communist rule increased commensurately with the power of the federation. During the latter part of the 1980s, the communists in Yugoslavia had used the federation as a mechanism to preserve their power and to oppose devolution or liberalization in the constituent republics. The army, party and civil service recognized and acted upon their interdependency to secure their survival, and each had supported the others to repel reform movements in the republics. For example, Slovenia's early attempt to limit party control and to pluralize its political system was opposed so forcefully and crudely by the army and federal civil service that Slovenia's political leadership could not contemplate negotiation and compromise with the Federation. It was compelled to chose between federal party solidarity or solidarity with the Slovenian nation. For Slovenia, reform and democracy could only occur outside party and federal constraints (Vodopivec, 1992).

In contrast to Yugoslavia, the Czech and Slovak republic institutions were not the initial carriers of change and reform, but even there, republic leaders emerged as the protectors of the transformation against a federal state whose communist dominated bureaucracy could not be trusted. The results of these open elections highlighted the fact that the reformed Communists were the only major political party with substantial support in both republics and with a claim as the only federal party (Pehe, 1992a). This outcome encouraged both the Czech and Slovak non-communist political leaders to fear the possibility of a return of communist rule so long as they remained members of the same federation. Again, anti-communism and anti-federalism had become linked to the politics of post socialist transformation.

In retrospect, it is easy to understand why the new elites did not view the federal institutions favorably or even as neutral elements in the new society. Federal structures were staffed by communist functionaries; and they had been impediments to the transformation process. In addition, in contrast to the experience of the unitary communist states, federal communist systems had other alternatives for governance. These republic institutions more closely matched the needs of the new elites and were more secure from the threat of a potential communist comeback. For the new leaders, the federal institutions were perceived as potential Trojan horses whose patronage would unnecessarily endanger their newly won autonomy; and from their perspective, the federal institutions were not essential to the well-being of the nation.

B. Impact of Ethnicity and National Self-determination

A second issue dooming the continuance of federalism in the post socialist states was the insistence that ethnic identity be the guiding principle for the federal system (Sheehy, 19920. Unlike Anglo-Saxon federations, a major organizing element of the socialist federations was to provide the appearance of self rule for nationalities or distinctive ethnic groups. For Czechoslovakia, the primary emphasis was on the preservation of Slovak identity. For the Yugoslav federation, the principle was also to provide ethnic national autonomy within a republic boundary for certain recognized nationalities and to protect minority rights of members from other ethnic groups within the framework of the Federation.

Both the central European socialist federations made exceptions to the principle of self-determination. The Czechoslovak federation excluded federal status for Hungarians who largely resided in the Slovak republic, and the Yugoslav system restricted and later eliminated autonomy for the overwhelmingly Albanian population in Kosovo. Both federations ignored the Gypsies who could not lay claim to a specific territory, and the Yugoslavs created the republic of Bosnia for the exceptionally ethnically mixed area in the center of the country.

Ethnicity was also extremely important in the governance of both republics. In Yugoslavia and to a lesser extent Czechoslovakia, ministerial posts, diplomatic assignments, military ranks, etc. were distributed with ethnic quotas in mind. The 1974 Yugoslav constitution routinized and legalized the process when it mandated a predetermined ethnic rotation of major leadership assignments and a collective decision-making process.

Federal authorities in both Czechoslovakia and Yugoslavia propagated a mythology which solemnly proclaimed that each ethnic group had voluntarily and temporarily suspended their rights to self-determination and had freely chosen membership within the federation. For Yugoslavia, the AVNOJ declaration on the resistance forces during the second world war provided the legal framework in which deputies from each of the ethnic groups pooled their sovereignty into the new socialist federation.

Rather than bind the federations together, the ethnic quotas and federal mythologies served to drive the ethnic groups apart and to accentuation divisions. Unpopular federal decisions were justified on the basis of the nationality compact, and instances of individual incompetence served to reinforce ethnic stereotypes or to pander to ethnically based conspiratorial theories. In Yugoslavia, educational curricula, mass media, transport, social service legislation and numerous other public polices diverged from republic to republic without serving any rational principle save ethnic separateness. Each republic protected and articulated the rights of its ethnic group and relied on the federation only to protect its members in other republics. Thus, as the republics achieved additional autonomy and the powers of the federation waned, ethnic minorities within the republics became increasingly disenchanted and fearful for their future (Varady, 1992). More importantly, as support for the communists and federation weakened among the elite in the republics, the minority groups sought allies from their ethnic kindred in other republics and sought union with them rather than cooperation with the majority ethnic group within their host republic.

Demonstrations and riots by the Albanian population in Kosovo in 1981 underscored the seriousness of the situation in Yugoslavia. Demands for autonomy and republic status by Albanians in Serbian-held Kosovo could only be met by relegating Kosovan Serbs to minority status in their ancestral homeland, an unacceptable outcome to the leadership in the Serbian republic. It was this failure by the Serbs to accommodate the Albanians which induced the Slovenians to worry about a democratic future in a Serb-dominated and increasingly non-pluralist federation, and it eventually underscored their demands for separation from the Federation (Goati, 1993). During the latter 1980s , as the republics assumed more responsibilities and power, minorities in other republics, particularly Serb minorities in Croatia, feared assimilation by the dominant ethnic group and undertook destabilizing actions against the republic governments (Markotich, 1993).

Following the Second World War, the concept of federating ethnic nations together seemed reasonable. Prior to the war, the small ethnic states had been easily threatened by their larger neighbors and had been blocked from equitable entry into the larger European markets. By 1990, however, a federation no longer provided significant external trade or defense advantages, and the successful experience of such small states as Denmark, Belgium, Luxembourg, and Portugal highlighted how it was possible for small states to prosper without endangering their political sovereignty.

The drive towards European unity undermined the founding rationale for federations in small states such as Czechoslovakia and Yugoslavia. In Slovenia, Croatia, Macedonia and even Serbia, the new elites effectively argued that the dissolution of the federal republic would strengthen ethnic identity at home and encourage ethnic prosperity abroad. Correspondingly, Czech leaders could argue that entry into the European Community would be simplified and facilitated by ejection of the lesser developed Slovak republic from its membership application (Wolchik, 1994).

C. Role and Orientation of the New Political Elites

One of the peculiar aspects of the dissolution of the socialist federal republics was that the new political elites were much more committed to the dissolution of the federations than were the general populace. Public opinion polls in Czechoslovakia before and following the federal breakup underscored substantial majorities of the population in both republics favoring the maintenance of federal ties. As little as one third of the populace favored dissolving the federation, but the leaders of both the Czech and Slovak ruling parties pushed for the breakup rather than engage in efforts to form a coalition government (FBIS, June 30, 1992). Attempts by Mr. Havel, then president of the Federation, to hold a referendum on the issue were strongly resisted by party leaders, particularly in Slovakia, who feared that the results of the referendum would undermine their rationale to dissolve the federation. In brief, The federation of Czechoslovakia broke up despite popular will, not because of it.

In Yugoslavia, the situation was more complex but essentially similar to the Czechoslovak case. Until 1990, few outside the republic elites favored dissolution and most preferred negotiations and a new confederal compact. Among the populace, many families, particularly in Bosnia, feared the consequences of dissolution along ethnic national lines. Intermarriage among ethnic groups was common, and the economic and commercial advantages of inter-ethnic association were substantial. Nevertheless, the new anti-communist leaderships had articulated their programs on the basis of ethnic independence and opposition to federal (i.e. Serbian) rule and domination. In Slovenia, Janez Jansa, later defense minister for independent Slovenia, achieved prominence and hero status by his opposition to federal army authorities. Croatia's Franjo Tudman had capitalized on Croatian nationalism an employed nationalist symbols in order to differentiate his party from the reformed communists. Tudman's Croatian Democratic Community (HDZ) benefitted from a divided left and swept into power with approximately 40 percent of the vote, two thirds of all parliamentary seats, and the militant opposition from the Serb minority in the republic (Grdesic, 1992). Serbia's Slobodan Milosevic achieved the same result by benefitting from the boycott of the elections by the Albanian population in Kosovo.

In Yugoslavia, both Slovenia and Croatia held referenda on sovereignty, but it was the understanding at the time that there would be negotiations leading to confederation. Again, it was the political leaders in the new republics, with the exception of Kiro Gligorov in Macedonia, not the populace, who steered their republics towards immediate separation. Following the referenda, it was the republic leaders, not the masses nor business elites, who stonewalled good faith negotiations.

The history of most federal formations suggest that the regional elites play a major role in federal state formation, and that the populace is ambivalent or hostile to the proposed arrangements. In the case of the failed socialist federations, however, it was the republic elites who sought breakup despite ambivalence or opposition from their constituents.

In the socialist federal cases, it appears that the exhaustion of mass politics and the unique circumstances contributed to the demise of the federal compact. Not only were the new regional elites anti communist and anti system, they were also divided and shared few commonalities with one another. Contrary to the popular mythology, the communist parties in the socialist federations did not mount a sustained resistance. they essentially collapsed like a house of cards and the opposition movements never coalesced for a protracted struggle. In some cases, the new regional elites were direct heirs to the communist regimes (e.g. Serbia, Slovakia, Macedonia). In other cases, they were national front parties (e.g. Demos in Slovenia and Civic Forum in the Czech lands) or aggressively ethnic nationalist (e.g. HDZ in Croatia). The opposition to the Communists in Czechoslovakia or in Yugoslavia never banded together, cooperated or proposed a common program of action.

The new regional political elites tended not to gravitate toward a federal toward a federal style of governance or advance pluralist principles. They seemed uncomfortable with pluralism and with the give and take of federal style politics (Siber, 1993). Unlike the experience of Solidarnosc in Poland, the new political leaders in the federal states had never associated together nor did they struggle for power over a long period of time. The republic elites in the federal republics achieved their aims and garnered public support because of their separateness and courage in opposing the communist federal regimes. The new leaders had also matured in a communist system that excelled in co-option as a prelude to absorption, and many had survived because of their refusal to be coopted or to accept compromise. Their success, in other words, could be attributed to their steadfastness to principles, not to their skills at compromise (Kasapovic, 1992). For these leaders, cooperation, compromise, co-option and coercion were synonymous. Integrity and independence were the models that had defined the character of political opposition, a model not conducive to the give and take of political federalism. Again, the advantages of the federation were depreciated in value while the problems and corruption of the central regimes were blamed on federal structures and priorities.

D. Absence of Inter-Republic Political Activity

Most conceptual analyses of federalism conclude that democratic federal arrangements can only exist in an environment supportive of interest group politics. As James Madison argued 200 years ago in the *Federalist Papers*, federalism's primary advantage was to control the effect of faction and to prevent a tyranny of the majority over the minority. In the East Central European federations interest groups and socio-political organizations had little autonomy or legitimacy. They were transmission belts for Party policy, and forty-five years of communist rule had atrophied politics independent of the Party and had emasculated institutions not controlled by the state.

The socialist societies, in other words, were mass societies, hostile to factions and independent political movements, and their experiences with independent social activity, particularly activities which crossed republic borders, were extremely limited. Even environmental groups which organized within the republics and their nascent Green parties in both Yugoslavia and Czechoslovakia failed to cooperate and to develop a common program and common organizational structure. In the struggle for freedom, the republics struggled alone.

While poor communications and language difficulties played a role in explaining the absence of cross-republic organization, the lack of trust and real danger of repression from the federal authorities forestalled cross-republic organization. There were few incentives and many risks for those segments of the population whose interests crossed republic borders and who sought broad-based federal movements or activities. The successful model of resistance in the federal republics were republic-based and mass-based. Interest groups lent support, but did not play critical roles in the transformation process and did not coalesce across republic lines.

Compounding the difficulties of cross-republic interest group activities were the wide variations in the transformation process across republics in the two federations.. The Slovak experience, for example, lacked the spontaneity and humanism of Prague's's new awakening. In Yugoslavia, Slovenia had developed a multi-party framework well in advance of any of the other republics, and Slovenia pioneered the transformation through a unique mechanism for accommodating the Slovenian communist party into its grand coalition. Croatia's turn from communism lacked many of the democratic overtones associated with Slovenia, and Serbia failed to undertake any serious democratic reform. Given the disparity in experiences across the federal republics, it would have been very difficult for any of the new leadership groups to coalesce across republic borders, despite any latent commonalities of interests. In fact, from the perspectives of the elites, those who supported federalism could only be perceived as sympathetic to the communist cause and enemies of the populist revolt against the Communist regime.

E. International Disincentives

The decision to federate is often influenced by national security concerns and fear of potential military threats against the sovereignty of the potential federal members. Strength in unity has often been used as a major contributing factor and prop for successful federations. In Yugoslavia, for example, Tito had often made the point that Croatian, Slovenian, Macedonian or Serbian independence against potential expansionism by Germany, Italy, Bulgaria or Hungary could only be guaranteed by federal associations. Correspondingly, the Czechoslovak Federation was conceived as a defense against expansionist German or revisionist Austrian tendencies.

For both Czechoslovakia and Yugoslavia, the end of the Cold War removed any credible military rationale for continued federation. Yugoslavia's policy of nonalignment, a core ideological principle of the Yugoslav socialist regime, became meaningless with the breakup of the eastern bloc. For Czechoslovakia, the military concentrations of power following World War II meant that the additional security benefits derived from federation were marginal at best. Since no external force threatened the sovereignty of the smaller nations, there was no logical reason to pursue federal arrangements for security purpose.

With the success of the European Economic Community, national economic interests could logically be enhanced by dissolution of the small federations. Czechs, Slovenians and Croats all felt that their chances for eventual membership into the Community would be enhanced if they could shed the burden of association with their more economically backward partners such as Slovakia, Macedonia, Bosnia etc. From the perspective of the developed federal partners, the benefits derived from the respective federations paled in comparison to the potential market benefits of early entrance into the European Community. From their perspective, the continuance of the federal system would mean that they would continue to bear a disproportionate burden of the military costs of the federation, receive disproportionately less of the externalities associated with the military; and they would be hindered in negotiating new ties with Western Europe.

F. Socialist Regional Development Policy and Federalism

Federal systems can retain support if the commercial and economic interests in the federal republics are convinced that the economic benefits of association outweigh the costs, and if these groups feel that they have some control over the decision-making process in the distribution of federal costs and benefits. In both Socialist Yugoslavia and Czechoslovakia, however, federal authorities appeared to rely more on coercion, Party politics, and central decision-making. Economic principles in formulating and implementing developmental policies played a decidedly secondary role (Bombelles, 1991). Regional developmental policies were perceived as politically-biased and arbitrary, and both recipients and grantors perceived themselves as victims in the relationship (Milosevic, 1989). The net result is that influential components of the economic and commercial sectors in all the federal units perceived that there would be more economic advantages from independence and dissolution than from continuance of the federal bonds.

Czech commercial elites, for example, resented subsidies to the state-run heavy industries in Slovakia, particularly those associated with armaments. Reciprocally, many Slovaks tended to perceive that the shock therapy policies of the federal state and demilitarization of the economy disproportionately threatened their basic economy (Wolchik, 1994). In Yugoslavia, Slovenians resented the distributive policies of the development fund which took scarce capital from Slovenia and applied it to support inefficient industries in Bosnia, Macedonia and Serbia. Many Croats criticized the Federation for controlling the hard currency earned from its profitable tourism sector. Among the less developed Yugoslav republics, Macedonia resented Slovene control over raw material processing of Macedonian goods, and many Bosnians felt that they were relegated to the role of a raw material provider for the other republics. The lesser developed republics were convinced that they were exploited, and that the developed republic received a disproportionate amount of the value added. In short, both the developed and underdeveloped republics in both Czechoslovakia and Yugoslavia perceived that independence would generate more commercial benefits than they would lose from continued association.

Although reasonably objective studies have concluded that the federal attempts to redistribute wealth and build balanced economies generally conformed to equality driven values, the lack of local control and involvement in the collection, distribution and planning of development funds under socialism meant that regional developmental policies never developed any supportive constituencies (Hugelin, 1987). From the perspective of the less developed republics, the rush to market economies resurrected concerns of the abandonment of equality concerns and the reintroduction of exploitative capitalism. This fear of renewed exploitation was seized upon by the former communist parties and it became an issue that the new ruling elites could not ignore.

SUMMARY

In summary, the federal systems in both Yugoslavia and Czechoslovakia were not able to survive the transition from socialism. The close identification of the Party to the federal idea, the linking of nationality-ethnicity to federalism, the lack of inter-republic solidarity among the republic elites, the relatively poorly developed interest group structure, the withering of the military threat, and the failure to build an economic constituency all doomed the federal systems to collapse following the exodus of communist authority. It is not accidental that none of the socialist states proposed the adoption of federalism, and that none of the federal systems under socialism retained the federal idea after the collapse of communist authority. There were simply few incentives and many powerful disincentives to the concept of federalism following the communist collapse. Thus, while the decisions to disband the federation were, from a rational economic perspective, lose-lose decisions, the political environment in which the decisions occurred would not permit a more objective consideration of the federal option.

II. CONTRASTS BETWEEN THE DISSOLUTION IN CZECHOSLOVAKIA AND YUGOSLAVIA

For political observers, the contrast between the pre-negotiated and peaceful breakup of Czechoslovakia and the vicious degenerative disintegration of Yugoslavia is stunning. Although it is comforting, we should not ascribe the difference to the innate humanism of Vaclav Havel and the nationalist myopia represented by Slobodan Milosevic. While the personalities and behavior of the leaders are important, other systemic, cultural-historical, social and political factors need to be taken into account.

Several factors suggest themselves as possible contributors for explaining the contrast between the collapse of the federations in Czechoslovakia and in Yugoslavia. First, the Serbs, the largest national group in the Federation, had propogated a national mythology as the defender of the Yugoslav idea and as the core ethnic group in the Federation. Neither the Czechs nor Slovaks assumed that role in the Czechoslovak federation. Second, the number of federal units in Yugoslavia and their often competitive and violent historical experiences contributed to a deep hostility that was reinforced by the clash of civilizations represented in the area. Third, the Czechoslovak Party did not fragment into warring republic units prior to the collapse of the communist monopoly of power. In Yugoslavia, in contrast, the unity of the Party and variation among republic Communist parties were often greater than differences among parties within the republic following multi-party elections. Fourth, the Yugoslav National Army functioned as a military arm and defender of the socialist regime and it resisted the transformation process. In Czechoslovakia, the military undertook a much less significant political role. Finally, the Yugoslav federation faced dissolution at a time when the international community remained wedded to the concept of permanent borders. By its actions, it encouraged the federal authorities in Yugoslavia to stand firm and resist secession. In the Czechoslovak case, the international community was uninvolved and did not pressure for one outcome over another.

A. Defenders of the Federation

When one compares the politics and mythology of statehood for Czechoslovakia and Yugoslavia, one is confronted with a major disparity in viewpoints and approaches. Czechoslovakia's mythology of federal statehood is described as a marriage of convenience and a practical accommodation for the two small nations which constituted it. The formation of the state following World War I was not preceded by a Czechoslovak national movement nor by extensive popular agitation for dual nationhood (Obrman, 1993). Following the formation of the Federation, Slovaks may have perceived their identity threatened by the larger and more robust Czech nation, but the Czechs did not respond with a national vision embracing the absorption of Slovakia's national identity. Few Czechs lived in Slovakia, and the ethnic borders between the two nations were substantially stable (Pehe, 1993).

There is a striking contrast between Czechoslovakia and Yugoslavia with respect to each of their historical memory and interpretation of the formation of the state. Serbs viewed themselves as the core of the Yugoslav federation, a Piedmont of the South Slavs, and as the natural leaders of the Federation. It was a Serb monarch who headed the first Yugoslav state, and it was the Serbian military which made the enormous sacrifices during World War I that led to a unified Yugoslavia. The other nations within Yugoslavia, however, saw themselves as co-equal partners and this contrast in views between the centralist Serbian perspective of Yugoslavia and the more pluralist view of the smaller nations provided constant tension within the Federation.

For many Serbs, Yugoslavia was an intermediate form of Greater Serbia, a situation historically analogous to Prussia and the German state or the Piedmont and Italy (Mackenzie, 1994). For Serbian nationalists, those who opposed a centralized Yugoslavia were agents of Germany, Turkey, Italy or other allegedly imperialist power (Milosevic, 1993). For non Serbs, Serbian centralism threatened their national identity and existence.

The contrast between Yugoslavia and Czechoslovakia is made even more problematic because each of the Yugoslav republics, with the exception of Slovenia, hosts significantly large ethnic minorities within their borders. Serbs constitute approximately 15% of the Croatia's population; 40% of Serbia's population are of Albanian, Croatian, Hungarian or other non-Serb origin; and Albanians were one quarter of Macedonia's population.

Under the socialist federation, minority rights were protected by the federation; and to secure these rights, minorities often enrolled in the republic's Party, police and civil service in disproportionately high numbers. One result is that the communists governments of the republics were often heavily staffed by ethnic minorities, particularly in Croatia, Kosvovo and the Vojvodina (Markotich, 1993). Thus, when the new nationalist parties assumed power in the republics, the first victims were the communist cadres, many of whom belong to one of the republic's ethnic minorities.

Following the nationalist victories in the republics, each of the minorities felt threatened and excluded from the political and governmental life of the republic. Ethnic minorities, particularly Serbs in Croatia, were isolated from the political mainstream and felt abandoned by the Federation. These groups often formed the core of the resistance movements in the republics, demanded political autonomy and sought support from their ethnic brethren in other republics. Under such circumstances, the threshold for ethnically based civil violence was very low.

Yugoslavia's complex and intermingled ethnic patchwork, coupled with the emergence of a Serbian nationalist movement committed to the preservation of the status quo, helped to create an extremely volatile situation in many parts of the former federation. Serbs were called upon to defend their co-nationalists in other republics while the nationalist governments in the other republics were committed to uprooting diversity in their realms.

The exclusionist policies of all theses governments forced confrontation and demands for renegotiation of the borders. Both Serbs and non-Serbs felt their identity threatened.

B. Multiple Poles and Multiple Historical Legacies

As a two unit federation, Czechoslovakia had solved its major ethnic problems with the expulsion of the Sudetenland Germans after World War II. Historical relationships between Czechs and Slovaks were not exceptionally bitter, and interactions among the two nations were relatively infrequent. In addition, Czechs and Slovaks shared the same religious affiliations and possessed similar cultural backgrounds. Thus, in this bipolar federal context, negotiations between these two groups were relatively simple; differences were not as deep; and division of resources and assets were comparatively straightforward (Pehe, 1992b).

The dissolution of Yugoslavia occurred in a multipolar context with six republics and two provinces participating in the discussions. Compared to Czechoslovakia, the policy agenda of the dissolution was much more complex and depended upon considerable reservoirs of trust and statesmanlike behavior. Unfortunately, the Serbs, Croats, Macedonians and Slovenians had not cooperated well during the federation and had not built up that necessary bank of trust. The Communists had argued that only they could avoid a repetition of ethnic violence and created a co-dependency to reinforce that view (Job, 1993). Cultural differences among the nations were enormous and included Christian Orthodox, Roman Catholic and Islamic cultural heritages who were in basic value conflict with one another (Huntington, 1993). Even basic cultural values and historical experiences such as the Enlightenment were not universally shared; and in recent history, many of these nations had engaged in barbaric atrocities and massacres against the others.

Within this context of mistrust, hatred and misunderstandings, multiple and often conflicting perceptions accompanied the negotiations prior to the secession of Slovenia, Croatia, Bosnia and Macedonia. Serbia, for example, had initiated a trade boycott against Slovenia in a misguided attempt to force Slovenia's capitulation. Later, Serbia's government raided the federal treasury and seized its foreign exchange holdings to cripple Croatia's struggling economy. Croatia's new nationalist government exacerbated tensions by refusing to guarantee minority rights in its republic and by re-introducing symbols associated with the war-time fascist regime. Bosnia's Muslim-Croat coalition adamantly refused to grant veto authority to Serbs within the republic, and Bosnian Serbs appropriated for themselves all the weaponry of the former Yugoslav national army.

In contrast to Czechoslovakia, the entire negotiation process in Yugoslavia was protracted and non-directive. Serbia, as the defender of the Federation, refused to contemplate the breakup and appropriated the federal assets for itself. Slovenia and later Croatia presented ultimata to the Federation with timetables that precluded serious discussions. Each republic fervently believed that the others were acting in bad faith and whenever any two federal units held private discussions, the others believed that they were the intended victim.

The distrust, particularly towards Serbia, fed and grew upon the increasingly authoritarian and imperialist policy of the Serbs in Kosovo. In the latter 1980s, under pressure from Serbia, the Federal authorities suspended civil rights and basic freedoms of the Albanian majority in Kosovo province. Croats and Slovenians not only disagreed with this policy, but they deeply resented that their investment funds for the underdeveloped regions were being used in the province to build up the economic infrastructure designed to maintain minority Serb rule. Their fear which found receptive ears among the non-Serb population, but rejected by Serbs, was that Albanian repression would be followed by repression in all non-Serb republics (Kovacevic, 1993). Serbia's Kosovan policy, more than any other factor, poisoned the federal negotiation process.

Complicating the negotiation climate even further was the realization of sharp divisions in the ideology, goals and orientation of the respective republic governments. Serbia and Montenegro were led by their former Communist parties and were committed to a nationalist communist vision. Croatia's government was conservative nationalist and committed to eviscerating remnants of communist rule. Slovenia's government was a government of national union, and Bosnia's government was an unabashed shifting coalition of ethnic-based political chieftains. Throughout the dissolution, each side claimed that it was virtuous and that they could not negotiate with the other. Each side believed that negotiations would only deepen their losses and that conflict was preferable to discussion. Willingness to negotiate was perceived as a sign of weakness and a political liability for any of the leaders.

C. Fragmentation of the Communist Party

At the conclusion of the 1980s, Czechoslovakia's Communist Party faced its final crisis and lost power as a single entity. The collapse occurred in a remarkably short period of time and was largely absent from public view. Throughout the ordeal, the Czech and Slovak Parties functioned as one, and republic-based communist factions did not emerge until after the first multi-party elections in the Federation. Once the resistance of the Party was crippled at the top, the Party structure ceased active resistance and acquiesced in the results. The Czechoslovak Communist Party, to its credit, did not advocate or engage in acts of sabotage or illegal resistance; it simply withered away and atrophied in a wave of idealistic popular euphoria.

Yugoslavia's Party behaved much differently than was the case in Czechoslovakia. Since Tito's death in 1980, the League of Communists acted as a lose association of republic party organizations. Each Party developed its own political agenda and its own style of governance. Each republic, particularly after the Serbian inspired putsch in Vojvodina and Montenegro in 1988, operated essentially autonomously and often in open conflict with the other republic parties. Gradually, each of the republic communist parties adopted nationalist populist programs and attacked the others to retain its power at home (Seroka, 1992).

With Yugoslavia's rotating Party chairmanship, conflicts rapidly became apparent as different coalitions of republics jockeyed for power with one another. In violation of Party rules, the Serbs under Milosevic pressured to suspend the normal rotation and exclude the Croatian party from its federal leadership posts. In 1989, the federal Party officially collapsed with the walkout of the Slovenian and Croatian delegations.

In marked contrast to Czechoslovakia, the rump federal Party called for resistance by true Party members against the fragmentation of the Party. Attempts were made to initiate "true Party organizations" in Slovenia and Croatia, and army officers were encouraged to work through the Party to restore Party unity and discipline.

Negotiations became more strained in this volatile environment. The surviving communist parties, such as Serbia, refused to negotiate with the non-communist leaders in the other republics. In the non-communist republics, the new governing coalitions reneged on agreements negotiated prior to their entry into power. Complicating matters even further was the absence of Slovenian and Croatian deputies in the federal parliament and the insistence by the federal parliament to recognize only deputies elected earlier under the single-party communist elections. In brief, in its final days, Yugoslavia had no legitimate and institutionalized mechanisms in which binding and legitimate agreements could be made.

D. The Military's Role in Defense of Socialism

Any comparison between the Czechoslovak and Yugoslav federal dissolution must be struck by the radically different role undertaken by the national defense forces in the federation. In Czechoslovakia, the primary military problem associated with dissolution was the logistics of the process, including officer placement, pension payments, and equipment distribution. The Czechoslovak armed forces did not work to oppose the Velvet Revolution and it stayed in its barracks throughout the crisis. The Czechoslovak officer corp was noticeable thought its silence and its lack of activity to mobilize on behalf of socialism and the socialist federation.

In Yugoslavia, the military, particularly since 1968, played an active political role in defense of the state and socialist self-management. In the events leading up to the armed intervention, the Yugoslav National Army actively supported the Serb viewpoint on the federation, federal authority and federal institutions (Mlakar & Svarm, 1993. It arrested Slovenian dissidents and tried them in military tribunals, and whenever possible, and it backed the unity and discipline of the Party. Throughout the crisis, the Communist Party organization was strongest within the military ranks, particularly among the officers. The Party relied on the army to protect the Party, self-management and the Titoist system (Bebler, 1992).

Following the multi-party elections in Slovenia and Croatia and the adoption of independence referenda by these republics, the new governments quickly recognized that the YNA would not remain in its barracks and that the army was committed to preserving the federal state and socialism. Both Slovenia and Croatia hastily reorganized their self-defense militia to counteract the army and then set into motion the prospects of armed conflict within the republics. The new nationalist republics, prior to their announcements of sovereignty, encouraged their co-nationals to desert the Yugoslav army and prohibited the drafting of their citizens into the Yugoslav army. YNA barracks were placed under siege and ordered to surrender their arms. A peaceful resolution of the conflict became improbable.

The major difference between the interventionism of the YNA and neutrality of the Czechoslovak armed forces lie in the YNA's constitutional role as defenders of the state. The Yugoslav army originated as an armed force of the Party during World War II. It reinforced this view during the crisis with Stalin when it worked to preserve Marshall Tito's regime against the Comintern. In the 1974 constitution, it was pledged to defend socialism and the socialist system; it could undertake many of the roles of a police force; and it perceived itself as the last bastion in defense of Tito's way.

E. The International Community

A major stimulus to the violence accompanying the collapse of the Yugoslav federation was the encouragement which federal authorities received from the international community. When the Yugoslav crisis initially developed, the world powers, particularly the United States, had opposed any changes in the sovereignty of Yugoslavia and had committed itself to preserving the borders of the Federation. Just as in Africa and Asia, the world community feared the precedence of encouraging border changes following internal political disputes. The international community quietly backed the Federal Yugoslav authorities to maintain the Federation, and it initially opposed Slovenian and Croatian secessionist attempts (Weitz, 1992). The reluctance of the global powers to countenance change encouraged the Federal authorities to avoid making serious concessions, and it pushed the secessionists to more extreme measures as a mechanism to win world public opinion support (Gow, 1993). The debacle which followed, although not the responsibility of the world community, might have been prevented had a more farsighted policy been employed.

In the interim between the Yugoslav dissolution and the proposed Czechoslovak breakup the world community acknowledged the folly of unquestioning support for borders and the status quo. When Czech and Slovak leaders began their discussions, the collapse of the Soviet Union reinforced the necessity for caution in the world community and re-emphasized the need for non-intervention and neutrality. In contrast to Yugoslavia, the world leaders would not get involved to prevent the Czechoslovak dissolution and risk another Yugoslav-type conflict.

CONCLUSION

The events of the last few years underscore the difficulty which non-democratic federal systems have in making a transition to a more open political process. The communist regimes had used the federations as transmission belts to secure their rule, and they failed to grant these institutions the autonomy to build internal constituencies in their support. In addition, the linkage of ethnicity to federalism compounded the weaknesses of the federations so that ethnic groups and nations felt compelled to seek independence and protection outside the federal umbrella. Finally, the European political and economic environment and movement towards unity had shifted to the point that the economic rational calculus no longer supported the formation and maintenance of small federal entities.

Compared to Czechoslovakia, Yugoslavia's dissolution had been exceptionally violent and destructive. Much of this can be attributed to Tito's policies of decentralism and fragmentation of power; some can be attributed to the inherent weakness in a multi ethnic state with wide economic disparities and enormous variations in culture and historical experiences. Some must be attributed to the failure of leadership and petty political rulers; some to the politicization of the armed forces; and some to the innate conservatism of the world community faced with new choices and new policies.

The major lesson from the experiences of Federal Yugoslavia and Czechoslovakia is that federal systems depend upon the support of the people and upon those who govern the people. Federal institutions are critically weakened when they cover for authoritarian rule or when they are used by one group to dominate another. Federalism without rule of law and respect for minorities is an illusion, and federalism without mutual and guaranteed respect for all political subjects is a recipe for disaster. Under such circumstances lose-lose decisions are likely to occur.

REFERENCES

Bebler, Anton. "Political Pluralism and the Yugoslav Professional Military," in Jim Seroka and Vukasin Pavlovic (eds.) *The Tragedy of Yugoslavia: The Failure of Democratic Transformation*. ME Sharpe: Armonk, New York, 1992, pp. 105-140.

Bernhard, Michael. "Civil Society and Democratic Transition in East Central Europe," *Political Science Quarterly*, Vol. 108, no. 2 (Summer, 1993): 307-321.

Bombelles, Joseph T. "Federal Aid to the Less Developed Areas of Yugoslavia," *East European Politics and Societies*, Vol. 5, no. 3 (Fall, 1991): 439-465.

Butorova, Zora. "The Hard Truth of Democracy in Slovakia," *East European Reporter*, Vol. 5, no. 1 (January-February, 1992): 62-67.

Foreign Broadcast Information Service. "Polls Show Most Czechs Favor Common State," *FBIS-EEU-92-126* June 30, 1992, p13.

Franck, Thomas M. *Why Federations Fail.* New York University Press: New York, 1968, pp. 167-199.

Goati, Vladimir. "Smrt Civilnog Drustva," *Nedeljne Informativne Novine*, January 1, 1993: 24-25.

Gow, James. "One Year of War in Bosnia & Hercegovina," *RFE/RL Research Report*, Vol. 2, no. 23 (June 4, 1993):1-13.

Grdesic, Ivan. "1990 Elections in Croatia," *Croatian Political Science Review*, Vol. 1, no. 1 (1992): 91-99.

Hueglin, Thomas. "Legitimacy Democracy and Federalism," in Herman Bakins and William Chandler (eds.), *Federalism and the Role of the State*. University of Toronto Press: Toronto, 1987.

Huntington, Samuel P. "The Clash of Civilization?" *Foreign Affairs*, Vol. 72, no. 3 (Summer, 1993): 22-49.

Job, Cvijeto. "Yugoslavia's Ethnic Furies," *Foreign Policy*, Vol. 92 (Fall, 1993): 50-74.

Kasapovic, Mirjana. "A Country by Any Other Name: Transition and Stability in Croatia and Yugoslavia," *East European Politics and Societies*, Vol. 6, no. 3 (Fall, 1992): 242-259.

Kovacevic, Miladin, "Neodlucni i Neopredeljeni", *Vreme*, November 15, 1993: 16-17.

Mackenzie, David. "Serbia as Piedmont and the Yugoslav Idea 1804-1914." *East European Quarterly*, Vol. 28, no. 2 (Summer, 1994): 153-182.

Markotich, Stan. "Ethnic Serbs in Tudjman's Croatia," *RFE/RL Research Report*, Vol. 2, no. 38, (September 24, 1993): 28-31.

Milosevic, Milan. "Barometar," *Vreme*, June 21, 1993: 26-28.

____________. "Izgubici sa Svakih Strana," *Nedeljne Informativne Novine*, February 2, 1989: 16-18.

Mlakar, Mirko and Filip Svarm. "Fantomska Vojska," *Vreme*, June 21, 1993: 34-36.

Obrman, Jan. "The Czechoslovak Elections," *RFE/RL Research Report*, Vol. 1, no. 26 (June 26, 1992): 12-19.

__________. "Havel Challenges Czech Historical Taboos," *RFE/RL Research Report*, Vol. 2, no. 24 (June 11, 1993): 44-51.

Pehe, Jiri. "Czechoslovak Elections Create Deadlock," *RFE/RL Research Report*, Vol. 1, no. 25 (June 19, 1992): 26-31.

_______. "Czechs and Slovaks Define Post Divorce Relations," *RFE/RL Research Report*, Vol. 1, no. 45 (November 13, 1992):

_______. "Slovaks in the Czech Republic a New Minority," *RFE/RL Research Report*, Vol 2, no. 23 (June 14, 1993): 59-62.

Rusinow, Dennison. "Yugoslavia: Balkan Breakup?" *Foreign Policy*, Vol. 83 (Summer, 1991): 146-159.

Seroka, Jim. " Variation in the Evolution of the Yugoslav Communist Parties," in Jim Seroka and Vukasin Pavlovic (eds.) *The Tragedy of Yugoslavia: The Future of Democratic Transformation.* ME Sharpe: Armonk, NY, 1992: 67-88.

Sheehy, Ann. "The Ethnodemographic Dimension," in Alastair McAuley (ed.), *Nationalism and Economic Decentralization*, Leicester University Press: Leicester, 1992.

Siber, Ivan. "Structuring the Croatian Party Scene," *Croatian Political Science Review*, Vol. 30, no. 2 (1992): 111-129.

Varady, Tibor. "Collective Minority Rights and Problems in Their Legal Protection: The Example of Yugoslavia." *East European Politics and Societies*, Vol. 6, no. 3 (Fall, 1992): 260-283.

Vodopivec, Peter. "Slovenes and Yugoslavia," *East European Politics and Societies*, Vol. 6, no. 3 (Fall, 1992): 221-241.

Weitz, Richard. "The CSCE and the Yugoslav Conflict." *RFE/RL Research Report*, Vol. 1, no. 5 (January 31, 1992): 24-26.

Wolchik, Sharon. "The Politics of Ethnicity in Post Communist Czechoslovakia," *East European Politics and Societies*, Vol. 8, no. 1 (Winter, 1994):153-188.

Chapter 13

SOS AND THE CRIMINAL JUSTICE SYSTEM

Ramsen Isaac

INTRODUCTION

The current state of the criminal justice system is one that needs, requires, and demands the attention of both liberals and conservatives. If "Justice For All" is, our credo, the present system fails to provide it. If offering a system that will offer fair and speedy trials is to be one of our goals, then a new solution found.

This paper is an attempt to provide a Super Optimum Solution (SOS)to under-staffing of public defenders and assistant prosecutors in the criminal justice system of the United States of America. While there is a need for competent public defenders and assistant prosecutors available for both civil and criminal cases, in our society, there is also a need to save taxpayer money. Conservatives and liberals both would like to have the best criminal and civil justice system in the world, one that is high-staffed with competent lawyers; conservatives and liberals also would like to get the most "bang for their buck" when paying the bill comes in the form of taxes. Conservatives value savings of tax dollars more than they value paying top-dollar for America's best attorneys. Liberals value the fairest, best-staffed justice system even if it costs more, because money is not as important when, dealing with people's lives.

SUPER-OPTIMUM SOLUTIONS IN TABLE FORM

In a country that recognizes the reality of scarcity, these two contradictory goals must be reconciled. Often, this is done by compromise, whereby a "neutral position" is adopted. Often both parties ate left dissatisfied with the system they inherit. The claim that Super Optimum Thinking makes is that both sides will come out ahead of their best expectations. Therefore, in reference to the justice system, an SOS solution would be one that, simultaneously saves tax dollars and has more competent, well staffed public defender's, offices and states attorney offices as well.

SOS's are not Cure-all solutions, but they are better than the traditional compromises that take place in government arenas today. SOS's often have feasibility problems; these will be discussed in order to decide on the best, most realistic SOS.

Below, is a generalized chart of the under-staffing problem in the form, of a traditional SOS table.

GENERALIZED CHART OF THE UNDER-STAFFING PROBLEM

Goals / Alternatives	C Save tax $	L More competent attorneys/ more access	Weights C	Weights L	Weights N
C $0 Civil: volunteer Crim: assigned rotation	4	2	14	10	12
L $600 Civil: gov't salaried Crim: gov't salaried	2	4	10	14	12
N $300 Civil: volunteer Crim: Gov't salaried	3	3	12	12	12

p.w.Generalized Chart of the Under-Staffing Problem.doc

This table represents the goals and alternatives that conservatives liberals and neutrals (moderates and/or compromising conservatives and liberals) have, chosen to deal with problems of under-staffing and under competence in the American justice system.

Conservatives prefer the alternative of rotating lawyers for criminal work and having civil lawyers only on a volunteer basis. This would cost the state, thus the taxpayers, nothing, as lawyers would bear the expense. Since this alternative does well on the conservative goal, the number 4 (out of 5) is given to how well the alternative does. Liberals, however, would not rate this alternative well (2) because it doesn't necessarily satisfy the competence prong of their goal, and it doesn't provide for access since civil cases would still be on a volunteer basis.

By the same token, the liberal alternative of spending a great amount to salary government lawyers for both civil and criminal proceedings does very well (4) in meeting the liberal goal of access and competence, but does poorly (2) on the conservative goal of saving taxes ($600 million, is an arbitrary figure).

As stated before, what usually happens in the traditional Public policy setting is a compromise" this, is exemplified by the neutral position. Since criminal proceedings are deemed more important to the well-being of our justice system, and our people (it is unconstitutional to deprive a poor person of a criminal lawyer if he or she wants one), criminal proceedings will have salaried lawyers, and civil proceedings will have volunteers. In this situation, the neutral, and often adopted position scores a 3 on both the liberal and conservative goals; neither side is happy with what they got but each side was appeased in a certain way, and frustrated in another.

The next portion of the table is the weights that are assigned to each alternative. Each horizontal row (alternative) of scores is weighted to see how the alternative does on a Scale of 1-3, multiplied by that score, and then added to the next horizontal score. For example, for this first row, conservatives would rate their alternative a 3 (3 x 4 = 12) and liberals would rate the conservative alternative a 1 (1 x 2 = 2); added together, these come up to a 14 for the conservative weight. Each alternative is weighted in reference to the respective group. When the chart is complete it is clear that any SOS must score more than 14 on all weights and over 3.5 on the rated alternatives.

Specific SOS Solutions (In Class Examples)

There are many possibilities for SOS solutions; two were offered in class. The first was a combination of salaried base attorneys and coordinating volunteers through a clearing house of training sessions. This solution requires the stimulation of volunteers through creative means. Requiring attorneys to report the amount of hours they donated to charity, then printing the names of those who didn't contribute is one way of stimulating volunteers. Allowing attorneys whose practices are too time consuming or too profitable to pay other attorneys to take their required hours wouldn't unnecessarily burden all attorneys.

The second SOS is contracting out. This involves offering contracts to firms that would take on the responsibility of defending and prosecuting criminals for less than the amount it costs right now. For example, if it costs the state and the people $600 million per year to run the nation's public defender's offices and the state's attorney's offices, the government would announce that it would offer a contract to the firm(s) that could do the job for $525 million or less. The contract could be fragmented into regional pieces of the settled price. So a $500 million contract could be divided into 5 pieces: Midwest, East Coast, West Coast, Southwest, and Southeast. There are many different ways that a contract can be divided.

As mentioned before, an SOS is not a cure-all. Every SOS that we come up with will have its own problems and difficulties. I see four potential problems with the first SOS: 1) the vagueness of stimulating volunteers for the service program, 2) training costs plus salary costs may cost a considerable amount of money (the difference in savings from a purely salaried base may be negligible) , 3) the length of some civil cases, especially those against large corporations are prone to lasting many years; having the case passed from lawyer to lawyer might not give the quality of legal aid to the people that this proposed system is designed to help, and 4) getting lawyers that do not want to be practicing in a certain field but feel obligated to do it, or can't afford to pay some other lawyer to do it.

Stimulating volunteers through humiliation and public display of the names of attorneys who did not volunteer might work for some lawyers, but there are probably lawyers that could sleep very well at night despite this creative tactic. Furthermore, lawyers are a relatively powerful group; it is easy to envision a collective movement against this kind of tactic.

Keeping the costs low and obtaining high quality "products" is important in SOS's. Training a tax lawyer to effectively counsel a person on a product liability case is not hard, but it takes the time of the government salaried lawyers, which could be use to do directly help those in need of legal assistance.

Having the case passed around would be a serious degradation of a client's legal problem. Having a couple of lawyers that will only be doing 20 hours of work a year is not conducive to the assistance of a client, especially in civil cases. If civil cases will now be covered by the right to counsel, we should expect that the case load will seriously increase.

As said before, lawyers are powerful people in our society, and if such a system was instituted, at the very least, it would seem that lawyers would want to do service in their given field, and not in whatever happened to be the high-case category for poor people.

The second SOS that was offered in class was contracting out. This SOS is an attempt to bring the efficiency, cost-effectiveness, quality, and competition of the market place to the public sector. Let's say that the city of Chicago asks for bids from law firms for all the public defenders and state's attorneys. One way it would work is that many firms would bid for each arm of the justice system in Chicago. For example if the city spent $10 million for each side, each year, city officials might decide that if a bid could be gotten for $9 million for each side, then savings would be decent enough to go ahead and contract out. Law firms bid and the best bid for under 9 million is taken for each side.

The second best bidder is given position as alternate; if the winning bidder is not able to fulfill the obligations of the contract, the second firm is ready to take the place of the first firm. This also insures that winning company's actions will be watched by the city and the alternate. Watchdogs watch more vigorously when there is a buck to be made.

There is a severe problem with this SOS, however. How is the city to judge the actions of the 2 winners who oppose each other? There must be a system of accountability in place. This problem is not easily solved in this case because we are dealing with 2 opposing groups who are trying to carry out their mission: to prosecute and defend, successfully. A potential system of accountability must not judge the firm by the amount of cases it wins and loses. This kind of score-keeping would say nothing about the intricacy of each case or whether or not justice was done. If such a system was in place, the firms might get overzealous and just concentrate on winning the case instead of serving justice. Before contracting out can be used in this context, this fundamental problem of accountability must be addressed.

SPECIFIC SOS SOLUTIONS (NEW EXAMPLES)

The following three SOS solutions are ones that I have generated. I will elaborate on each one according to its problems. Finally, I will choose the best SOS of the six presented, explaining why I think it is the best choice for our justice system.

The first newly generated SOS is adding a requirement of an extra year of law school as an intern for the state. The way this could possibly work is that students could compete to work and be trained in the different areas of civil and criminal defense and prosecution. Each student would be paid a living stipend (just enough to get by: rent, food, transportation) and would work with full-time salaried government employees.

There are many benefits to this system. First, it doesn't affect all lawyers, thus making it more feasible with lawyers as a group. This internship becomes a rite of passage in the process of becoming a lawyer. Second, this is an excellent opportunity for students to get into a field that they are interested in and actually handle cases. Hands-on experience will put their legal education into a better, more practical perspective. Third, hands-on experience improves the market value of each student by offering training for which companies would rather not put up the cost. Fourth, this training and work helps society by educating every lawyer about the needs and values of the poor in our society. Fifth, the benefits society derives from this is so much greater than the cost incurred by the government and small group law students. The sheer number of law students that would participate would allow for civil cases to be included in our constitutional provision of meeting the legal needs of the poor. In other words, access would greatly improve.

There are problems with this solution. First, it's going to be hard to get the American Bar Association to adopt such a requirement; it might be met with harsh criticism and backlash, hurting the legitimacy of the ABA. Second, this might not meet the conservative goal of saving taxes. Providing a living stipend might increase the cost of the legal system, though the benefits derived would be great.

The second SOS is offering to forgive government law school loans in return for service to the community. For example, if a student owed $100,000 in loans, he or she could choose to work for a year as a public defender and be forgiven of a fifth of the loan ($20,000). Offering this type of incentive might spur people to serve the poor law after law school, since most students come out of law school up to their neck in debt.

The benefits of this system are 1) there is a large market for potential people to participate since the number of debt owners is high among law graduates, and 2) it would provide more access for cheaper than the salary of a regular long-term, full-time government employee.

The problem is that this would work well only in a time where the market is flooded with lawyers. If there are jobs, unless one had a specific interest in a public service field, one would not take a forgiveness of $20,000 over a $40,000 a year job.

Also there would be the problem of supporting oneself while working to forgive the loan. If a living stipend is given, this is an extra cost; it may be just as expensive for the government to pay the debt owner as the full-time employee (or the cost difference may be).

The third SOS is positioning work for the government as a loan requirement. For example, if a student wants to borrow money to go to law school from the government, he or she must agree to work for a year in the public sector for free immediately after finishing his or her studies. A living stipend would be included for that year, but it would be counted as part of the loan.

The benefits of this system are the following: 1) Again, there is a large market for candidates because most law students take loans out to finance their education, 2) the person gains hands-on experience in carrying out a lawyer's everyday tasks, 3) one can compete for the area by which one is most interested, and 4) access is provided for by the excessive numbers of loan carriers, and 5) this will only affect an even smaller group of people than a rotation list, or the addition of a fourth year of law school.

The problem with this SOS is that it may have the affect of spurring candidates to seek out other means of financing their legal education. For example, banks might begin competing with the government on a large scalc for the loans. This is a possibility, though it is unlikely, as no one has money like the government.

TALLYING UP THE SCORES

Below is a table of how each SOS alternative would score and weight on conservative and liberal goals:

HOW EACH SOS ALTERNATIVE WOULD SCORE AND WEIGHT ON CONSERVATIVE AND LIBERAL GOALS

Goals / SOS Alternatives	C Save tax $	L access/ competence	C	L	N
Stimulate volunteers	4.0	4.0	16	16	16
Contracting out	4.0	4.0	16	16	16
Extra year	3.5	4.25	15.75	16.25	15.5
Forgive loans	2.5	4.0	11.5	14.5	13
Loans Requirement	4.5	4.0	17.5	16.5	16.5

p.w.How each SOS alternative.doc

The scores that each SOS received are estimates based on the above information (benefits, problems, etc.). The weights were derived in the same way the weights in the initial chart were derived. For example, conservatives would weight their score higher (3) than the liberal score (1). Neutral scores are multiplied by 2.

It is obvious that the SOS "forgiveness of loans," in its present form, is not an SOS because the conservative weight (11.5) fell under a 14, as did the neutral weight (13). All the other SOS's are true to the definition of an SOS; all sides come out ahead of their best expectations.

From this chart, it seems that the loan requirement SOS would be the best SOS, because it scores higher for all weights than any other SOS. Even though one other liberal goal (extra year of law school) scored higher in the initial scores, it is the weighted ones that are the most important in deciding on an SOS. The reason for this is because each ideological side does not live in a vacuum, and all sides' ratings must be taken into account. If there was only one side, there would be no need for SOS thinking, or more accurately, no alternative to compromise would be needed.

CONCLUSION

Using public service as a loan requirement is the best SOS for saving tax dollars and providing a large number of competent lawyers simultaneously. Shifting loan conditions and other market and demographic factors might require a different SOS. This solution also helps the lawyers that it requires to serve by giving them practical experience. This raises their market value after the service requirement is fulfilled. Because of the number of loan recipients is large, both civil and criminal caseloads can be met. Handling civil cases will require the state to erect a screening process that will eliminate any abuses of assistance.

This paper has hopefully shed some more light on the effectiveness of Super Optimum Solutions through the generation and processing of new alternatives. Generating SOS's requires creative effort that is in large need in our public policy making arena. SOS's main point has been to offer hope and real alternatives in public policy that outshine the present policies. If "Justice For All" is a real concern of public policy makers, then it is clear that there is a plethora of Super Optimum Solutions that can bring criminal and civil justice to even the poorest of Americans.

Chapter 14

ANTITRUST LAWS AND SUPER OPTIMUM SOLUTIONS

Christy Meredith
University of Illinois

I have spent the Spring semester of 1993 working at the Federal Trade Commission in Washington, DC. The majority of the work I did this semester involved gathering information from cases involving mergers and acquisitions over the past fourteen years. In order to demonstrate how I think the work I have done relates to Super Optimizing Solutions, I would first like to explain the project I was involved in and its relation to the Federal Trade Commission.

The Federal Trade Commission is an independent regulatory agency that was created by the Federal Trade Commission Act passed by the United States Congress in 1914. At the head of the agency are five Commissioners who are appointed by the President of the United States, with the advice and consent of the Senate. Each Commissioner serves a seven year term. No more than three Commissioners may belong to one political party. One commissioner is named Chairman of the Commission. The President may appoint a new Chairman if it is deemed necessary.

The purpose of the Federal Trade Commission is to regulate any unfair business practices. It was created to enforce the provisions of the Sherman Act of 1890 and the Clayton Act of 1914. Part of the reason the Federal Trade Commission was created was because Congress felt that an independent agency would be better able to develop special knowledge and skill in antitrust laws and economics than the courts or Congress could (Bork, 48). The Federal Trade Commission was given the power to order the cessation of unfair methods of competition. Its two major areas of concern are antitrust and consumer protection.

The Bureau of Consumer Protection oversees practices such as false or misleading advertising, while antitrust cases are overseen by the Bureau of Competition. Antitrust cases commonly involve attempts by a company or a cartel to monopolize a market or mergers between two or more companies that may have the effect of lessening competition. Unfair pricing policies, such as price fixing or tying arrangements, also fall under the Federal Trade Commission's jurisdiction. Generally, price fixing cases are considered to be per se illegal, while a rule of reason is applied to tying arrangements.

This is because tying arrangements can often result in new efficiencies and, therefore, should not always be considered unfair.

In addition to the Bureau of Competition and the Bureau of Consumer Protection, there are three other main divisions within the Federal Trade Commission: the Bureau of Economics, the Office of the General Counsel, and the Office of the Executive Director. The Bureau of Economics researches economic problems for the Federal Trade Commission and, sometimes, for other agencies or Congress. One of the duties of the Bureau of Economics is to advise the attorneys in the Bureau of Competition and the Commission what effects mergers or other business practices may have on various markets. The Office of the General Counsel advises the Commission on legal issues and may be called upon to represent the Commission in court. The Executive Director oversees various activities of the Commission.

In addition to the office in Washington, DC, there are several regional offices across the country. The purpose of these offices is to assist the Federal Trade Commission in gathering information about and prosecuting cases in the geographic areas in which they are located (Wagner, 39-47).

The Federal Trade Commission may receive cases from complaints received by consumers, the competitors of a company, or by regulations that require companies to give the Commission notice when they take certain types of action (e.g. acquiring another firm). When deciding whether to pursue a case, the Federal Trade Commission considers various aspects of the case. Some of the things the Commission considers are the size and importance of the industry to which the company belongs, the size of the company compared to other firms in the industry and the number of firms operating in the industry, and the amount of time it will take to investigate the complaint. Sometimes the Commission will pursue a case if it involves certain areas of law that need clarification (Wagner, 58-9).

When a company is investigated for a possible trade violation, a series of steps must be taken before formal charges can be made. For example, in an antitrust case, the facts of the case are investigated by economists in the Bureau of Economics and attorneys in the Bureau of Competition. At a meeting with the commissioners, both bureaus present their findings and give their recommendations as to what action the Commission should take. The commissioners then vote on whether or not they should pursue the case any further. Usually, a complaint against the companies involved is issued by the Commission. The complaint specifies the actions the companies have taken, the markets that are affected by those actions, and what effect those actions may have on commerce. Sometimes the case will be heard by an Administrative Law Judge. When this happens, the judge's decision will be reviewed by the Commissioners. The Commissioners then decide to uphold, dismiss, or modify the judge's order (Wagner, 63-73).

I have been working on a project for the Bureau of Economics and the Compliance Division of the Bureau of Competition. The Compliance Division is responsible for making sure that companies follow the orders given to them by the Federal Trade Commission. The project involves summarizing files from old cases for a study that will determine whether the types of orders the Commission has given in the past have been followed and whether they have been effective in restoring competition to the market.

More specifically, the Federal Trade Commission wants to determine if ordering firms to divest certain assets where there is a chance that a merger between two companies may reduce competition is effective at restoring the relevant markets to their pre-merger levels of competition.

Prior to 1976 the Federal Trade Commission would search for possible antitrust violations after two companies merged together or one company acquired another. By this time, it was often too late to restore pre-merger levels of competition or to provide the market with any type of effective relief. It was then decided that, if the companies are a certain size, they should first obtain the approval of the Commission before they are allowed to merge. In order to allow the Federal Trade Commission to act more quickly in antitrust cases, Congress passed the Hart-Scott-Rodino Antitrust Improvements Act of 1976. The Hart-Scott-Rodino Act states that companies of a certain size must notify the Commission before completing a merger. Guidelines issued by the government help the Commission to determine whether a merger will cause a substantial change in the structure of the relevant market. A specific product and geographic market must be affected. The guidelines state that mergers which will significantly increase market concentration may be subject to investigation. Factors that may affect concentration include the number of sellers in the market and barriers to entry. Some mergers may be allowed if it can be shown that the merger can increase efficiencies, increase competition, or result in lower consumer prices. A merger can also be justified by a failing firm defense. A failing firm defense is applicable if the firm to be acquired is likely to withdraw from the relevant market and is unable to find another buyer (Horizontal Merger Guidelines, S-3 - S-4, S-13). If there is a possibility of violating antitrust laws, several types of relief can be ordered.

One common remedy involves ordering the acquiring company to divest one or more of its subsidiaries where it is determined that the effect of the company's acquisition of another company may substantially lessen competition in the relevant market. For example, a company that produces soap and paper may acquire another company that produces soap and bread. If it is determined that the acquisition will give the acquiring company too much power in the soap market, that company may be required to divest the soap division of one of the companies. In order to assure that the assets are divested to a buyer deemed suitable to the Federal Trade Commission, the divestiture must be approved by the Commission. In this process, the Commission evaluates whether the prospective purchaser of the divested assets could gain control of a large part of the market or fail to successfully operate the assets. Either could have the effect of reducing competition relative to prior the merger.

In my job, I read through divestiture orders from 1979 to the present. The information I sought included what was required to be divested, whether or not it was divested within the time the Commission had ordered, and to whom it was sold. I believe the Federal Trade Commission intends to use this information to find out what has happened to the companies since they were divested. Then, it may determine whether ordering divestitures is an effective form of relief.

In this paper I would like to consider why antitrust laws were adopted and whether or not they have the effect intended by Congress. I also wish to look at various forms of relief, particularly divestitures, and their effectiveness. Also, I want to determine if the problems involving antitrust cases and their remedies may be addressed by Super Optimizing Solutions.

Before addressing these problems, I would like to consider the basic premises of Super Optimizing Solutions. The goal of Super Optimizing Solutions is to find a way to settle a dispute so that opposing sides exceed their initial expectations. It may be considered a win-win situation. In order to find a Super Optimizing Solution, it is first necessary to define each side's goals. Next, alternatives for reaching those goals are presented by each side. The Super Optimizing alternative may combine different aspects of the liberal and conservative alternatives and goals. For example, it may use key aspects of each alternative. The Super Optimum Solution may include the goals that are most important to each side, or it may try to avoid using what each side particularly dislikes in the other side's goals. In another case, a Super Optimizing alternative may involve looking at the problem in a new way and coming up with a solution that had not been considered by either side before. The relationships between the alternative and how well they reach the various goals are then determined and scored. These scores are weighted, and the alternative that receives the highest scores in each of the totals columns is the alternative that should be chosen as a solution to the problem. A true Super Optimum Solution will receive the highest total scores (Nagel, 4-7, 13-16).

To find a Super Optimum Solution to the problems created by monopolies, it is first important to understand how pricing decisions are made in the absence of monopolies, and why antitrust policies were adopted.

The antithesis of a monopoly is a state of pure competition. Pure competition is characterized by a large number of small sellers producing a homogenous product for a large number of buyers, no barriers to entry into or exit from the market, and all buyers and sellers possess the same knowledge. No single firm is able to influence the operations of the market.

Producers want to sell as much of their product as they can for as high of a price as they can. A graph can be made to show quantity producers are willing to supply to the market at each price. (P=price; Q=quantity; S=supply)

Table 1. The Quantity producers are willing to supply at each price

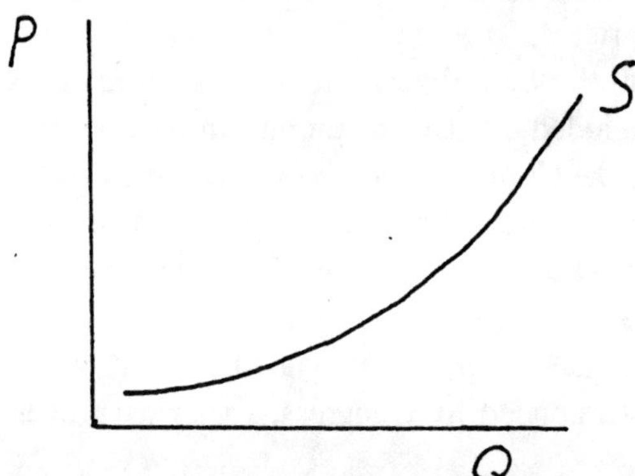

It can be seen that as the price of the product rises, producers are willing to make and sell more of the product. As the price falls, producers will bring a smaller quantity of the product to the market. Firms may produce smaller quantities when there are lower prices because they do not receive enough income to justify spending more on production. If producers are able to receive higher prices for their products, they will be willing to produce more. They have a greater incentive to produce and sell their product.

A similar graph can be made showing the demand consumers have for the product. Consumers are willing to buy more of a product at low prices than they will buy at high prices. As a consumer possesses more and more of a product, the value associated with one more unit of the product declines. (D=demand)

Table 2. The demand customers have for the products

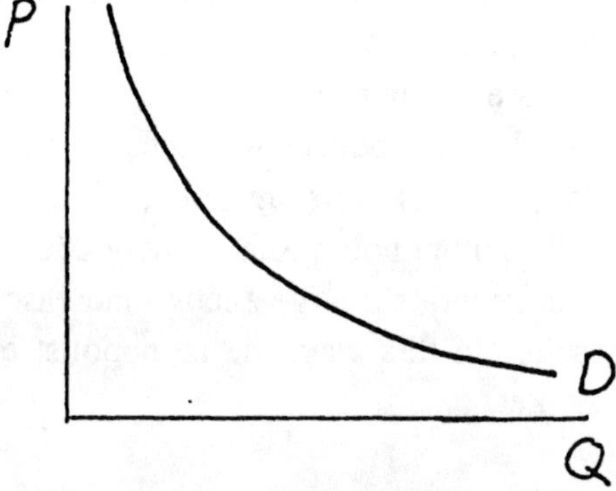

In a market characterized by perfect competition, the price of the product and the quantity produced and sold are set where the supply and demand curves cross. The market is considered to be in a state of equilibrium. Producers are receiving the price they want for the quantity of the product that they are supplying to the market, and consumers are paying the price they want for the quantity of the product they are receiving. Neither side has an incentive to change the price charged or quantity bought (Atkinson, 35-58). (Q'=quantity sold; P'=price paid for the goods)

Figure 3. The market in a state of equilbrium

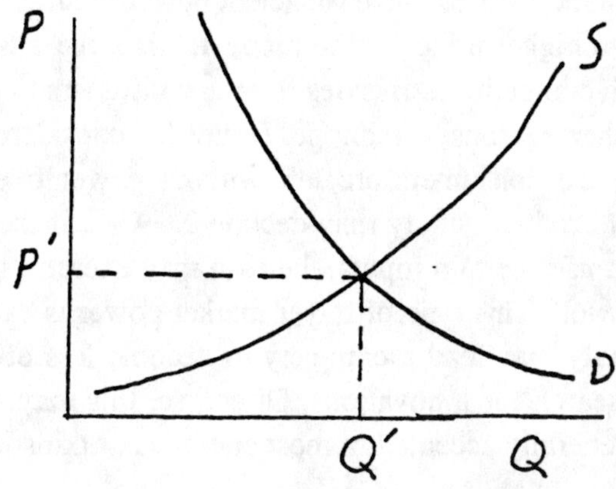

Antitrust laws try to preserve competition in the market. In order to preserve competition, antitrust laws try to prevent monopolies, or, if a monopoly already exists, to break it up or regulate it 1. A monopoly exists when there is only one seller of a product. A group of sellers combining their actions to act as one seller may be able to act like a monopoly. One example of a group of sellers acting together is a cartel, an arrangement in which the various companies act with explicit combined action. Nonexplicit combined action is referred to tacit collusion. If there is only one person or company selling a product that seller may choose to sell the product at any price. Other sellers may be prevented from entering the market because they lack the materials, capital, or other resources necessary to produce and sell the product. It is assumed that businesses want to maximize their profits. A firm with monopoly power will be able to control the output of the product, which, up to a certain point, will also allow the firm to control the price charged for the product. With competition, the price will be set where the supply and demand curves cross. A monopolist can lower the supply available. This will raise the price. If the price consumers are willing to pay rises at sufficiently to make up for the smaller quantity of goods sold, the producer will receive extra profits. Also, the total production costs will be lower if fewer units are made, which will also add to the profits received by the monopolist. The monopoly producer may continue to restrict output until a reduction in output does not generate a large enough increase in the price of the goods sold to cover the smaller sales. In this way, the monopolist can extract the maximum profits available from the market.

I. Natural Monopolies Generally are not Broken Up, But are Regulated by the Government.

Natural monopolies, usually the result of large economies of scale, exist when it is more efficient for one firm to produce the commodity than it is for several firms to do so. Electric utilities are an example of a natural monopoly. It should also be noted that patents are considered legal monopolies and are allowed by the government in order to encourage innovation.

A case like this is good for the monopolist, but generally is not considered to be good for consumers. if consumers do not have sufficient power to affect the price charged, they may be forced to pay a higher price for the product. Also, there is not as much available as there would be with competition. Besides forcing consumers to pay a higher price for a product, there are other reasons a monopoly may be considered bad for consumers. Without competition, the consumers are left without power over other aspects of the product besides price. Product quality may decline 2. Also, if the monopoly producer is the only producer that uses certain inputs, the firm may exercise control over the market for those products as well. This type of buyer market power is called a monopsony. The existence of a monopoly may lead a company to become less efficient. Also, they may lack a motivation to search for innovations. Of course, this may not always be true, but these arguments are generally accepted in most countries (Atkinson, 478-493).

II. If the Quality Declines Too Much, Demand Might Disappear.

If a monopolist wants to maximize profit, the quality will only diminish to the extent that is profitable. Still, it may be argued that competition would force higher quality standards

In addition to the economic costs of monopolies to a society, various political arguments have been presented as reasons to prevent monopoly power.

One political argument is that a monopoly takes money from consumers and gives it to the monopolist. It is a case of taking from the poor and giving to the rich. However, it may be argued that the monopolist does not keep all of the money taken from consumers, as it is necessary to spend large amounts of money on capital and labor inputs in order to gain monopoly power.

Another political argument states that a monopoly or any cooperation among firms in an industry will lead those firms to seek protection from the government at the expense of the public. With fewer firms, it should be easier to organize to attempt to influence the government. Firms may seek price controls, government barriers to entry, and tariffs or other taxes on substitute products. Yet it is not clear if the fact that an industry is highly concentrated makes it easier for the producers to obtain governmental protection. In fact, there are many highly competitive industries that receive government protection. For example, the agricultural industry, which is close to perfect competition, receives price supports and direct subsidies from the federal government and some protection from foreign producers.

A third political argument against monopolies is sometimes called the Populist policy. This policy would limit the powers of large companies with the goal of advancing the interests of small businesses. Inherent to this policy is the belief that small businesses are somehow better than large ones. This may be argued for competitive and efficiency reasons or sentimental ones. Many people believe that bigger businesses have an unfair advantage over smaller businesses in setting prices, negotiating contracts, and in other areas (Posner, 8-22). Others may feel that big business may be harmful to individuality, entrepreneurial spirit and ambition, and pride in and a feeling of responsibility for communities. One of the major problems with this policy is that it puts the welfare of small producers before the welfare of consumers. In fact, this is the attitude that the courts have often expressed when deciding antitrust cases. Some courts have read various antitrust statutes as being attempts by Congress to protect small businesses rather than attempts to protect consumers. Dangers that can arise from this type of attitude include relegating business relations to the courts rather than leaving them to negotiations among the companies themselves, and protecting smaller, more inefficient businesses at the expense of the larger businesses and consumers. As a result of this policy, industries may become fragmented and more inefficient than they would be with fewer, larger firms (Bork, 53-54). A paradox is created by this argument. Large firms often started out as small firms that were able to successfully provide what consumers value through competition. If the firms are too successful at competing, they may be punished. It is often complained that although antitrust laws were designed to help consumers by protecting competition, they often act to protect competitors, not consumers. As with the two previous arguments, there is no conclusive evidence to either prove or disprove this idea.

However, these are among the ideas that led to the passage of the first antitrust laws in the United States.

During most of the nineteenth century, business in the United States was, basically, not regulated by the government. Rapid industrial growth, faster, more efficient production methods, and the great influx of immigrants to produce and consume products led to the growth of large companies. With no restrictions on their actions, firms fought to gain control of their markets. Some companies merged into one, others formed trusts and worked together to set output levels and prices. Some businesses grew so large that they were able to drive all of their competitors out of business. For example, a large company could sustain losses in one geographic area without being in danger of going out of business, because they still received income from other geographic markets. The firm would be able to charge such low prices that its competitors could never match them. Then, once all of the competition was gone, the remaining firm could raise prices to almost any level it wanted, as the consumers had no where else to go to buy the product. If a company was large enough, it could also demand low prices from its suppliers. If the monopoly is the only purchaser of the products of the suppliers, the suppliers' businesses may suffer. With no competition, product quality might decline. Also, the firm could have control over the labor market in many cases. It may have been the only employer in the area.

As monopolies and trusts grew, people began to question their power and the abuses they practiced. A growing contrast between the few wealthy people and the many poor added to criticism of the large companies. In the late nineteenth century and early twentieth century, a wave of reform swept across the country. People demanded changes in economic, political, and social systems. The growth of labor unions and written accounts of the corruption present in big businesses probably added to the public feeling against large companies.

Around 1885, many state governments began to pass legislation against trusts. In 1890, the federal government passed the Sherman Antitrust Act. The Act states:

Section I. Every contract, combination in the form of trust or otherwise, or conspiracy, in restraint of trade or commerce among the several States, or with foreign nations, is hereby declared to be illegal . . .

Section II. Every person who shall monopolize, or attempt to monopolize, or combine or conspire with any other person or persons, to monopolize any part of the trade or commerce among the several States, or with foreign nations, shall be deemed guilty of a misdemeanor . . . This was the first major step in the government's regulation of business (Concise Dictionary of American History, 868-9).

The passage of the Sherman Antitrust Act may be seen as a Super Optimum Solution to a problem. The solution for this problem is illustrated in Table A on the following page.

Criteria ---- ----- ------- Alternatives	Conservative Goal: Business Profits	Liberal Goal: Protect Consumers	Neutral Goal: Economic growth/ strength	Neutral Totals	Liberal Totals	Conservative Totals
Conservative Alternative: No regulation	4	2	4	20	18	22
Liberal Alternative: Government Control of Business	2	4.5	3	19	21.5	16.5
Neutral Alternative: Regulate some businesses	3	3	3	18	18	18
SOS Alternative: No attempts to monopolize or actions in restraint of trade	4.6	4.8	4.6	28	28	28

TABLE A

In this case, the conservatives are concerned with what will happen to business. Their goals are business growth and profits. These can be considered important goals for various reasons. Business and economic growth are important to the country. While this was always true, it may have been especially important during the late nineteenth century. When industrialization and the invention of new products were growing throughout the world. It was important that the United Stated develop industries, so that it could keep up with the growth occurring in the rest of the world. Of course, those who already controlled large businesses wanted to maintain control of these businesses and the profits they received from them. Freedom from any governmental restrictions was the most desirable alternative for them. Opponents of governmental interference would argue that any attempts at regulation would impede economic growth. By not allowing large firms to operate as they had been, economies of scale would be lost and industry production costs would rise. This would lead to lower business profits, which could impede a company's ability to invest in new technologies and the production of new and improved products. Lower profits might also mean that the companies could not afford to employ as many people as they had before, or they might have to pay lower wages to all of their employees. If the businesses are hurt, consumers are also hurt. Higher production costs would mean higher prices for the products. Also, the costs associated with paying for an agency to regulate businesses would have to be paid for by higher taxes. It would not matter if the public was taxed directly to pay for the agency or if the businesses were taxed instead, as the businesses would only pass as much of the tax as they could on to the consumers in the form of higher prices for their products. Conservatives could argue that government regulation of businesses would hurt not only the businesses (their main concern), but that it would hurt the labor and consumers as well.

A liberal goal would be to protect consumers. Liberals might argue that, left to itself, business took advantage of consumers. Large companies were able to force smaller companies out of business. As a result, the wealth of the nation ended up in the hands of a small group of people. The great disparities between the rich, so-called robber barons around the turn of the century, and the living conditions of the factory workers could be a persuasive argument. Not only were the large companies able to control the output and prices of goods, but the could also control the wages paid to workers. The public well-being was dependent on the actions of the large companies. If allowed to continue growing as the were, the abuses of the large companies would only increase and the working class would be hurt more and more. Liberals would argue that the government should be more concerned with the well-being of all of its citizens, rather than just the well-being of its largest companies and its few, wealthiest citizens.

Economic growth is a neutral goal. To achieve growth, a strong economy must also be a goal. This goal can be considered a neutral one, because both liberals and conservatives want to have a strong economy that will provide benefits to society. It is already a part of both the liberal and the conservative goals. Conservatives are mainly concerned with benefits received by businesses, while liberals are concerned with benefitting the general population and especially want to help the poorer segment of the population. The neutral view is somewhere between these two goals. A general state of economic well-being, characterized by a strong, expanding economy, would encompass and benefit businesses, labor, and consumers. The neutral goal realizes that goals of conservatives and liberals are related, and that the biggest problem for policy-makers is how to find a balance between the two sides. First, the stability of industry is important. Without a healthy economy, consumer goods, services, and jobs would, not be available. For this reason, it is in a society's best interest to ensure that its businesses are able to develop, grow, and prosper. However, if they act too selfishly, they may end up hurting themselves. They must have workers, and the workers must be able to buy the goods that are produced. For this to happen, the products must be available at a reasonable price, and the workers must be paid a high enough wage to buy the products. Industry and the general population are mutually dependent upon each other. Finding a balance between the power each side has is necessary. The liberal and conservative goals and alternatives simply have different ways of looking at the problem - each goal emphasized different aspects of the problem - and at solving the problem. Liberals believe the government can balance the power between businesses and consumers, while conservatives prefer market solutions to government solutions.

The problem becomes deciding how the balance between the powers of businesses and consumers is reached. Should it be left to the market to decide, or should the government assume the role of acting to set a balance?

The conservative alternative to solve the problem is no regulation. A belief that, left to itself, a free market will automatically achieve the best possible balance between the number and kinds of goods produced and the prices that are charged for those goods. Also, all resources will be distributed and used in the most efficient way possible. The firms that are the most efficient producers are the ones that will survive.

This is where the problem develops for liberals. The end result of no government restrictions on business practices could be that several industries end up being controlled by one or a few large companies. This is what happened in the United States at the end of the nineteenth century. The amount of control these companies have over inputs, outputs, and prices can be so great that entry into the market by new firms is difficult.

An extreme liberal alternative that might be suggested to solve this problem would be for governmental control of all businesses. This alternative depends on the belief that the government can best decide how to allocate resources, set production levels, and set prices. If firms are not allowed monopolistic profits, the great disparities present between the few rich and the many poor may not exist.

A neutral proposal would fall somewhere in between the conservative and liberal alternatives. The neutral alternative calls for some government regulation. It could be the regulation of certain key industries - such as fuel, food, and medicine. The government may want to ensure that at least the basic necessities are available at a price that can be paid by all. The main problem with this kind of policy is that without economic profits, there is no incentive for producers to enter the industries that would be regulated. Entry into unregulated markets that have the potential for higher profits would be more desirable. If a policy of regulating industries were to be implemented, the government would have to provide incentives to businesses to enter these industries. In fact this is the case that exists in some industries, such as electricity.

For this paper's consideration of this problem, at the time the Sherman Antitrust Act was passed, government regulation of monopolies was the Super Optimum Solution. The government does not concern itself with all industries and the profits that are made in each industry. It is not responsible for making all of the country's economic and production decisions. Nor does it allow companies complete control to manipulate the markets. Following an antitrust policy, the government would concern itself with cases where competition is substantially lessened.

In order to see how that goals and alternatives relate to each other, and to determine which alternative provides the best solution, weights are given to each relationship. In this case, a score between 1 and 5 is given to the relation between each goal and alternative, with a 5 representing the most desirable situation, and a 1 representing the least desirable situation.

Comparing the conservative goal of achieving maximum business profits with the conservative alternative of no regulations of any type yields a relationship score of 4. No regulation provides the greatest opportunity for businesses to maximize profits. However, this may only be true for large businesses. Smaller businesses may be driven out by larger ones and may be unable to maximize their profits in the face of aggressive competition from larger business. It is for this reason that this combination does not receive a 5.

When the conservative goal is measured against the liberal alternative of government control of businesses, a value of 2 is assigned to the combination. A relationship score is received because the alternative does not provide an effective way to reach the goal. With government control, businesses may have restrictions on them that prevent them from being able to maximize profits. Another possibility is that the businesses are all owned by the government, rather than by individuals. A result of either situation is that there are no incentives for the businesses to do well. If the businesses are not fairly rewarded for their efforts, they will lose the incentive to make those efforts.

If the conservative goal of maximizing business profits is compared with the neutral alternative of regulated some business a higher score is received than the one given for comparing the conservative goal with the liberal alternative, but it is still lower than the score received when the conservative goal is put with the conservative alternative. Regulating some businesses still allows the industries that are not regulated to pursue the goal of maximizing profits, but some industries would still find themselves restricted. In this case, certain incentives would have to be provided by the government to induce companies to enter the regulated industries, otherwise, businesses would avoid the industries that were regulated in favor of industries that were not restricted in any way.

The alternative provided by the Super Optimum Solution receives a score of 4.6 when matched with the conservative goal. Because the Super Optimum alternative receives a higher score in this column than the conservative alternative does, the alternative meets the requirement that the solution meet or exceed the best expectations of conservatives. The alternative given by the Super Optimum Solution is to make illegal attempts to monopolize or act in restraint of trade. Under this alternative, businesses are still allowed to act freely to pursue profits as long as they do not conspire to create a monopoly or otherwise restrain trade. It is better at meeting the conservative goal than instituting complete government control of business, as the liberals would propose, and still allows the conservative goal of generating business profits to be met. It is also superior to the neutral alternative of regulating some business, because it does not have to decide which industries must be regulated. It is able to look at individual cases and decide if action is necessary.

The next step is to determine how successfully the various alternatives meet the liberal goal of protecting consumers from unfair business practices.

The conservative alternative of no regulation only receives a 2 in this category. With no regulations, businesses may engage in anti-competitive practices that may end up hurting consumers in the forms of higher prices, lower quality, and less selection. This alternative does not receive lower than a 2, because the free market should still impose some restraints on the actions of firms. For example, if prices are too high or quality too low, a company's sales and profits will suffer even with monopoly power, as consumers may refuse to buy its products. However, the free market may not be as successful at protecting consumers as the implementation of some regulations may be at protecting them.

When the liberal goal of protecting consumers is paired with the liberal alternative of government control of business, the combination receives a score of 4.5. This is a good way to protect consumers and to ensure that no unfair practices occur. However, it would be impossible to stop all unfair business practices. In some cases, the government may be even more corrupt than private firms. Also, consumers might still end up being hurt as a monopoly would exist in this case, the only difference being that it would be under the control of the government.

Comparing the liberal goal with the neutral alternative of regulating some businesses generates a score of 3. This is in between the first two scores in the liberal column. This alternative will provide some protection for consumersf but it will not stop all harmful business practices. In fact, it may be difficult to determine if a practice is harmful. In some cases, a practice which causes no harm may be prosecuted.

The Super Optimum Solution's alternative receives a score of 4.8 when paired with the liberal goal of protecting consumers. This is better than the previous alternatives because the government is allowed to watch all industries rather than being confined to overseeing only a certain few. Also, because the government does not have its own monopoly in each market, consumers can still receive the benefits that are provided by competition.

The final goal to be considered is the neutral goal of economic growth. This goal can be met fairly successfully by the conservatives' no regulation alternative. Without interference, businesses will continue to maximize profits and grow, helping to strengthen the economy.

The liberal alternative scores lower on this goal. If restrictions are put on businesses, or if they are not owned by the private sector, they may have less incentives to reinvest and grow. In time, this could weaken the economy.

The neutral alternative also receives a 3 on this goal. It is likely that this policy could also lead to less growth, as investors are left without incentives to put money into the regulated industries where profits would be lower. A lack of investment in these industries may slow down growth and weaken the economy. Growth may slow down in unregulated industries as well, as the threat of later regulation would diminish incentives to invest in the unregulated industries.

Once again, the Super Optimum alternative receives the highest score for the column. Although monopolies are not allowed, businesses are still allowed to grow by responding directly to market incentives such as consumer demand and production costs. The economy may also be helped because this policy protects small businesses and competition.

The next step in analyzing the relationships between the goals and alternatives is to calculate the neutral, liberal, and conservative totals for each alternative. This is done by using a weighting system. To calculate totals for conservative alternatives the relationship score for conservative goals is multiplied by 3, while neutral goals are multiplied by 2, and liberal goals by 1. The conservative goals receive the highest weight, while the liberal goals receive the lowest when calculating the totals for conservative alternatives. For liberal alternatives the liberal goals would be multiplied by 3 while the conservative goals would be multiplied by 1. Neutral and Super Optimizing alternatives multiply everything by 2. It can be seen by the totals in the table that the conservative total is the highest one for the conservative alternative, and the liberal total is the highest one for the liberal alternative. However, the highest totals are received by the Super Optimizing Solution, which receives 28 for a total in the neutral, liberal, and conservative columns.

By studying Table A, it can be determined that placing restrictions on monopolies and other actions in restraint of trade is the best solution. It is the Super Optimum Solution because it meets the 5 criteria necessary to be a Super Optimum Solution, which are:

1. It receives the highest score on the conservative totals
2. It receives the highest score on the liberal totals
3. It wins by a sufficient margin that it is probable that it would still be the winner even if errors were made in weighting or calculating the totals
4. It can be successfully executed
5. It makes meaningful substantive sense, (Nagel, 77).

After these totals are reached, a what-if analysis is done to determine whether or not the Super Optimum Solution remains the best choice if a new goal or alternative is introduced. An important goal for the solution to any problem is to be economically feasible or affordable to society. The costs of the solution should not outweigh its benefits.

For this problem, the costs of any solution include the direct, monetary costs needed to run a government program to oversee business practices. This can be measured by the new taxes which must be imposed on the population to run the program or by the money that must be taken from other programs to run the new one. Indirect costs include the costs imposed on society by the policy that is chosen. The costs of a monopoly include the higher prices consumers pay and reduced output. Costs of breaking up monopolies may be the profits lost by businesses.

The effect that the goal of economic feasibility has on the various alternatives can be seen in Table B.

--- Criteria ----- ------ ------- Alternatives	Conservative Goal: Business Profits	Liberal Goal: Protect Consumers	Neutral Goal: Economic growth/ strength	Neutral Goal: Costs	Neutral Totals	Liberal Totals	Conserv-ative Totals
Conservative Alternative: No regulation	4	2	4	3.5	27	25	29
Liberal Alternative: Government Control of Business	2	4.5	3	2.5	24	26.5	21.5
Neutral Alternative: Regulate some businesses	3	3	3	3	24	24	24
SOS Alternative: No attempts to monopolize or actions in restraint of trade	4.6	4.8	4.6	4	36	36	36

TABLE B

The conservatives' alternative of no regulation receives a 3.5 for economic feasibility. While there are no costs that must be paid for by the goverment (which means costs paid for by the firm, shareholders, and taxpayers), the cost to society in higher prices and restricted output may be greater than the cost of a program.

The liberal alternative receives the lowest score in this category. This alternative would impose higher costs on the government than any of the other alternatives would. However, it may be argued that these costs are made up for in the form of lower prices, and that excess profits are taken from businesses and given back to consumers.

The neutral alternative scores in between the conservative and liberal alternatives. This alternative imposes the costs of governmental regulation, and the costs that business wrongdoing imposes on society are still present in the unregulated industries.

The Super Optimizing alternative receives the highest score. There is the cost of regulation, but if the alternative can successfully meet its goals, the total costs to society will be reduced.

When the revised totals are calculated, the Super Optimizing alternative still receives the highest scores.

It would seem that an acceptable compromise had been reached with the passage of the Sherman Antitrust Act of 1890. In fact, today it is generally accepted that monopolies and other types of business arrangements that may harm competition are wrong and should be regulated and punished by the government. However, it took many years for the government to take full advantage of the powers given to it by the Sherman Act. Other regulations followed to clarify areas where the powers of the government and the rights of the businesses were unclear. Also, the problems of how best to break up the monopolies and restore competition to the markets arose. There is still controversy over the best way to enforce the various laws and obtain relief for violations of the laws.

Although the various antitrust regulations passed covered areas such as price fixing, price discrimination, tying contracts, and other illegal actions, this paper will mainly focus on monopolies, particularly market power gained as a result of a merger or acquisition.

Section 1 of the Sherman outlaws contracts, combinations, and conspiracies in restraint of trade. Section 2 of the Act outlaws monopolization and attempts to monopolize. A part of the compromise between the two sides of the debate can be seen in the language of the Act. The language is brief and focuses on actions that are done with the intent of illegally gaining market power. A lot of room is left to the courts to determine each case on its own merits and the economic consequence of the case, and to decide the best way to interpret and enforce the law. It was Congress' intent that monopoly power resulting from growth through mergers should be illegal, while growth that was the result of greater efficiency should not be illegal. After all, a major purpose of the Sherman Act was to promote efficiency and competition. The means by which the power is achieved should be an important factor in determining the legality of a company's market power. This raises a problem as to whether certain types of actions that may appear to be wrong - such as large expansions or exchanging price information - should be per se illegal even if the result of these actions may be to increase efficiency and promote competition.

In its first decade of enforcing the Sherman Act, the Justice Department initiated ten civil and five criminal cases under the Act (Posner, 25). Probably, this was not as much activity as supporters of the Act had hoped for. Despite the seemingly small number of cases brought under the Sherman Act in its first decade, by the end of the nineteenth century the Supreme Court had established certain principles to guide enforcement of the Act. One of these was the principle that cartels and other types of price fixing arrangements were illegal, even if it could be claimed that the fixed price was a reasonable price. The Court stated that any attempts to fix prices should not be allowed. The only reasonable, efficient price was the price decided by a market operating without pricing constraints (Posner, 24).

In interpreting the Sherman Act, the Supreme Court adopted a "rule of reason" by which to judge cases. The effect of this rule was that not every act that could conceivably decrease competition was per se illegal. Rather, each act must be examined on a case by case basis. It may persuasively be argued that the courts adopted the goal of maximizing consumer welfare as the goal of antitrust legislation. Protection of the conservative goals may appear to be lost in the application of antitrust laws as they have been applied to cases since the laws were passed.

The vagueness of the Sherman Antitrust Act and public belief that the courts were not using their power to enforce the Act led to subsequent legislation intended to clarify the government's powers under the Sherman Act. In 1914, Congress passed the Clayton Antitrust Act to supplement the Sherman Act. The preamble to the original bill stated that the intent of the legislation was to forbid practices not covered by the Sherman Act. Certain practices were declared illegal, with the understanding that not declaring a practice to be illegal did not mean that the practice was legal. Practices mentioned in the Act include price discrimination, price fixing, exclusive dealing, and stock acquisitions. The Clayton Act was also passed in order to prevent the creation of trusts, conspiracies, and monopolies. The intent of this part of the legislation was to avoid the problems inherent in trying to find a remedy to the problems caused by trusts by preventing the trusts from ever being created. Section 7 of the Clayton Act addressed this problem:

That no corporation engaged in commerce shall acquire, directly or indirectly . . . another corporation engaged in commerce, where the effect of such acquisition may be to substantially lessen competition . . . or tend to create a monopoly of any line of commerce. The 1950 Celler-Kefauver amendment to the Clayton Act changed section 7 of the Clayton Act into an antimerger law.

Congress also passed the Federal Trade Commission Act in 1914. The belief behind the passage of the Federal Trade Commission Act was that an agency created to oversee antitrust cases and other cases involving unfair business practices would become skilled at handling those cases and would be better able to understand and oversee the cases than Congress or the courts could. The Federal Trade Commission Act created the Federal Trade Commission and gave it the power to issue cease and desist orders against what it termed "unfair methods of competition".

Section 2 of the Sherman Act and Section 7 of the Clayton Act have been used to break up and prevent not only monopolies, but also companies that may be seen to have an unfair advantage over their competitors because of their size or market power. This is especially true where a company has power in a highly concentrated industry. There is a belief that it is easier to engage in unfair business practices in a highly concentrated market that it is to do so in a less concentrated market. If there are only a few firms in an industry, it will be easy for those firms to engage in practices such as price fixing. If there are a large number of firms in the market, it will be harder for those firms to set prices. This is why the agencies charged with enforcing antitrust laws monitor mergers and acquisitions. A result of a merger may be to reduce the number of competitors in a certain market, giving one firm more control power in the market and making it easier for the firms that remain in the market to try to control what happens to supply and prices.

A successful form of relief for any case would be relief that can remedy whatever anticompetitive harm may have been caused and prevent it from happening again. A type of relief often sought in merger cases where there may exist an anticompetitive concern is divestiture. Divestiture attempts to undo the harm caused by an acquisition by returning the market to premerger concentration levels. If the government's policies for pursuing relief under merger cases are clear and the antitrust authorities follow their own guidelines, and if firms believe and understand the guidelines, the government may also be able to prevent other companies from completing mergers that may have the effect of harming competition. However, if enforcement of the guidelines is misdirected (e.g. it ignores efficiencies), government actions may have the effect of discouraging procompetitive mergers.

In fact, the government has tried to make its stance clearer. In 1992, the Department of Justice and the Federal Trade Commission issued guidelines to be used in pursuing horizontal merger cases. Among other things, the agency prosecuting a horizontal merger case is to consider how the merger will affect market concentration, barriers to entry and likely likelihood that the merger will be successful (Horizontal Merger Guidelines, S-3 - S-4)). If both agencies follow the same, clear set of guidelines for pursuing cases, misdirected actions may be avoided, and companies will have better information to use to guide their actions.

In order to increase the speed in which divestitures or other forms of relief may be completed, the Hart-Scott-Rodino Antitrust Improvements Act of 1976 stated that in cases of mergers and acquisitions involving assets valued at over $15 million, the companies involved must file pre-merger notification with the Federal Trade Commission and obtain prior approval from the Federal Trade Commission before completing the merger. A preliminary injunction may be sought in federal court to keep one company from acquiring another if there is a possibility that such an acquisition may reduce competition. An investigation of the acquisition is conducted, and a Complaint is issued to the respondent company. The next step, if a settlement is not reached, is to bring the matter before an administrative law judge. The judge hears the case and issues an Initial Decision. Depending on the administrative law judge's decision, the respondent or the Federal Trade Commission's attorneys may appeal the decision to the Federal Trade Commission. The commissioners hear the case and issue a Decision and Order. If the respondent objects to the decision of the commissioners it may appeal the case to a federal appellate court.

In merger cases, the Federal Trade Commission often issues a divestiture order as an attempt to restore the relevant product and geographic markets to their pre-acquisition states. In order to be considered successful, the divestiture should achieve certain goals. First, it is important that the divestiture be completed as quickly as possible. The longer it takes to accomplish a divestiture the harder it may become to separate the assets required to be divested from the rest of the company. A lengthy divestiture process also prolongs the loss to society of the restricted output that resulted from the merger.

Before 1976, companies did not have to wait for prior approval, and the Federal Trade Commission would have to try to find a remedy after the merger had been completed. Under the Hart-Scott-Rodino Act, the Federal Trade Commission may obtain a divestiture agreement from the companies before the property has changed hands. This should make it easier to complete a divestiture.

In addition to meeting time requirement, a successful divestiture should involve the divestiture of assets that are related to the area of competitive concern. For example, if the market affected by a merger is grocery stores in a certain geographic area, it is more effective for the respondent to divest one or more grocery stores in that area than to require the divestiture of a store in another area or a warehouse that may supply some of those stores. Similarly, the divestiture of one store where ten stores were acquired may not be effective.

Because the goal of divestiture orders is to restore competition and return the market to premerger levels of concentration, the ideal purchaser of the divested assets would be a company that is a new entrant to the relevant market. Divestiture to another firm with a large market share may do little to remedy the problem of concentration in the market. Finally, it is important that the divested assets are able to remain a viable, competitive force in the market. If the divested company goes out of business the condition of the market has not been improved and may become even worse. For this reason it is important to ensure that the divested assets are capable of being operated as a business entity and that they are divested to a firm that will be able to successfully run the business.

The success of divestitures as a form of relief has been debated since it was first used in early antitrust cases. In a 1911 case against the Standard Oil Co., a holding company that owned several operations to was ordered to dissolve into a several smaller companies, with shares in the companies going to the stockholders of the holding company 3. Although the intended effect of this order was to increase competition, it actually did little to achieve this goal. Instead, the effect of the order was to substitute a series of small, regional monopolies that did not compete with each other for one large, national monopoly. Due to stock turnovers, John D. Rockefeller was able to retain control over the companies.

III. Standard Oil Co. of New Jersey v. United States, 221 U.S. 1 (1911).

Another 1911 case, involving American Tobacco, also ordered a divestiture 4. American Tobacco was broken up into three companies. The largest of the new companies still had a 37% share of the market. The three new companies still colluded with each other for a number of years after they had been broken up.

IV. United States v. American Tobacco Co., 221 U.S. 106 (1911).

There have been other cases where the part of a company ordered to be divested comprised only a small part of the company's operations, the result being that the divestiture had little effect on the company. Also, some companies were ordered to divest operations that were becoming or soon became obsolete. The end effect of these divestitures was to help the companies. Other firms have been able to remain the dominant firm in the market despite being forced to divest some of their assets (Posner, 85-7).

Economist Robert A. Rogowsky argues that the'structures of the Federal Trade Commission and Department of Justice are partly to blame for the problems in enforcing antitrust laws and obtaining relief. The decisions made by the staff attorneys responsible for conducting investigations, litigation, and settlement are affected by the reward system present in the agencies. For most of the attorneys, an agency job is seen as a way to gain experience and recognition before entering private practice. Because of this, the attorneys want to generate as many cases as possible and to resolve them as quickly as possible. Rogowsky believed that the attorneys' goal becomes not improving consumer welfare, as would be expected, but rather to maximize his or her own gains. If an attorney's goal is to maximize the number of cases he or she successfully prosecutes, that attorney will be attracted to cases involving smaller companies where it may be easier and less time consuming to obtain a settlement. Longer cases that have a bigger impact on consumers' welfare may be ignored. It is possible that if the government decides to prosecute a large firm, the large firms may agree to sign trivial consents to get rid of the government and negative press. It is doubtful that the relief is effective in these cases or that it has an effect on the future actions of businesses. Because it is easier to show that a settlement has been reached than it is to show if the settlement has been or will be successful, often not a lot of energy is spent on finding an appropriate form of relief, and little analysis is done to evaluate the effectiveness of the relief. This practice is not challenged at higher levels of the agencies, as the higher levels are also concerned with visible output which is the way to gain budget increases (An Economic Study--o-t Antimerger Remedies, 142-62).

Rogowsky conducted a study that evaluated the effectiveness of the relief of a sample of 104 divestiture orders in merger cases prosecuted by the Federal Trade Commission and the Department of Justice 1986 to 1980. The relief in each case was categorized as successful, sufficient, deficient, or unsuccessful. Rogowsky considered a successful relief to be a divestiture that established the acquired firm as an independent, viable, competitive force within a reasonable amount of time. Sufficient relief included divestitures in which the divested entity may not be able to sufficiently meet the requirements of a successful divestiture. Rogowsky considered relief to be deficient if only a partial divestiture of the acquired assets that raised anticompetitive concerns occurred, or if some type of continuing relation between the company and the divested assets (such as a marketing agreement) existed. Unsuccessful cases included orders in which the divestiture offered little or no structural relief, or the divestiture was made to an unacceptable purchaser (The Economic Effectiveness of Section 7 Relief, 191-8).

Applying these criteria to the sample, Rogowsky determined that twenty-one of the divestitures offered successful relief, fourteen divestitures offered sufficient relief, twenty-six divestitures offered deficient relief, and thirty-seven cases offered unsuccessful relief (The Economic Effectiveness of Section 7 Relief, 216).

According to Rogowsky, significant structural relief was realized in only one-third of the cases studied in his investigation. Some of the reasons successful relief was not reached include only a partial divestiture that failed to return the market to its premerger level of competition, a lengthy divestiture process which minimized the effect of the divestiture once it was completed, and divestiture of assets not related to the area of competitive concern. Rogowsky concludes that the federal government's administration of antimerger laws has been largely unsuccessful and has done little to advance the economic welfare of the United States (The Economic Effectiveness of Section 7 Relief, 228).

Kenneth G. Elzinga, of the University of Virginia, believes that structural relief is required in merger cases. To him, the effects mergers have on markets must be remedied because a merger will result in additional market power for one firm. Because the merger changed the structure of the market, the relief must also change the structure of the market. If a merger has anticompetitive results, relief is obtained by ordering the divestiture of the acquired firm. Further, the divested firm must be able to continue operating at the level of productivity it possessed before the merger took place. Time is also an important element, as each day the acquiring firm holds the assets it gained from the merger, the firm is receiving benefits and exercising market power that it did not have before the merger. Also, because market conditions may change during adjudication and divestiture efforts, divestiture may no longer be feasible (Elzinga, 45, 75).

Elzinga also conducted a study to determine the effectiveness of the relief ordered in merger cases. Considering the independence and viability of the divested firms were able to achieve, he determined the success of thirty-nine divestiture cases. Six cases were found to be successful, four were sufficient, eight were deficient, and twenty-one cases were rated as unsuccessful (Elzinga, 48). When the time it took to complete a divestiture was added, three cases were rated as successful, one as sufficient, four as deficient, and thirty-one as unsuccessful (Elzinga, 51).

Despite the criticism the Federal Trade Commission has been receiving in regards to the way it handles merger cases, divestiture is still the most common form of relief used to remedy the effects of mergers. The project I worked on this semester involved gathering information to be used for a study for the Federal Trade Commission to determine whether past divestitures have been successful. The remainder of this paper deals with possible solutions to obtaining effective relief in merger cases.

Table C shows goals and alternatives for finding effective merger relief.

For this problem, the conservative, liberal, and neutral goals remain the same as they were for the previous controversy. Conservatives still concern themselves with what will happen to business. Business growth and profits are important. Liberals want to protect consumers from high profits and monopolies. Economic growth and a strong economy are still important considerations for any solution.

The conservative alternative in this situation is to allow mergers to take place without the government trying to prevent the mergers from happening or trying to interfere once the merger has been completed. Conservatives want businesses to be allowed to grow with minimal interference from the government. one of the methods by which businesses grow is through mergers and acquisitions. Although an acquisition of one company by another may lead to fewer competitors in a market, this does not mean that all mergers have an adverse effect on the market. One of the most important things to consider when reviewing a merger case is whether the merger brings greater efficiencies to the company and the market. By acquiring another company, a firm may be able to realize economies of scale which would lead to lower costs and lower prices. This would benefit rather than hurt consumers.

The liberal alternative is to protect consumers, competition, and small companies by not allowing any mergers to take place. The goal of this alternative is to keep a large number of competitors in the market. However, this may not necessarily be achieved by forbidding mergers to take place. Rather than being acquired by a stronger firm, weak firms would go out of businesses. The end result may still be a few large firms dominating the market.

The neutral alternative is to allow mergers to take place, but to make firms behave as if the merger had not occurred. Each company, even though they share the same owner, will continue to operate separately from thc other. If each company is still competing for market share, prices may remain low. This alternative would most likely decrease the number of mergers, because there would be little incentive for one firm to acquire another. A major reason one firm acquires another and is able to make a profit by doing so is that greater efficiencies are possible when the resources of the two firms are combined. If the firms are unable to combine their resources, little reason remains for the companies to merge.

Criteria ---- ----- ------- Alternatives	Conservative Goal: Business Profits	Liberal Goal: Protect Consumers	Neutral Goal: Economic growth/ strength	Neutral Totals	Liberal Totals	Conservative Totals
Conservative Alternative: Allow mergers/no action	4	2	4	20	18	22
Liberal Alternative: No mergers allowed	2	3	2	14	15	13
Neutral Alternative: Allow mergers/ behave as if no merger	3.4	2.5	3	17.8	17.8	17.8
SOS Alternative: Divest with clear guidelines/ better orders/ better enforcement/ time	4.2	5	5	28.4	28.4	28.4

TABLE C

The alternative given by the Super Optimum Solution calls for continuing the practice of ordering divestitures, but to implement some changes in the current system. First, although remedies must be determined on a case by case basis, clear guidelines should be set to guide the actions of the Federal Trade Commission and the Justice Department when the agencies order divestitures. One of the goals of the guidelines should be to first determine whether the merger will have an adverse effect on the market. If it is determined that this is the case, a full divestiture of the acquired assets in the affected market should be ordered. orders should ensure that the divested assets will be able to operate independently of the firm ordered to divest them. The divested business should be able to establish itself as a viable competitor that will be able to remain in the market. It is important that the assets not be sold to a company that already has a large share of the market. A new entrant is the best purchaser of the divested assets. It is necessary that the government be willing to spend the resources needed to achieve a successful solution. If the government wins a case without ensuring that adequate relief is ordered, the resources spent prosecuting the case have only been wasted. Also, time is important, as it may be impossible to undo the effects of a merger if too much time is allowed to pass before the divestiture is completed. Another part of the Super Optimum Solution may be to take further precautions to ensure that mergers that will have an anticompetitive effect on the market are not allowed to take place. A good policy to follow is to allow mergers that will create efficiencies, and not to allow mergers that will restrict output (Bork, 61). An additional goal for the Super Optimizing Solution would be to improve the method by which cases are reviewed. It is important to avoid errors in which truly anticompetitive mergers are allowed to take place. It is equally important to avoid wasting resources by prosecuting mergers which are not anticompetitive.

Once again, the goals and alternatives are compared. Pairing the conservative goal of business profits with the conservative alternative of allowing mergers without interference from the government yields a score of 4. if companies are allowed to merge they will be able to achieve economies of scale and other efficiencies which will lead to an increase in profits. However, the combination of the conservative goal and the conservative alternative does not receive a 5 because smaller businesses may be hurt by this policy. Also, growth does not always bring higher profits. For example, a company may not realize any gains by combining two unrelated businesses, because the businesses will not be able to share resources.

The relation between the conservative goal and the liberal alternative of not allowing any mergers at all receives a 2. Because this will restrict their growth, businesses will not be able to maximize their profits. Although this policy may save smaller companies from the threat of takeover, it cannot ensure that they will be able to compete with other companies.

A score of 3.4 is received when the conservative goal is paired with the neutral alternative of allowing mergers to take place, but requiring companies to behave as if the merger had not happened. Although businesses may receive additional profits from the new firm, if they are not allowed to combine the resources of both firms they will lose the full potential for increased profits.

When the conservative goal of increased business profits is paired with the Super Optimizing alternative of better enforcement of divestitures, a score of 4.2 is achieved. This alternative allows efficient mergers to take place. These mergers will increase business profits. If clear guidelines for allowing mergers and enforcing divestitures are set, and if the Federal Trade Commission and Department of Justice are consistent and follow these guidelines, businesses will be better able to decide if a merger will be allowed. Businesses will be able to avoid wasting time and other resources on completing mergers that will be challenged, and then defending those mergers.

The liberal goal is now compared with each alternative. A score of 2 is given to the combination of the liberal goal of protecting consumers and the conservative alternative of allowing mergers. In this case, firms are allowed to grow without restrictions. This is likely to lead to monopolies. Even if the end result of the mergers is not a monopoly, it is likely that markets will come to be dominated by a few large firms. If this happens, the likelihood of collusion among the firms increases. It will be easier for firms to act together to fix prices.

Although monopolies are more easily avoided when mergers are not allowed, the liberal alternative of no mergers receives only a 3 when paired with the liberal goal of protecting consumers. There is not guarantee that one company will not gain control of the market by methods other than taking over competitors. A low score is given because consumers as well as producers lose out on the gains that may be achieved by mergers which increase efficiency. Consumers will not be able to benefit from lower prices that may result when firms are allowed to combine resources to achieve more efficient, cheaper production methods.

An even lower score is received when the liberal goal is paired with the neutral alternative. Because firms are not allowed to integrate businesses acquired through acquisitions with the rest of the company, the cost savings generated by an acquisition or a merger cannot be realized by the company or passed on to consumers. Although this alternative may prevent firms from exercising power over the market, it takes away incentives firms may have to grow.

The highest score is received when the liberal goal is paired with the Super Optimizing alternative. This alternative allows consumers to share in the gains achieved from the increased efficiencies that are the result of allowing mergers to take place. Because mergers that would be anticompetitive in nature are either not allowed or are remedied by a quick, full divestiture, consumers are not hurt by monopolies.

Finally, the neutral goal of economic growth and strength is compared to each alternative. When combined with the conservative alternative, the neutral goal receives a score of 4. This alternative allows producers to grow and to receive the benefits, such as a reduction in production costs, that are achieved through mergers. These benefits may be passed on to consumers in the form of lower prices. In this case producers are allowed to act in their own best interest. Unfortunately this may not always be in the best interest of the economy as a whole (e.g. a firm with monopoly power may restrict output which results in a loss to society). This fact keeps this combination from receiving a higher score.

A score of 2 is given to the combination of the neutral goal and the liberal alternative. Not allowing firms to grow will have bad results for both producers and consumers. Because producers are not able to act in ways that can reduce costs, they are not able to pass savings on to consumers. Although small firms are protected from being taken over by large firms, there is no guarantee they will be able to successfully compete with the large firms. They may go out of business. Because other firms are prevented from buying the firms that fail, the resources of these firms are wasted. If another firm is allowed to acquire the failing firm, the resources of the failing firm will not be wasted.

Allowing mergers while making firms act as if a merger has not taken place does little to help the economy. Substantial growth cannot be achieved if the resources of the two firms cannot be combined and used together.

When the neutral, liberal, and conservative totals for each alternative are calculated, it can be seen that the Super Optimum Solution receives the highest score in each column. This is the alternative best able to meet each of the goals. The Super Optimum Solution protects consumers from monopolies and collusion between companies, but it allows mergers that will achieve efficiencies. Resources will be allocated to the firms best able to use them. The benefits achieved from economies of scale and other efficiencies can be passed on to consumers in the form of lower prices. If an anticompetitive merger takes place, the government will have clear guidelines and goals to guide the method by which relief is ordered and the effects of the anticompetitive merger can be minimized.

In order to truly qualify as a Super Optimum Solution, it is necessary to see how the totals change when another goal or alternative is added to the chart. In this case, the neutral goal of economic feasibility, or controlling the costs of the chosen solution, is added.

When the new goal is compared with the conservative alternative, it receives a score of 3.5. Although there are no direct costs are imposed on society, such as higher taxes to pay for a regulatory agency, consumers may be subjected to other costs. For example, if only one or a few firms are able to exercise control over a market, they may set high prices or restrict output. These costs, in the form of higher prices, may outweigh the costs that would be imposed by higher taxes.

A 2.5 is given to the combination of the neutral goal and the liberal alternative. In this case, society will have to pay a government agency charged with overseeing business to ensure that no mergers take place. Also, because businesses are not allowed to merge, the benefits that could be achieved by mergers which increase efficiencies are lost, which is a cost to society.

A low score is also received when the new goal is paired with the neutral alternative of allowing mergers but requiring companies to behave as if the merger had not taken place. A government agency will be needed to regulate the companies to make sure that the assets received from the merger are not combined with assets already owned by the company. The cost of losses associated with not being able to achieve the savings that may be gained by combining resources is added to the regulatory cost imposed on society.

--- Criteria ----- ------ ------- Alternatives	Conservative Goal: Business Profits	Liberal Goal: Protect Consumers	Neutral Goal: Economic growth/ strength	Neutral Goal: Costs	Neutral Totals	Liberal Totals	Conserv-ative Totals
Conservative Alternative: Allow mergers/no action	4	2	4	3.5	27	25	29
Liberal Alternative: No mergers allowed	2	3	2	2.5	19	20	18
Neutral Alternative: Allow mergers/ behave as if no merger	3.4	2.5	3	2.5	22.8	22.8	22.8
SOS Alternative: Divest with clear guidelines/ better orders/ better enforcement/ time	4.2	5	5	4	36.4	36.4	36.4

TABLE D

The Super Optimizing alternative receives the highest score in this column. Although there are costs involved in regulating businesses, if the guidelines are followed and only efficient mergers are allowed, the benefits of the policy should outweigh its costs. Efficient mergers are allowed, and anticompetitive mergers are not allowed.

When the totals are calculated, the Super Optimum Solution remains the alternative with the highest totals in each column.

Although the United States government has passed several statutes to try to balance the power that producers and consumers exert over markets, the problems have not all been solved, and it is unclear how much of a difference the legislation has made. There is still controversy over what type of a role the government should take in regulating markets. Several factors must be taken into consideration: the rights of both consumers and producers, as well as workers, how the regulations affect what these groups will do, and how the government's actions affect the economic growth and stability of the country. Increasingly important is how requirements the government imposes on American firms and foreign firms operating in the United States affects the United States' competitiveness in world markets.

I think that Super Optimizing Solutions can be used to address these problems. The Super Optimizing method of problem solving can be used not only to decide whether to pass new legislation to deal with monopolization and other unfair trade practices, but also to determine the best way to enforce the laws that government agencies are currently charged with enforcing.

References

Atkinson, Lloyd C. Economics: The Science of Choice. Homewood, IL: Richard D. Irwin, Inc., 1982.

Bork, Robert H. The Antitrust Paradox: A Policy at War with Itself.. New York: Basic Books, Inc., 1978.

Concise Dictionary of American History. Wayne Andrews, ed. New York: Charles Scribner's Sons, 1962.

Department of Justice and Federal Trade Commission Horizontal Merger Guidelines Antitrust & Trade Regulation Report. Vol. 62, No. 1559. Washington: The Bureau of National Affairs, Inc., 1992.

Elzinga, Kenneth G. "The Antimerger Law: Pyrrhic Victories?"

The Journal of Law and Economics. Vol. 12, 1969: 43-79.

Nagel, Stuart. Super-Optimizina Policy Analysis.

Posner, Richard A. Antitrust Law: An Economic Perspective. Chicago: The University of Chicago Press, 1976.

Rogowsky, Robert A. "The Economic Effectiveness of Section 7 Relief". The Antitrust Bulletin. Spring 1986: 187-233.

Rogowsky, Robert A. An Economic Study of Antimerger Remedies. Ann Arbor, MI: University Microfilm, International, 1983.

Wagner, Susan. The Federal Trade Commission. Washington: Praeger Publishers, 1971.

Chapter 15

SOS AND THE MERCURY PROBLEM IN BRAZIL

James A. Day
University of Illinois

Thousands of desperate men migrate westward into rugged territory to search for gold. They work feverishly, often standing shoulder to shoulder in shallow water panning for bits of treasure. This description could easily fit the nineteenth century California gold rush in the United States. However, this same scenario can also be seen nearly one hundred and fifty years later, in a country thousands of miles away. Brazil is currently about fifteen years into a gold rush reminiscent of the one that had Americans flocking to the hills of California in the mid eighteen hundreds. Hundreds of thousands of impoverished Brazilians have been lured to westward by the discovery of gold in the Madeira River Basin and Pantanal wetlands of central-western Brazil (see figure 1). Covering parts of two states, Rondonia and Amazonas, the Madeira Basin's waters nourish the Amazon rainforests. The Pantanal wetlands lie primarily within the states of Mato Grosso and Mato Grosso do Sul. Because of the significance of these two ecological treasures, there is great concern regarding the impact of contamination from mining operations.

The Madeira is a large river, carrying between five and twelve million gallons of water per second, depending on seasonal variations (Pfeiffer 239). By biological standards, the Madeira is classified as highly productive, creating a bountiful fishery upon which a great proportion of the local population is highly dependent (Pfeiffer 241). Perhaps the state most directly dependent upon the Madeira's waters is Rondonia. Its capital, Porto Velho, lies directly on the river (see Figure 2). A state of about 1.2 million inhabitants (Sanches 100), Rondonia lies along the western edge of Brazil, bordering Bolivia (see Figure 1). In a country where seemingly every state has its share of natural wonders, Rondonia manages to stand out above the rest. Rondonia represents the convergence of two of the world's most treasured natural resources. The Amazon rainforests dominate in the northern portion of the state and the Pantanal wetlands lie to the south. Rondonia covers almost 100,000 square miles of tropical rainforests,

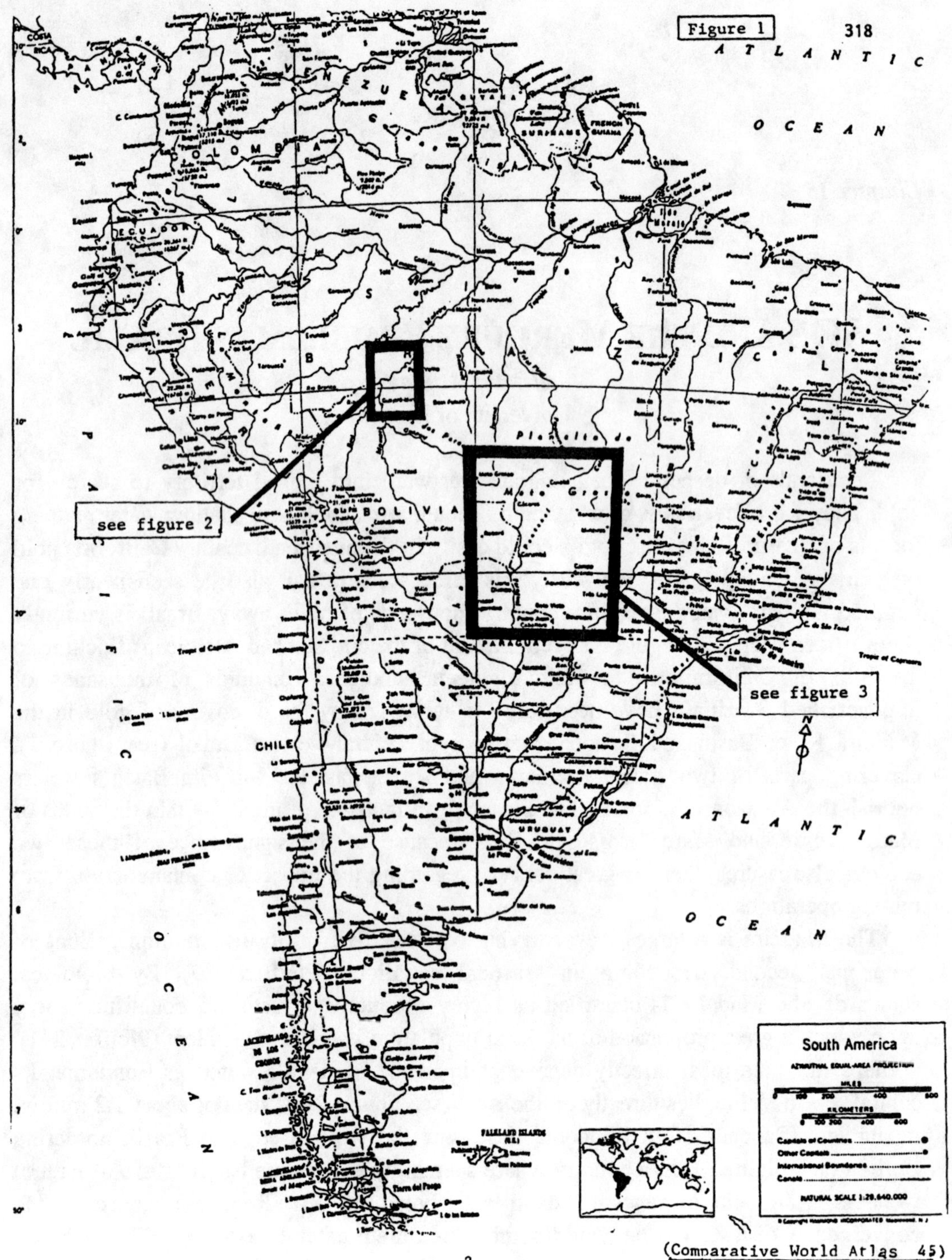

(Comparative World Atlas 45)

marshlands, and complex river ecosystems (Sanches 91). This represents an area nearly twice as large as Illinois. Its residents are highly dependent upon these ecosystems for their subsistence. As in much of northern and western Brazil, the fishing industry is of paramount importance.

After the Madeira flows through Rondonia it enters the state of Amazonas. Amazonas is Brazil's largest state, covering over 600,000 square miles (Sanches 91), more than twice the size of Texas. It is here in Amazonas that the Madeira flows into the Amazon, the largest river in the world. The Amazon discharges 50 million gallons of water into the Atlantic Ocean every second (Sanches 94).

Because its waters nourish the rain forest, merge with the Amazon, and eventually reach the ocean, the influence of the Madeira to the north of Rondonia is substantial. On the other hand, the influence of the Pantanal extends far to the south. The Pantanal is a 54,000 square mile nature preserve ("Gold-Diggers" 8) that extends into both Bolivia and Paraguay (see Figure 3). The Paraguay River, which originates in the Pantanal, flows south through Argentina and eventually empties into the Atlantic Ocean. About the same size as Illinois, the Pantanal is the largest wetland in the world. This unique ecosystem has one of the world's greatest concentrations of wildlife, including unique varieties of alligators, cayman, jaguars, capybara, and the jabiru stork ("Gold-Diggers" 8). Luiz Marques Vieira, of Embrapa, the government-run Brazilian agricultural research institute, claims that the Pantanal's complex ecosystem will be completely disrupted by contamination ("Gold-Diggers" 8).

As is the case in much of Brazil, water is obviously the common link among all the areas and ecosystems I have described. The people of the rainforest and Pantanal regions are highly dependent upon these water-based ecosystems for their subsistence. But now the water, the lifeblood of these regions, is threatened. Beginning in earnest around 1980, the Brazilian gold rush now involves more than 650,000 people ("Price" 23). Most of these prospectors, called "garimpeiros," are organized in small nomadic bands. While lacking the large-scale machinery and support of the larger, more established mining operations of the southeast regions, these garimpeiros currently manage to produce 70-90% of all the gold annually produced in Brazil ("Fool's Gold" 14). The activity has been centered around the Madeira River, primarily along a 180 mile stretch from Porto Velho to Guajara-Mirim (Pfeiffer 239) (see Figure 2), yet as more and more aspiring miners flock to the region, the gold rush is annually extended to new, previously unmolested waters.

The seemingly unending flow of new prospectors is partly fueled by the other great problems of Brazil. Much of the northeastern region of Brazil is plagued by a lack of availability of productive land for agriculture. This shortage is due to two problems. First, the historically agricultural region is plagued by drought. Compounding this problem is a system of land ownership whereby thousands of acres of fertile land are held by large enterprises, or "latifundarios," which allow only a small portion to be farmed at any given time, yet refuse to sell the other viable land.

While many prospectors come from these suffering rural regions, still others come from the great cities of the southeast. The phenomenon of "rural exodus" has seen

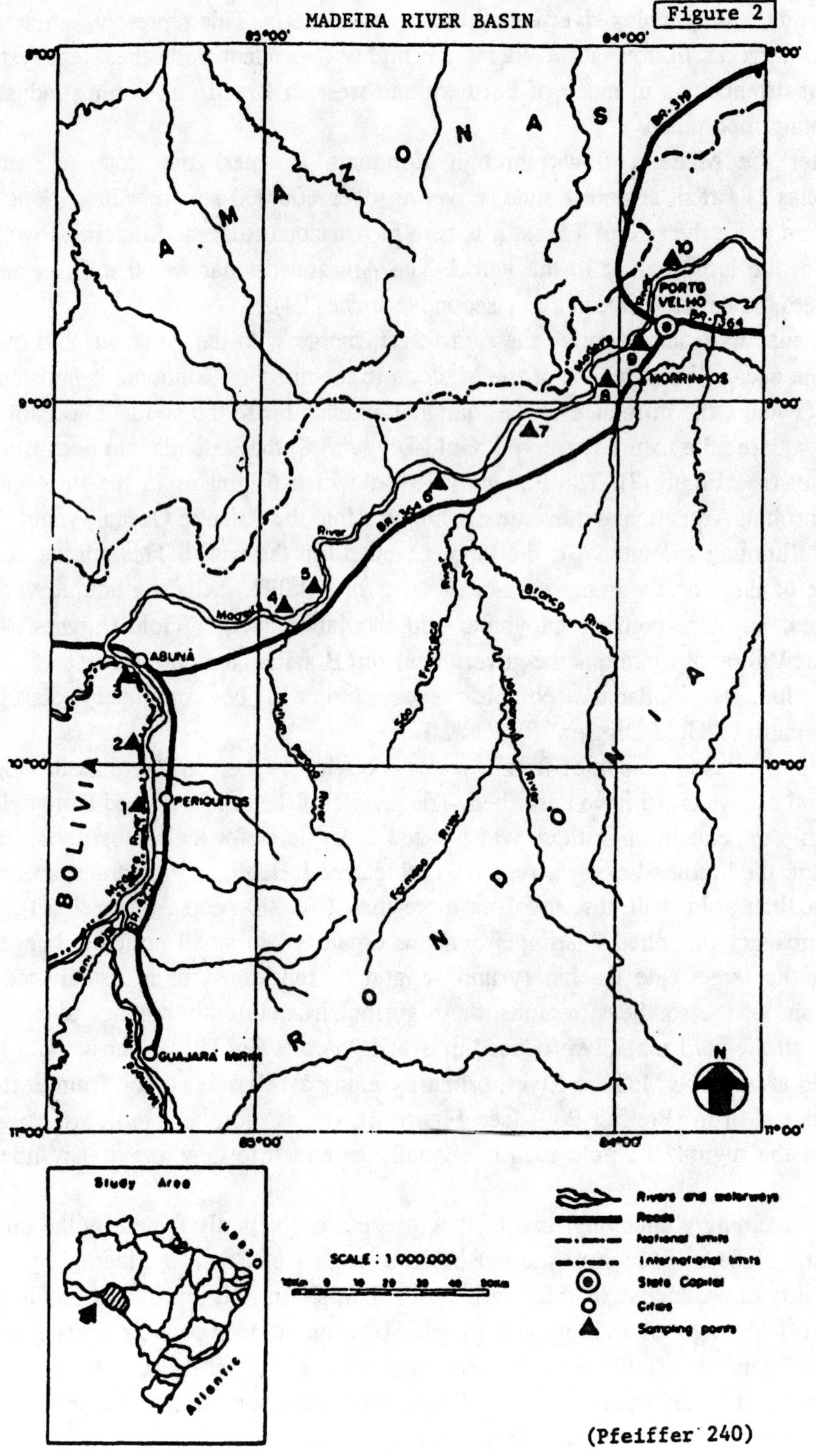

(Pfeiffer 240)

PANTANAL

Figure 3

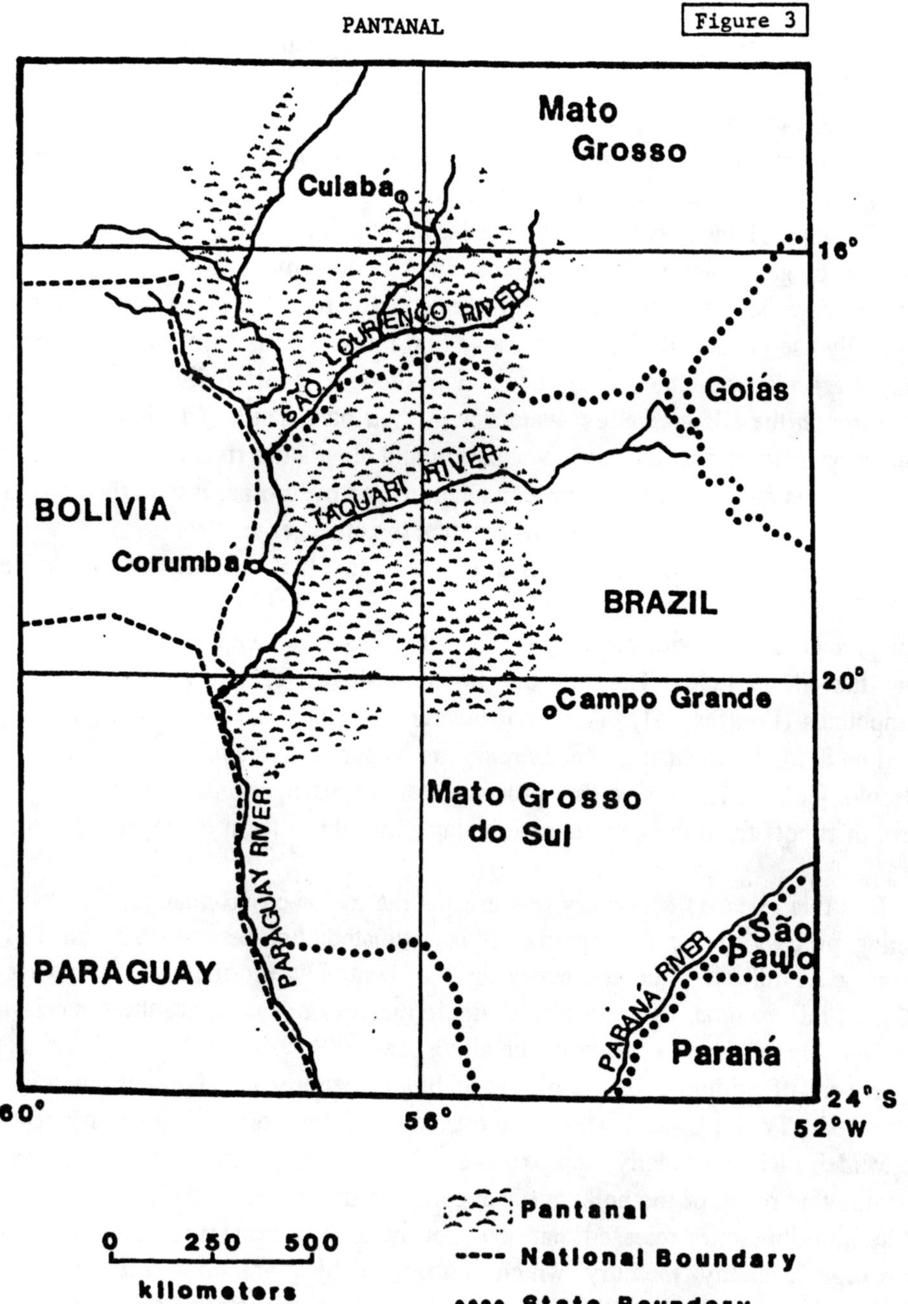

millions of Brazilians leave the struggling agricultural regions for the newly industrialized cities of Sao Paulo and Rio de Janeiro. Upon arriving in the cities, they often find that there is in fact no need for uneducated, unskilled workers. Often with nothing to return to, many remain in slum-like "fazelas." This situation of despair leads many to follow the lure of gold and head west.

These problems in both the rural and urban economies of Brazil have spawned a new industry of gold mining. The dire hardships faced by many of the prospectors have led them to feverishly pursue gold with little concern about their methods. The garimpeiros generally use boats and divers to remove bottom sediments from the river beds (Pfeiffer 241). Larger operations employ mechanical dredges, while individual prospectors often sift through the silt in shallow waters with their bare hands (Chisholm 36). While this collection process destroys river vegetation and clouds the rivers' waters with silt, these are problems the river ecosystems can adapt to and overcome. It is in the second stage of the mining process that severe environmental threats emerge.

This second stage of the gold mining process involves refining the gold-laden silt that is dredged from the river beds. In order to extract the gold from the silt, the miners first amalgamate the silt with mercury (Malm 11). This is accomplished by pouring mercury over the silt particles. The mercury bonds with the gold, removing it from the silt compounds (Pfeiffer 241). This gold-mercury complex is then burnt, generally with a hand-held torch, releasing the mercury as vapor and leaving behind only the gold ("Fool's Gold" 14). During this process, mercury escapes into the environment in the form of runoff from the amalgamation stage and in the form of vapor from the burning stage.

It is this release of mercury that creates the major environmental threat of the gold mining process of the garimpeiros. It is estimated that between 90 and 120 tons of mercury are released into the ecosystems of central western Brazil each year (Nriagu 389). Of this volume, 45% consists of liquid mercury released into the rivers, while 55% consists of particulate released to the atmosphere ("Price" 23). In the Pantanal, Brazil's department of mining claims ten tons of liquid mercury are released annually into the watershed ("Fool's Gold" 14). Of the estimated 32 tons of liquid mercury released into the Madeira River annually, approximately 23 tons are carried by the water down river, meaning that much of the pollutant is exported to the Amazon (Nriagu 389). The portion of the liquid mercury released that does not travel downstream reacts with sediments to form organic methyl mercury, which is absorbed by plankton and algae and eaten by small marine animals ("Fool's Gold" 14). After entering the food chain at this level, the toxic mercury begins its passage up the chain, becoming highly concentrated in high level predators, most notably fish and humans.

Evidence of this contamination of the food chain is indisputable. In the Pantanal region, Luiz Marques Vieira of Embrapa, the Brazilian government's agricultural research institute, reports, "We already have a serious public health problem and something should be done," ("GoldDiggers" 8). Embrapa says that there are more than 250 orold mining ventures operating in the Pantanal itself. In order to assess the impact of these activities, Vieira has measured the level of mercury contamination in more than 1000 fish, mollusks, and birds. More than a quarter of the specimens contained mercury at levels beyond the World Health Organization's "safe" limit for mercury contamination ("Gold-Diggers" 8). Some of the specimens collected by Vieira contained more than twenty-five times the acceptable limits for mercury. While most of the specimens found to contain hazardous levels of mercury were from the areas near the mining activity, Vieira reports finding levels exceeding the WHO standards in specimens obtained as far downstream as the city of Corumba, more than 375 miles from the primary mining area of Pocone ("Gold-Diggers" 8) (see figure 2).

While scientific evidence clearly indicates mercury contamination in the Pantanal region, evidence supporting claims of contamination in the Madeira River ecosystem is even more conclusive. A study published in Forest Ecology Management surveyed mercury levels in river water and sediments, forest soils, fish, and humans in the Madeira watershed region. Regarding water, sediments and soils, the study found that while seventy percent of the samples from the region contained mercury levels within the normal range, thirty percent indicated abnormally high mercury contamination levels (Pfeiffer 242). Some of the samples contained mercury at a level more than one hundred times greater than the average in the control areas. The complete results of the tests on water, sediments, and soils are listed below (Pfeiffer 243).

TABLE 1
Mercury concentrations in water, sediments and soils from the Madeira River Basin

Sample	Madeira River	Forest Rivers	Control Area
Water (mg/1)	0.2-5.1	0.4-9.5	<0.04
Bottom sediments (mg/1)	0.05-2.62	0.2-19.83	0.19
Soils (mg11)	0.03-0.18	0.1-0.95	0.1

Based on these widely varying results, the authors concluded that mercury contamination in soils and sediments seems to concentrate in "hot spots," often near areas that indicate no abnormal presence of mercury. This abnormal distribution of contamination poses unique dangers to the local population, since testing can easily miss a small area of concentrated contamination. This factor may lead to a false sense of security when a test indicates a lack of contamination in a certain area. The authors also concluded that because soil contamination was discovered in remote forest areas where no mining had occurred, the estimated 55% of mercury that is released to the atmosphere during the refinement process must be absorbed by water particles and redistributed in the form of toxic rain (Pfeiffer 243). This discovery further expands the sphere of influence of the mercury contamination in the Madeira.

The study also measured mercury levels in the edible fish of the region. The results of these measurements are listed below (Pfeiffer 243).

TABLE 2
Mercury concentration in fishes (parts per million)

Origin	Popular name/Scientific name	Mercury(ppm)
Madeira River	Filhote (Brachyplatystoma)	0.5
(Porto Velho)	Corimata (Prochilodus nigricans)	0.21
	Dourado (Salminus)	1.43
Madeira River	Filhote	1.47
(180 km down river Corimata from mining area)		0.10
Jaci Parana	Tucunare (Cichla)	0.47
(Tributary)	Pintado (Pseudoplaty stoma)	2.70
Jamari River	Pintado	0.07
(Control area)	Pirarucu (Arapaima gigas)	0.17
	Jatuarama (Brycon)	0.08

note: Maximum permissible concentration for human consumption, 0.5 ppm

These results indicate that contamination in the region can reach more than fifty times the maximum permissible level allowed by Brazilian government regulations. Because the local population is highly dependent upon the fish population for subsistence, this contamination is likely to be passed on to the local population.

This transference of mercury contamination to the local population is verified by the results of the study of human hair samples taken from area residents (Pfeiffer 244).

TABLE 4
Mercury contamination ranges for human hair samples (mg/g)

Sample Origin	Concentration
Madeira River	1.0-26.7
Mato Grosso	0.04-6.3
Amazonas	10.0-29.0
Rio de Janeiro	
Vegetarian diet	0.74
Common fish diet	3.0-6.4
No regular fish diet	1.2-2.7

note: The World Health Organization level for acute mercury poisoning is 50.0 mg/I

Obviously, the threat of mercury contamination in both the Pantanal and Madeira watershed is very serious. Enormous volumes of mercury are entering these ecosystems every year. The evidence of this contamination and the resulting contamination of animals and humans is indisputable. The mobility of the contamination via water and air further exacerbates the problem. Because the problem (1) involves disparate views on how to address it, (2) has a profound impact, and (3) encompasses both public and governmental concerns, the problem of mercury contamination in central-western Brazil is ideal for super optimum analysis. This type of problem involving conflict between economic and environmental interests in developing countries is becoming increasingly common, and this trend is likely to continue.

Super-optimum solution (SOS) analysis involving finding a solution that simultaneously exceeds the initial best expectations of both liberals and conservatives. The following overview of the basic concepts involved in SOS analysis is based on information taught by Stuart S. Nagel in political science courses at the University of Illinois and detailed in his books *Global Policy Studies* and *Public Policy Controversies and Win-Win Solutions: Economic, Social, and Technology Issues.*

For a policy alternative to be super-optimum, it must best achieve the goals of two separate parties. In SOS analysis these two parties are generally classified as "conservative" and "liberal." The two parties generally share a common set of goals, yet each assigns a different relative level of importance to each of the goals.

A simple example often employed by Nagel to illustrate SOS methodology is the minimum wage controversy. Table 5 presents this controversy in the form of a of the standard super-optimum analysis chart. An SOS chart displays the parties' goals in vertical columns, the policy alternatives in horizontal rows, the relations (or scores the alternatives achieve in relation to the goals) in the cells where columns and rows overlap, and total scores for the alternatives at the far right (Global Policy 22). In this case, both liberals and conservatives share common goals of paying a fair wage and not over-paying to the extent that employers cannot afford to maintain their original number of employees. While the two parties agree that each of these goals is important, they disagree on which is more important. Liberals place a relatively higher weight on the first goal and a relatively lower weight on the second. The conservatives, on the other hand, consider the second goal to be more important.

Based on the weights they have assigned to the goals relating to this issue, the liberal alternative may be to require a minimum wage of $4.40 an hour, whereas the conservative alternative might be a minimum wage of $4.20 an hour. The liberal alternative would score higher on the "fair wage" goal, while the conservative option would score higher on the "avoid over-payment" goal. In Table 5, these scores are indicated by a value of between one and five, with five indicating that the alternative is highly conducive to the goal and one indicating the alternative is highly adverse to the goal.

In order to reach a super-optimum solution in the dispute, an alternative must be created that can better achieve liberal goals than can the $4.40 alternative and simultaneously better achieve conservative goals than can the $4.20 alternative. In many cases like this one, the parties involved see the conflict as a tradeoff, where any gain by one side results in a corresponding loss by the other. This perspective causes the parties to be skeptical of any super-optimum solution. This unwillingness to look for super-optimum solutions generally leads to a neutral or compromise position that allows both parties to come out above their worst expectations yet below their best expectations. In this case such a neutral position may consist of a minimum wage of $4.30.

TABLE 5 Sample SOS table- The minimum wage problem

GOALS / ALT'S	L Decent Wages C=1 L=3 N=2	C Avoid over-payment C=3 L=1 N=2	Totals N	 L	 C
C $4.20/hour	2	4	12	10	14*
L $4.40/hour	4	2	12	14*	10
N $4.30/hour	3	3	12	12	12
SOS $4.41/hour to worker, $4.19 from employer, $0.22 wage supplement	5	5	20	20	20

5= highly conducive
4= mildly conducive
3= neutral effect
2= mildly adverse
1= highly adverse

* Highest scoring alternatives when not considering the SOS alternative

In this case a super optimum solution would consist of a government supplement of twenty two cents per hour to a minimum wage of $4.19 per hour paid by the employer. Thus the employer would pay even less than the conservative best expectation ($4.20), yet the worker would receive more than the liberal best expectation ($4.40). As indicated in Table 5, this alternative is truly super-optimal, as it achieves the highest total score on both liberal and conservative totals.

While the government and taxpayers would appear to be the losers in this scenario, they would in fact benefit as well. The government and taxpayers would gain (1) the money saved that would have been paid in public aid to those hired under the supplement plan, (2) an increase in gross national product corresponding to the increase in affordable labor, (3) better role models for the children of those people employed under the plan, and (4) an improvement of labor pool skills that could be gained by requiring businesses to provide on-the-job training to workers for whom they wish to be subsidized (Public Policy 2).

In this example, a super-optimum solution was reached by using a third-party benefactor, the government. Other common methods developed by Nagel to facilitate reaching super-optimum outcomes include (1) expand available resources, (2) set higher goals than the ones the parties had considered best, (3) create large benefits for one side at minimal cost to the other, (4) combine alternatives in cases where alternatives are not mutually exclusive, (5) eliminate or reduce the source of conflict, and (6) develop a well-rounded package of alternatives that could satisfy both liberal and conservative goals (Public Policy 4).

Nagel's super-optimum solution methodology can easily be applied to the mercury contamination problem in central-western Brazil. The first step in the super-optimum decision-making process is to determine the inputs that will be included on the SOS table.

The first of these inputs to determine are the conservative goals and alternatives. The first of the conservative goals is to maintain profitability for the garimpeiros. This goal is evidenced by some members of the Brazilian government. One such governmental official is Flavio Perri, Brazil's national Secretary of Environment. Environmentalists in both Brazil and the United States consider Perri to be more pro-business than pro -environment. They cite speeches Perri has delivered in which he called for increased economic activity in the Amazon region. In September 1991, Perri stated that under his direction, the Brazilian government's environmental regulation branch would "open up the Amazon region to economic exploitation" ("Amazonian Exploits" 8). Speaking in Rio de Janeiro, he elaborated, "the Amazon is there to be exploited. It cannot be mummified" ("Amazonian Exploits" 8). Perri indicated that he considered the economic benefits of cattle-raising, agriculture and mining to be important enough to merit consideration despite economic concerns. In its report on the speech, New Scientist claims that Perri's goal of sustaining economic profitability of mining in the Amazon basin is supported by state governments in the region ("Amazonian Exploits" 8).

TABLE 6 The Brazilian mercury contamination problem

ALT'S \ GOALS	C Maintain Profits	C Avoid Tax Cost	L Reduce Pollution	N Quality of Life	Totals C	Totals L	Totals N
C Unrestricted Mercury Use	4	2	2	2	24*	16	20
L All-out Ban, Bomb	2	1	4	2	17	19*	18
N Partial Ban	3.5	1.5	3	2	22	18	20
SOS Subsidized Recycling Devices	5	4	5	5	42	34	38

* Highest scoring alternatives when not considering the SOS alternative

Conservatives in Brazil are also concerned with avoiding the high costs to the government and taxpayers that are associated with some liberal alternatives (Silva). They argue that with the severe poverty problems that currently face Brazil additional expenditures for the enforcement of restrictions on miners are not economically feasible. Thus the second conservative goal is to avoid cost to taxpayers and the government.

In order to best address these goals, conservatives have taken the position that the current practice of using mercury for refinement of alluvial gold should be allowed to continue without restrictions. This conservative alternative is naturally supported by the garimpeiros. Ironically, the other major proponents of this alternative are the residents of the areas where the mining is occurring. Conclusive evidence indicates widespread contamination of the soils, riverbeds, water, air, and fish of these areas. The toxic mercury is slowly progressing up the food chain and is now being detected at dangerous levels in some residents. Yet despite all this evidence that the mercury contamination that results from the mining process is accumulating in dangerous levels in their environment and in their own bodies, the residents of the mining areas support the conservative alternative of placing no restrictions on the use of mercury in the mining operations. Like Secretary of Environment Flavio Perri, they are willing to accept these consequences in order to reap the economic benefits of the mining activity.

The impetus for the area residents' support of the conservative alternative lies in the economic boost the area has experienced since the inception of the gold rush. Towns of up to 66,000 have appeared in the wilderness, complete with new airstrips, banks, hotels and other businesses (Chisholm 36).

On the other side of this divisive issue are the goals of liberals. In regards to the problem of mercury contamination, the primary liberal goal is to reduce or eliminate pollution in the area. This liberal goal is based on concern about the rain forest and wetland ecosystems that are affected by the contamination. This goal is reflected by environmentalists in both the United States and Brazil.

In order to accomplish this goal, liberals have supported the alternative of banning mercury use in mining operations and taking any necessary action to enforce this ban ("Fool's Gold" 14). They feel that this policy action is warranted by the threat to environment and health posed by the contamination problem. While mercury use in gold refinement is currently banned only on Indian reservations in Brazil, some liberal government officials who support the liberal alternative of a national ban have already displayed their willingness to enforce such restrictions at all costs. In 1990 miners were operating on islands that are property of the Yanoama Indians. When attempts to remove the mining presence in the area initially failed, the Brazilian government bombed the area (Dorfman 100). Because of the mobile nature of the garimpeiros and the dense forests and swamps in which they operate, enforcement of a national ban would probably require this same type of action from the Brazilian government but on a much greater scale.

On this controversial issue, there is one neutral goal that both conservatives and liberals find relatively important. This neutral goal is to improve the quality of life for area residents. While both conservatives and liberals agree on the importance of this goal, they do not agree on the best method by which it could be accomplished. Conservatives feel that the neutral goal of improving quality of life for area residents is most compatible with their goals of maintaining profits and keeping taxes low. Liberals also feel that their goals are compatible with the neutral goal. They feel that banning mercury use is the only way to prevent area residents from receiving unhealthy exposure to toxic mercury.

As is most often the case in policy disputes, the Brazilian government has adopted what can be characterized as a neutral alternative. This neutral alternative involves a compromise between the primary conservative and liberal goals. Whereas the conservatives want to allow the use of mercury and liberals want a national ban, Brazil now enforces the aforementioned partial ban that is limited to the lands of Brazilian Indians. Thus the neutral alternative involves doing a little of each of the other alternatives. In some places the Brazilian government allows the unrestricted use of mercury, and in some places the government enforces a ban at all costs.

Now that the goals and alternatives of the liberal, conservative and neutral perspectives have been determined, the input stage of super-optimum analysis is partially complete (see Table 6). The second step in the input stage in Nagel's super-optimum analysis process is to determine the relations or scores. This step involves assigning numerical values to represent how well each alternative does towards reaching each goal relative to the other alternatives. As in the sample SOS analysis detailed earlier, these relations are expressed on a one to five scale. On this scale, a five indicates that the alternative is very conducive to the goal. A score of four indicates that the alternative is moderately conducive; a score of three means a neutral relation exists whereby the alternative is neither conducive nor adverse; a two means the alternative is mildly adverse to the goal; and a one indicates the alternative is highly adverse to the goal.

In the context of the mercury contamination problem in central-western Brazil, the first goal to consider is the conservative goal of maintaining economic viability for the garimpeiros. In relation to satisfying this goal the conservative alternative of allowing unrestricted mercury use scores a four, indicating that this alternative is mildly conducive toward maintaining profitability. While this alternative would initially appear to be highly conducive to maintaining the profitability of the garimpeiros, under closer examination a score of five seems inappropriate. One reason that this policy alternative does not merit a score of five is that in the long run it will prove to be self-destructive. If this policy alternative were chosen, the contamination of the rain forest and Pantanal regions would continue. Eventually the problem will have become so bad that an all-out ban of mercury use in mining would be inevitable. Thus, while this alternative may be highly conducive to profits in the short term, it would virtually guarantee an eventual end to profitability that would be associated with a vigorously pursued ban.

Because the liberal alternative calls for this all-out ban to be pursued immediately, it scores much lower on maintaining profitability than the conservative alternative that would at least manage to stall implementation of the ban for a short time. However, this alternative is not highly adverse to profitability since its enforcement would likely not be entirely effective. This difficulty in enforcing an all-out ban is due to several characteristics of the garimpeiros. First, they live in migrant bands that are difficult to track down. This situation is further exacerbated by the heavy cover and rugged terrain that often characterizes the jungle and wetland areas where garimpeiros operate. Finally, the garimpeiros are economically desperate and will not give up their relentless pursuit of gold without a struggle. For example, in the city of Serra Pelada alone about 600 people have died in conflict between large mining companies, the Brazilian government, and the garimpeiros (Chisholm 36). Because an all-out ban would be difficult to enforce effectively, it receives a score of two (mildly adverse) rather than one (highly adverse) in regards to the conservative goal of maintaining profitability of the garimpeiros.

The neutral alternative of a partial ban receives a score of 3.5. This score reflects the fact that the current policy of enforcing a ban only on Indian lands has very little detrimental effect upon the economic viability of the garimpeiros. However, since the partial ban has driven the garimpeiros from some otherwise profitable areas, it receives a score slightly lower than that of the conservative alternative.

The second goal to consider is the conservative goal of avoiding cost to the government and taxpayers. Because it involves no action on the part of the Brazilian government, the conservative alternative of allowing unrestricted mercury use would appear to be highly conducive to this goal. However, because allowing unmitigated contamination would eventually lead to a public health problem severe enough to warrant a massive cleanup project, this savings would only be realized over the short term. The cost of health care for the garimpeiros and area residents could be extensive as well if contamination problems are allowed to worsen. Due to these long term considerations, the conservative alternative scores a two on avoiding cost to taxpayers.

Due to its inherent inability to be efficiently enforced, the liberal alternative of an all-out ban would also allow contamination problems to continue. Since this plan would also involve immediate costs related to enforcement attempts, it is even more adverse to avoiding costs to taxpayers than is the conservative goal. Due to these considerations, the liberal alternative scores a one in relation to the second conservative goal.

The neutral alternative of a partial ban would involve much less short term cost to the government and taxpayers than the liberal alternative, yet more than the conservative alternative which involves no immediate government action. Therefore the neutral alternative receives a score of 1.5, or midway between the respective scores of the conservative and liberal alternatives.

The third goal to consider is the liberal goal of reducing pollution. In relation to this goal, the conservative alternative of allowing unrestricted mercury use scores a two. The lack of pollution control guaranteed by the conservative alternative is only mitigated by the fact that this policy alternative will eventually lead to an all-out ban. Otherwise, the conservative alternative would have scored a one in relation to this goal.

The liberal alternative, while not entirely effective, would still be relatively successful in achieving the goal of pollution reduction. Because this alternative does a significantly better job reducing contamination than do the other alternatives, it receives a score of four.

The final alternative to consider in relation to the liberal coal is the neutral alternative of a partial ban. Because this policy would involve some aspects of both the conservative and liberal alternative, it receives a middling score of three in relation to the liberal goal. This score reflects the fact that the neutral alternative would be more effective at reducing pollution than the conservative alternative, yet less effective than the liberal alternative.

The final goal to consider is the neutral goal of improving the quality of life of the area residents. Because the conservative alternative would threaten the health of the area residents, it receives a two in relation to this goal. The conservative alternative avoids a lower score because it allows the area residents to retain the economic security provided by the mining industry.

While the liberal alternative does not ensure the maintenance of economic viability of the region as well as does this conservative alternative, it atones by more effectively addressing public health in the region. Therefore the liberal alternative also scores a two in regards to the neutral goal of improving quality of life for area residents.

The neutral alternative receives a score of two as well. This score reflects that the neutral alternative does relatively little to harm economic prosperity, yet also does very little to reduce pollution. As in the cases of the liberal and conservative alternative, these positive and negative effects help to cancel each other out. While a score of three may seem to be in order since no net effect is achieved, since the end result of having no net effect on an already troubling situation is not entirely desirable, each alternative receives a score of two in relation to the neutral goal of improving the quality of life for area residents.

Now that all the relational scores have been determined, the totals can be calculated (see Table 6). First the totals for the conservative perspective should be determined. In the Brazilian mercury contamination problem, conservatives tend to assign a relatively low weight to "reducing pollution," a middling weight to "improving quality of life," and a relatively high weight to "maintaining profits" and "reducing tax cost." These weights are represented on a scale of one to three, with three being the highest weight. To determine the conservative total scores, each of these respective weights is multiplied by the score listed under that particular goal. Thus the conservative total score for the conservative policy alternative is 24, or (3 x 4) + (3 x 2) + (I x 2) + (2 x 2). The conservative total for the liberal alternative is 17, or (3 x 2) + (3 x 1) + (I x 4) + (2 x 2). The conservative total for the neutral alternative is 22, or (3 x 3.5) + (3 x 1. 5) + (I x 3) + (2 x 2).

The liberal totals are calculated in the same manner. Liberals tend to assign a high weight to "reducing pollution," a middling weight to "improving quality of life," and a low weight to "maintaining profits" and "reducing tax cost." These weights yield liberal totals of 16 on the conservative alternative; 19 on the liberal alternative; and 18 on the neutral alternative.

The neutral weights are assigned a middling value of two for each goal. These weights yield neutral totals of 20 on the conservative alternative; 18 on the liberal alternative; and 20 on the neutral alternative.

After calculating all these total scores, the next step in Nagel's super-optimum analysis process is to check for internal consistency. As would be expected, the conservative alternative achieves the highest scores among the conservative totals, with the liberal alternative scoring the lowest. Likewise, on the liberal totals the liberal alternative scores highest, with the conservative total scoring lowest. Thus internal consistency is achieved in the SOS analysis of this problem (see Table 6).

The final and certainly most important step in Nagel's super-optimum analysis process is to determine a super-optimum solution. In this case the super-optimizing method Nagel calls "decreasing the source of the conflict" (Public Policy 21). Both *Environment* and *New Scientist* have reported that a device has been developed that would capture mercury used in the refinement process and allow it to be reused ("Price" 24) ("Gold-Diggers" 8). The SOS alternative would involve mandatory use of this device in gold mining operations in Brazil. The purchase of the devices would be subsidized by the Brazilian government. The relations of this alternative will now be discussed with regard to each goal in order to verify its classification as "super- optimum."

The first goal to be considered is the conservative goal of maintaining profits. In relation to this goal, the proposed SOS alternative scores a five. This score is achieved because the proposed SOS alternative is highly conducive to maintaining profitability of the garimpeiros. The mercury-capturing device would save the garimpeiros the expense of constantly purchasing mercury, since it allows the same mercury to be reused many times. More significantly, because the device would eliminate mercury loss to the environment, it would save the garimpeiros from the economic death sentence that an otherwise imminent ban on mercury use would effect. Because it would reduce the garimpeiros' operating expenses and ensure their continued opportunity to operate, the proposed SOS alternative is highly conducive to maintaining profitability.

The prospective SOS alternative also fares well in relation to achieving the second conservative goal, avoiding tax cost. While the SOS alternative would involve a significant initial investment on the part of the Brazilian government, it would avoid major long term costs associated with other alternatives. The immediate expense for the devices will certainly be much less costly than the cleanup and health care costs that would result from allowing contamination to continue. Furthermore, because the device was developed in Brazil and would be produced there ("Gold-Diggers" 8), this short term expense represents an investment in Brazil's economy. Because the Proposed SOS alternative achieves large long term savings with relatively minimal short term cost, it scores a four on avoiding cost to the government and taxpayers.

Since successful implementation of the SOS alternative would eliminate further contamination of Brazil's rain forest and wetland ecosystems, it scores a five on the liberal goal of reducing pollution.

As a result of the SOS alternative's ability to improve the public health conditions in the central-western region of Brazil while not adversely affecting the garimpeiro-dependent local economy, it scores a five on improving the quality of life for area residents. This score reflects the fact that under the SOS alternative the living conditions in the mining regions would be much improved relative to the conditions that would be created under the other alternatives.

With the relational values assigned, the total scores for the proposed SOS can be determined. The conservative total score for the SOS alternative is 42, or (3 x 5) + (3 x 4) + (I x 5) + (2 x 5). The liberal total is 34, or (I x 5) + (I x 4) + (3 x 5) + (2 x 5). The neutral total is 38, or (2 x 5) + (2 x 4) + (2 x 5) + (2 x 5). These totals for the SOS alternative are each the highest total in their respective column. Because the SOS alternative scores highest with the conservative, liberal and neutral weights, it is indeed worthy of the term "super-optimum."

The final step in Nagel's super-optimum analysis process is to test the SOS alternative's feasibility. Nagel offers six types of feasibility that must be examined-political, economic, judicial, administrative, psychological, and technological.

The SOS alternative should encounter no problems with political feasibility. Its ability to improve the quality of life of all involved in the contamination problem should guarantee its political support.

The economic implications of the plan were discussed in assigning a score to the SOS alternative in relation to the conservative goal of avoiding cost to the government and taxpayers. Since the initial investment would not be overwhelmingly large yet the long term savings would be substantial, the SOS alternative is economically feasible.

This SOS alternative involves no action that could be considered to be illegal or unconstitutional. Since nothing in the alternative could lead to its demise at the hands of the Brazilian courts, it is judicially and constitutionally feasible.

The next form of feasibility to consider is administrative- feasibility. Because the garimpeiros would be economically motivated to accept the plan, administration would be simplified. Distribution of the mercury recycling devices would be facilitated by the miners desire to obtain the devices. After the initial distribution, administrative duties would be minimal. For these reasons, the SOS alternative is administratively feasible.

There are no conceivable psychological constraints on this plan. No moral or social values would contradict the conditions that would be created under implementation of the SOS alternative. On the contrary, any moral concerns would likely create strong support for the plan. Therefore the SOS alternative is psychologically feasible.

The final type of feasibility and the one that first comes to mind in regards to this SOS alternative is technological feasibility. Technological unfeasibility often is the restricting condition in SOS solutions that rely upon the use of new devices or techniques. However, because the device involved in this SOS alternative already exists, the plan is technologically feasible.

The proposed super-optimum solution has fulfilled all requirements to be considered super-optimum. It scores highest in relation to the liberal, conservative, and neutral perspectives. It also passes all feasibility tests. As the deadly discase of mercury contamination further infects new areas of the rain forests and marshlands of Brazil each day, the Brazilian government is fighting symptoms when it holds the cure in its very hands. Until the Brazilian government adopts this super-optimum solution, the conditions for the garimpeiros and all the residents of central-western Brazil will be anything but optimal.

REFERENCES

Alho, Cleber J. R.; Lacher, Thomas E. Jr.; and Goncalves, Humberto C. "Environmental Degradation in the Pantanal Ecosystem." Bioscience 38 (Mar. 1988): 164-71.

Amazonian Exploits. *New Scientist* Sept. 1992: 8.

Chisholm, Patricia. "Death Along the Amazon." *Maclean's* 16 May 1988: 36.

Comparative World Atlas. New Jersey: Hammond, 1992.

Dorfman, Andrea. "Assault in the Amazon." *Time* 5 Nov. 1990: 100-1.

Fool's Gold: Refining With Mercury in Brazil. *Discover* Dec. 1986: 14.

Gold-Diggers Poison Brazil's Wild Paradise. *New Scientist* Sept. 1992: 8.

Malm, Olaf; Pfeiffer, Wolfgang C.; and Souza, Cristina M. "Mercury Pollution Due to Gold Mining in the Madeira River Basin, Brazil." *Ambio* 19 (Feb. 1990): 11-15.

Nagel, Stuart S., ed. *Global Policy Studies*. New York: St. Martin's Press, 1991.

Nagel, Stuart S. *Public Policy Controversies and Win-Win Solutions: Economic, Social, and Technology Issues*. Champaign, IL: Notes & Quotes, 1994.

Nriagu, Jerome 0.; Pfeiffer, Wolfgang C.; Malm, Olaf; Souza, Cristina M.; and Mierle, Gregory. "Mercury Pollution in Brazil." *Nature* 2 Apr. 1992: 389.

Pfeiffer, Wolfgang C.; Malm, Olaf; Souza, Cristina M.; Drude de Lacerda, L.; Silveira, E.G.; and Bastos, W.R. "Mercury in the Madeira River Ecosystem, Rondonia, Brazil." *Forest Ecology and Management* 38 (Feb. 1991): 239-45.

Price of Amazonian Gold, The. *Environment* 32 (Apr. 1990): 23-4.

Sanches, Arcenio, and Francisco de Sales, Geraldo. *Geografia*. Sao Paulo, Brazil: IBEP, 1992.

Silva, Rosangela. Personal Interview. 23 Apr. 1994.

Chapter 16

DEMOCRACY, DEVELOPMENT AND WELFARE STATE IN INDIA: A WIN-WIN POLICY ANALYSIS

Noorjahan Bava
University of Delhi South Campus, New Delhi - 110021, India

INTRODUCTION: INDIA'S DEVELOPMENTAL GOALS

Since Independence India has been pre-occupied with the pursuit of the four-fold goals of democracy, planned socio-economic development, nation-building and welfare state. These cherished values and objectives emanating from the Constitution of India have become the alpha and omega of public policies of the Government for the last fifty years.

The Constitution ordains that "The State shall promote the welfare of the people by securing and protecting as effectively as it may a social order in which justice - social, economic and political shall inform all the institutions of the national life" (Article 38). The Directive Principles of State Policy embody the objective of the State under the Republican Constitution, namely that it is to be a `Welfare State' and not a `Police - State'. These directives aim at the establishment of *economic and social democracy* pledged for by the preamble. They emphasize that the goal of the Indian Polity is not unbridled *laissez-faire* but a welfare state where the state has a positive duty to ensure to its citizens social, economic and political justice with the dignity of the individual and consistent with the unity and integrity of the Nation. By making them fundamental in the governance of the country, the founding fathers have enjoined upon all future governments in India the responsibility to find a middle way between individual liberty and the public good, between preserving the property and privilege of the few and bestowing benefits on the many in order to liberate the powers of all men and women equally for contribution to the common good. In order to achieve these grand goals of development, welfare and democracy the policy makers and planners of India have adopted two different sets of *win-win* policy packages - (i) the state - led, public sector dominated socialist model and (ii) economic liberalization or market - led Structural Adjustment Programme (SAP).

CONCEPTUAL FRAMEWORK OF STUDY

To talk of welfare/development/democracy is to talk atone of public policies in general and sectoral policies like social, economic, political and cultural development policies in particular. A clear normative foundation and a general interpretative framework together are necessary for the assessment of social policy. None has emphasized the need for this linkage better than Max Weber (1949:56-57).

"The distinctive characteristic of a problem of social policy is indeed the fact that it cannot be resolved merely on the basis of purely technical considerations which already assume settled ends. Normative standards of value can and must be the objective of dispute in a discussion of problem of social policy because the problem is in the domain of general cultural values".

LINKAGES BETWEEN WELFARE STATE, DEMOCRACY & DEVELOPMENT

The values of democracy, development and welfare state are very closely and positively correlated as the following pages would show. The relationship between these ideals can be hypothesized as follows:

1. Welfare state and development are closely linked as means and ends respectively.
2. Welfare state is a short term goal while development is a long term achievement.
3. Welfare state enhances and strengthens democracy.
4. Democracy being a goal of development, its achievement in political, economic and socio-cultural spheres constitutes all around development.
5. Citizen participation in all the interfaces of the decision - making process is the *sine qua non* of both democracy and development.

The value - loaded (Lin; 1976:189) umbrella concept of development is a multi-dimensional one involving normative, empirical, environmental, moral, legal, material, spiritual, individual, group, spatial and temporal aspects essential for human development (Bava; 1993:169). Development is measured by the extent to which the skewed distribution of factor ownership is corrected by the number of people who are lifted above the poverty line, by education, health facilities and housing provided to them, by the range of employment generation, by economic growth, price stability, political participation by the unorganized and disinherited majority and by cultural progress. (Malcolm: 283) For the purpose of this study *development is operationalised as removal of poverty, unemployment and inequality*. From Third World perspective (Islam and Henault; 1979: 253-678) development signifies the shift from industrialisation and urbanization to agriculture and rural development, from market determined priorities to state determined basic needs, from GNP per capita to individual/group welfare and from centralized planning to decentralised participative planning.

Given the fact that the concept Welfare State is a confluence of many philosophical streams - *conservatism, laissez - fairism, liberalism and Fabian socialism* - an undefinable abstraction" (Titmuss; 1976:145), there is no positive comprehensive philosophy or ideology that underlies the many polices and programms that form part of the Welfare State (Robson; 1976:12). However, it has been equated with a political system with *a high degree of responsibility for the welfare of the population* (Furnoss and Tilton; 1977:19), a kind of socio-economic system with a *dominant public sector* seeking to change the conditions and circumstances under which families live *but without basically changing society*. The two essential characteristics of a welfare state are its *intense individualism* which confers on the individual an absolute right to receive welfare and its *collectivism* that imposes a duty on the state to promote and safeguard the whole community (Marshall, 1963). Since the welfare state has not rejected the capitalist economy, it is a kind of capitalism softened by an injection of socialism - a mixture of semi-socialism and semi - liberalism (Thoens; 1966:127). The welfare state, in order to be worthy of name has to be at least a *social security state* with its assurance of a minimum standard of life (e.g. Britain before Thatcher) or at least the radically democratic and egalitarian *social welfare state* (e.g. Sweden) and not like "the corporate - oriented positive state" like the U.S. whose primary aim is to protect the holders of property from unregulated markets and from potential redistributive demands (Furniss and Tilton; 1977:15).

For operational purpose *the essence of a Welfare State lies in government protected minimum standards of income, nutrition, health, housing, and education and assured to every citizen as a political right, not as charity* (Wilensky; 1976:8-9).

Social development which is an integral part of economic development calls for human resource development. For, the human beings are the most precious assets and there all round development leads to the generation of human capital. The basic objective of the welfare state being the concern and care of the poor and needy in particular and promotion of welfare of all citizens in general, the concept, when translated into action can facilitate the upliftment of the poor and weaker sections of society from poverty, unemployment and inequality, thereby paving, the way for true development in society in the long run.

Economic development is concerned with how the *well-being (or welfare)* of people improves over time. The dominant approaches to the idea of well-being in welfare economics are fundamentally deficient. One approach based on utilitarianism focuses on "utility" and well-being is seen in terms of happiness/pleasure. The other approach sees well-being in terms of "opulence" and seeks to measure it by incomes, commodity possessions and affluence." Under the opulence approach, economic development is seen as expansion of the availability of goods and services. The focus on the growth of GNP per capita is an especially simple version of that approach. Under the utility approach, removal of inequality, exploitation, poverty, hunger, illiteracy and other deprivation is seen as rendered important only if - and to the extent that there is a net utility gain through that removal. It is this obsession with utility - judging the importance of everything in the scale of utility - that is fundamentally inadequate (Amartya Sen; 1986:175).

Under the *basic need* approach advocated by (Paul Streeton; 1981:21) "the basic needs concept is a reminder that the objective of development effort is to provide all human beings with the opportunity for a full life." The basic needs are also defined in terms of commodities i.e. "particular goods and services required to achieve results.

There are many factors that impinge on people's welfare: consumption of goods and services, their level of health, leisure, freedom rights etc. The greater the amount consumed, the higher is the level of welfare. If the process of economic development enables a person to consume more of at least one good, without requiring him to curtail the consumption of any other thing, then one can conclude that the person's welfare is improving (Mukheshwaran and Ashok Kotwal; 1994).

METHODOLOGY: A WIN-WIN POLICY ANALYSIS

At this juncture a brief explanation of the methodology that has been followed by the author will be in order. In order to achieve the goals democracy, development and welfare state, the policy makers and planners in India have adopted two different *win-win policy* packages which are popularly known as the *Nehruvian* (named after first Prime Minister of India, Pandit Jawaharlal Nehru) Model from 1947-1991 and the Economic Liberalization Model from July 24, 1991 onwards.

As evaluation of the impact of the two policy paradigms on the country's anticipated goals has been the principal objective of this study, both models have been subjected to a thorough going *public policy analysis* in the following pages. The *interdisciplinary field of public policy studies* focuses attention on the nature, causes and effects of alternative public policies addressed to specific social problems. (S. Nagel; 1984:1) Since *policy analysis by definition involves seeking to achieve or maximize given values or social goals rather than ignoring them* (S. Negal;1980:162), the policy analyst has to strictly adhere to the parameters of policy studies. These include (i) an obligation on the part of the policy analyst/evaluator to be "objective" in the sense of not allowing his/her own values or biases to influence the collection, recording, presentation and analysis of the data; (ii) at least a minimum level of acquaintance with the subject matter, tools, techniques and methods of various social sciences that impinge on public policy and (iii) skill for interdisciplinary research. Although methods of policy analysis consist of both quantitative and non-quantitative ones (Stuart Nagel, 1984:28); for the purpose of this study the interdisciplinary and multidisciplinary methodology involving a mix of philosophical, historical, legal, constitutional, political economy, political sociology, social psychology and management approaches combined with a sprinkling of statistics has been deployed. The adoption and application of a truly *integrated holistic systems approach* is imperative when one embarks upon evaluation of public policies for development (Lipset; 1972:xiii-xiv).

Win-Win Policy

A win-win policy is a public policy that is capable of achieving conservative and liberal goals simultaneously; it is not a compromise policy and above all it must the feasible in theory and practice (S. Nagel; 1995: 1-2).

Super - Optimum Solutions (SOS)

Those win-win solutions through which all major actors or parties gain are referred to as Super-Optimum Solutions (S. Nagel 1995: 1-2). They are a special form of win-win solutions in the sense that gain exceeds the best initial expectations of each side, and thus excludes a non-substantial gain.

Methodological Problem in Evaluation

The evaluation of the Nehruvian/socialist/public sector dominated (State - led) model is based on *project management* methods since all the eight Five Year Plan development programs, projects and schemes aimed at *micro* economic changes in the primary, secondary and tertiary sectors of the economy. On the other hand structural adjustment programme involved both *macro* economic changes through policy conditionalities aimed at stabilisation and micro economic reforms. Therefore the project management method is used only in respect of the latter whereas the evaluation of macro economic reforms is based on judgement in this paper. In fact the Brettonwood financial institutions are themselves in a quandary as far as the selection of the appropriate methodology for evaluating the SAP is concerned (Toye; 1995:13-42).

It is only after the *UNICEF Report on Adjustment With a Human Face* 1987, emphasized the need to protect the poor and vulnerable from the burden of the SAP that the "Social Safety Net" provision was included in the policies.

Bench Mark Data

Before the evaluation of the profile of India as a Welfare State begins it will do well to recall the bench-mark data about the country on the eve of Independence. As far as the basic needs of life in general, and food in particular are concerned, India was short of not only cereals but also of pulses and oil seeds. In 1945-46, the per capita availability of food grains had declined steadily from 195 kg 152 kg to per year! As far as cloth was concerned the per capita availability was 17 meters in 1951. After spending Rs. 100 crores (1000 million) in producing drinking water supply in 1971, as many as 3,25,000 villages out of a total of 5,76,000 villages were without this facility. On the housing front it was estimated that in urban areas alone which had only a little more than one crore (10 million) families, there was shortage of more than 18 lakh houses in 1951. In addition, 10 lakh houses were required for displaced persons from Pakistan.

In 1951, only 17 percent of the population was literate, and out of every hundred children in the school going age of six to eleven, only forty-three attended school, As far as health and medical facilities are concerned the position in India was thus:

- one doctor for 6300 persons against 1000 in U.K.
- one nurse for 43,000 people against 300 in U.K.
- one trained midwife for 60,000 women against 618 in U.K.
- one health visitor for 4 lakh against 4710 in U.K.

In short immediately after Independence India was one of the most underdeveloped countries in the world. Its per capita income was extremely low. Most people were engaged in over-crowded agriculture at a low level of productivity. There was no infrastructure for industrialization. Life expectancy was low and infant mortality high, inequalities between various sections of people, exploitation and oppression of women, scheduled castes and tribes existed.

Win-Win Policy I: State-Led Democratic Socialist (Nehruvian) Model

India adopted the strategy of development through *democratic planning* within the framework of a *mixed economy* to reach the Nehruvian vision of *socialistic pattern of society*. Rejecting the orthodox model of the western capitalist economies and the radical approach of the socialist command economies, India took the middle path of *"growth with equity"* based on the belief that developing countries like her where majority still live in rural areas and where the poor are concentrated, more governmental intervention and action than the orthodox (market economy) approach advocates is required if growth with equity is to be achieved. Plan after Plan reiterated India's faith in the growth with equity approach the chief components of which are: expansion of employment opportunities, corrections of market distortion through governmental policy and administrative action, emphasis on rural development, meeting basic needs of people, developing small/cottage/rural industries and new international economic order which will help the poor nations of the world to receive a fairer share of the world's wealth. The Indian State assumed a lion's share of responsibility to achieve a socialistic pattern of society and its multi-dimensional role as planner, policy-maker, catalyst, participant, regulator, manufacturer, importer, exporter, financier and distributor under the Industrial Policy Resolution, 1956 resulted in the growth and dominance of the public sector undertakings numbering 243 units with a capital investment of Rs. 178628 crore (1786280 million) as on March 31, 1991 vis-a-vis 5 PSUs worth Rs 29 crore (290 million) in 1951, and their control over the commanding heights of the Indian economy. The underlying rationale/philosophy of the expanding public sector was that the PSUs were expected to generate employment opportunities, generate surplus wealth, alleviate poverty, remove regional disparities, promote welfare and enable India to contribute to international understanding and peace.

IMPACT OF THE NEHRUVIAN MODEL

In a democracy everything that the government does has to be for the welfare of the people. Planning was started with a view to improve the quality of life of the people. *After four decades of planning for socio-economic development, welfare and nation building, India's experience is neither a run away success nor a dismal failure.* Indeed India to-day is a major industrial and military power. It produces a wide range of different industrial goods including sophisticated computers, military aircrafts, and automobiles. It has launched its own weather satellites into space. We have one of the largest pools of scientists and engineers in the world. India is self sufficient in food production.

Poverty Alleviation

Considering the critical importance of rural development for India our planners and policy-makers had given the highest priority to it in the National agenda right from the commencement of the era of planned development. A whole lot of programs ranging from the Community Development and National Extension Services, Panchayat Raj, IAAP, IADP, to special programs for weaker sections like the Small Farmers, Marginal Farmers and Agricultural Labourers Development Programme, Command Area Development Programme, Tribal Development, Hill Area Development Programme, Minimum Needs Programmes, Integrated Rural Development Programme, Integrated Child Development Programme, National Rural Employment Programme, Rural Landless Employment Guarantee Programme, Training Youth for Self Employment Programme, Jawahar Rozgar Yojana etc. had been implemented in order to achieve self-reliance, removal of poverty, employment generation and all round integrated development of rural/urban areas.

As Sukhmoy Chakravarty observes: While India had doubtless scored some success, but it had left number of people below the poverty line. The 32nd National Sample Survey showed that in 1977-78 the proportion of population in rural areas living below the poverty line was 51.2%, whereas the corresponding figure for urban areas was 38.2%. According to the 38th Survey (1983-84), the figures had nose-dived to 40.4% for rural and 28.1% in urban areas. This indicated the gross poverty that existed in the country, as the norm used for these purposes was based principally on caloric intake.

In terms of nutrition the average per person availability of cereals had gone up from 334 grams of 429 grams per day in (1986-87), though this is still not adequate to provide two square meals to the entire population. The per capita availability of oilseeds had remained static at 14 kg per year, while the availability of pulse, the main source of protein in India, had declined from 22 kg to 13 kg per year. *Thus the economic condition of half of the farmers of India who grew coarse cereals, pulses an oilseeds in the dry regions has not improved during the last four decades after independence.*

Employment

During 1947-90 period unemployment scenario of India was neither healthy nor sound. Vitiated by chronic unemployment both absolute and seasonal, the situation was quite grim. The position of unemployment within agronomy was further aggravated by wide underemployment with ten persons competing for every job opening and labor being mostly landless and disorganised, wages were poor and verged on exploitation. In the industrial, mining and infrastructural areas, the bulk of labor is unskilled, and education being largely non-vocational, there is large scale educated unemployment, wage differentials, deep-seated labor unrest and militant trade unionism (undermining production and productivity in the nation).

Since an overwhelming proportion of the Indian population lives in the villages, the bulk of the unemployment is rural. The backwardness of Indian agriculture and failure of land reforms, aggravate the situation. From 1970 onwards an additional 5 million was added to the rural unemployed. *The level of unemployment was very high all over the rural sector; it was equally rapidly rising in the urban sector, and public sector employment and public works programme-based palliatives had failed to check this additional alarming rise.*

The main factor causing the problem of unemployment had been identified as structural disequilibrium, distortions in planning, deficient employment planning, population explosion and faulty education cover.

Economic Growth

While independence certainly broke the spell of stagnation in India economy, *the national income showed a trend growth rate of 3.6 percent annum over the period of 1950-84*. India's macro economic performance had been only "moderately good" in the terms of GDP growth rates. Allowing for the fact that the better part of the entire plan period, population increased by *more* than 2% per annum, the growth in per capita income on an average basis had been somewhat *less* than 2% per annum. The rise in the domestic savings rate from around 10% of GDP in the early fifties to 23% currently was quite impressive. Secondly while India had to reckon with a fair measure of inflaction from time to time, the average rate of inflation had been a "modest" one by international standards. Most often they were triggered by harvest failures and brought under control without resort to large scale foreign borrowing. There are two major reasons for this success. One is the ability to maintain a rate of growth of food production of around 31 per cent ove the period as whole. The other is the financial deepening that was experienced by the country, which allowed domestic savings to go up in monitised form. As Nicholas Kaldor and others have emphasized in the analysis of Latin American inflaction, the proneness of these countries to inflation has been in large part due to their neglect of food grain agriculture. The policy of the Government to tackle the problem of inflation from both demand and supply side whenever inflation exceeded single digit coupled with political legitimacy (poor but an open democratic system is generally less tolerant of inflation than authoritarian regimes), it has, in the long run, helped to increase the savings rate by helping to maintain confidence in the standard of value. However, much of the saving had taken place in the housing sector and not in the public sector. Most of the public sector undertakings became white elephants.

While the trend growth rate of the industrial sector was 5 per cent per annum during 1950-84, that of agriculture was only 2.2 percent, same as the rate of population growth. Consequently the contribution of the industrial sector to the national income had increased from 15 percent in 1947 to 261 per cent in 1988, but it had not resulted in a significant increase in the percentage of total labor employed in industry, the change had been from 10 percent to 15 percent in 40 years. Consequently, the percentage of India's labor force employed in agriculture and allied activities had changed only from 74 to 66 in the same period.

Health Services

India is one of the very few countries that had from the very beginning planned health services as a part of general socio-economic development. The broad objectives of the health plans had been strengthening of the health infrastructure and complete eradication of diseases and their integration into basic health services. Health care system was coordinated with other nation building activities and was made a part of the community development programs and administered through a network of primary health centers, which formed the nucleus for a minimum of scheme of health services for the rural community.

During the First and Second Five Year Plans emphasis was laid on control of communicable diseases, improvement of environmental sanitation, organization of institutional facilities, training of medical and para-medical personnel, provision of maternity and child health services, and child health services, health education and nutrition and family planning. From the II Plan onwards greater emphasis on family planning had been laid by the Government. During the III Plan a shift in the approach took place from the narrow clinical to one of exclusive community education, provision of facilities near the homes of the people, and widespread effort in rural and urban community. The Family Planning Department was established in the Ministry of Health. The Medical Termination of Pregnancy Act was placed on the Statute Book in 1972. Since 1975-76 the Government has been actively implementing and expanding the Integrated Child Development Services (ICDS) which provides supplementary nutrition, immunization, health checkups, referral service, treatment of minor illness, nutrition and health education, pre-school education and other services. Out of the 5143 community development blocks in the country, the ICDS have been covered in 1551!

The experience of ICDS during the first twelve years indicated that it had the potential of bringing about a silent revolution - a profound instrument of community and human resource development. Its achievements include decrease in malnutrition and anemia, better nutritional assessments, significant decrease in preventable diseases, effective Anganwadi workers, fall in infant and child mortality and positive results of community participation. The health services also include Maternity and Nutritional Services to women. The central expenditure on the ICDS has increased over th year from 6.02 crore (60.2 million) in 1980-81 to 144 crore (1440 million) in 1987-88. There were 1054 rural projects and 497 tribal projects and 187 urban projects in the country covering 87.78 Lakh children in 1988.

The fruits of development had been neutralized by the failure of the family planning programme to arrest the population growth during the period under review.

Weaker Sections

The Constitution of India provides for the promotion of welfare of the weaker sections through socio-economic policies embodied in the Directive Principles of State Policy. Article 46 states: `The State shall promote with special care all the educational and economic interests of the weaker sections of the people and in particular, of the Scheduled Caste and Scheduled Tribes and shall protect them from social justice and all forms of exploitation.'

The weaker sections include not only the SCs and STs but also the physically the mentally handicapped, women, widows, orphans, socially and educationally backward classes, minorities and so forth. Although Article 17 of the Constitution declares that untouchability is abolished and the Untochability (offences) Act provides penalties for preventing a person on the grounds of untouchability from entering a place of worship, or taking water from a sacred tank, well or spring and enforcing all kinds of social disabilities, the implementation of the law has been very ineffective resulting in atrocities against SCs, STs, women and others which are on the increase. Though the SCs and STs enjoy constitutionally laid down reservation of seats in Parliament and State Legislatures, in public services and for admission in colleges and universities, after the Supreme Court judgement on Mandal Commission Report, OBC (other backward classes) have also been entitled for reservation not exceeding 27 percent in public employment.

The Ministry of Welfare of the Government of India administers several welfare programs for the SCs and STs, and the physically and mentally disabled. It provides financial assistance to organizations for disabled persons for the purpose of construction of building, purchase of furniture, equipment, salaries and allowances of the staff, books, contingencies, transport, publication of journal and maintenance charges, for purchases/fitting of aids of appliances and scholarship to various types of the handicapped - visual, hearing orthopedic and multiple, and mentally handicapped for studies under its scholarship scheme.

Although women constitute roughly 50 percent of the population of India and the Constitution guarantees the same fundamental rights that are bestowed on men, *women continued to suffer from serious social and economic disabilities. Their participation in various political, administrative and social institutions of national life and in the process of production is negligible.* Unless women are treated equally and their right to participate in the process of production, governance and administration is vigorously enforced and the social evils against them such, as dowry, child marriage etc. are removed, they will have to remain outside the orbit of development and its fruits. Thus participation of 50 percent of the (women) in the developments process which is not there needs to be corrected.

Social Security

The Constitution of India provides for social security and assistance in the case of unemployment, old age, sickness, disablement and other cases of want. It provides that the State shall within the limits of its economic capacity and development make effective provision for security, the right to work, education and assistance in the case of unemployment, old age, sickness and disablement. The welfare state in India has been strengthened by the enactment and enforcement of Retirement Benefit Act - Employment Provident Fund Scheme, Payment of Gratuity Act, 1972, Family Pension - Cum Life Insurance Scheme applying to employees drawing salary up to Rs. 1000 p.m. in every factory, mine, port, oil field, plantation, shops etc. employing ten or more persons. The state has passed a number of labor legislations regulating the conditions of work of employees which also provide for social security. For instance the Employees State Insurance Act 1948. It covers all power-using non-seasonal factories wherein 20 or more persons are employed for a period of 12 months except in mines and railway shed. The benefits include sickness, extended sickness, maternity, disablement, dependency and medical benefit.

There is no dearth of social security and welfare legislation in India. But the effective and efficient enforcement of these legal measures is far from satisfactory. The chief obstacles in the way of the full blossoming of the welfare state in India are: lack of welfare society, lack of will power, resources, and participation of people, corruption and inefficiency in social political, administrative systems, the new economic policy of the Government, poverty and low position of women and workers in the unorganised sectors, failure of the family planning programme to arrest the population explosion and illiteracy.

A comparison between India's record of performance at the developmental front with those of her Asian sisters leads to the startling revelation that although both India and South Korea had almost the same per capita income at about 7% that of the United States in 1950, it has gone up for South Korea to 25% in 1980 while it has remained virtually unchanged for India. Countries like Malaysia and Thailand have also shown superior performance than India with 25% and 15 percent respectively. The better performance of the Asian Tigers was attributed to the economic liberalization policy implemented in these countries.

By the end of 1990 not only India remained a very poor country, but also its income was unequally distributed as in many other countries of the world. The top 20 percent of the population in India had a share of more than 40 percent of the total consumption expenditure (income minus saving) while the share of the bottom 40 percent is less than 20 percent. The distribution of income was even more skewed than that of consumption expenditure. As a result the poorest in India, typically the landless agricultural workers are exceedingly poor. Even by the most conservative estimate over 35 percent of Indians were below the official poverty line in 1987. (The Sixth Five Year Plan defined an all-India poverty line as a per capita consumption expenditure of Rs.65 of 1977-78 prices in rural areas corresponding to a calorie intake of 2,100). According to the World Bank data of 1985, the poverty condition of India was worse than that of Sub-Sahara Africa. What is even more alarming is the fact that the percentage of population below the poverty line is higher and yet falling more slowly in India than in other less developed Asian countries like Indonesia, Malalysia and Thailand.

A significant percentage of the population is so poor that its basic needs like adequate diet, clean drinking water, and health care are not being satisfied as health indicators like child mortality and life expectancy reflect this fact. On the literary front India's performance is one of the worst in the world. In 1947, 19 percent of India's population could read and write. By 1985, this has improved to only 43 percent whereas during the same period China has improved the literacy rate from 30 to 70 percent, and South Korea from 32 to 95 percent. India's performance is especially shocking in the light of her achievement in higher education. While the slums lacking in drinking water and sanitation are increasing in metropolitan cities, thousands flee to cities every day from villages in search of better life. The stark reality and most oppressive fact of life in rural areas being the scarcity of employment opportunities India is far away from reaching the goal of a welfare state. The hypotheses of the study thus stand vindicated.

WIN-WIN POLICY II: MARKET-LED LIBERALIZATION / GLOBALIZATION PARADIGM OR SAP

India witnessed a *policy paradigm shift* to the Structural Adjustment Programme in 1991 when the Congress Government under Prime Minister P.V. Narasimha Rao assumed power. The same policy continued under the 13 party United Front Coalition Government as well. The SAP which is rooted in neo-liberalism was advocated by the World Bank and IMF as the international model of development for the Third World under the influence of the new monetarists (Friedman), the new political economy, Public Choice School (Buchanan and Niksanan) and the New Right who gave the clarion call for the rolling back of the State, reinventing the Government and establishment of the free market economy based on liberalization. The World Bank's World Development Report: The Challenge of Development 1991 called for a market-friendly development.

Components of Liberalization

1. Privatization of State and parastatal enterprises in order to reduce inefficiencies and government protected monopolies;
2. High interest rates and credit squeeze in order to reduce inflationary tendencies;
3. Trade liberalization in order to open up the internal market and expose local industry to world market competition and boost foreign trade exchange;
4. Domestic demand management leading to a lowering of State budgets and decreasing expenditure in the social sector;
5. Currency adjustment in order to improve the balance of payment by raising import prices and making exports more competitive;
6. Free-market prices in order to remove distortions resulting from subsidized food and fertilizers and from import taxes on luxury goods.

Liberalization can be either internal or external or both: *Internal liberalization signifies privatisation, marketisation and minimialisation of the state's economic role.* It calls for unfettered role for private enterprises and market forces and sustained withdrawal of the State from its regulatory, directly participative, enterpreneurial role. On the other hand, external liberalization denotes *globalization* in terms of import liberalization, exchange rate adjustment, generally devaluation of the currecy of the poorer, debter nations, free flow of foreign direct investment (FDI) induced by liberal incentives-tax concessions, political guarantees and unfettered activities of the MNCs on the basis of their unfettered reading of market signals and profit calculus and continued curbing of labor mobility. External liberalization provides increased space freely accessible to foreign capital, goods and services, finance and technology on favourable terms. The MNCs transcending the national barriers have become the vehicles of global economic hegemony with command over huge capital, technology, diversified and geographically dispersed production mix; huge R&D outlay, global markets in which Third World nations and former command economies are holding promising prospects (the emerging markets).

IMPACT OF THE LIBERALIZATION MODEL

In India the implementation of the Liberalization Policy since July, 1991 has led to decontrol, deregulation, privatisation/disinvestment of the public sector enterprises; and abolition of industrial licensing for all projects except in few strategic and environment concerned industries. As against 17 industries that were reserved for public sector investment under IPR 1956, now only 8 industries concerned with defense and strategic mattes are reserved. Foreign equity participation limit has been increased from 40 percent to 51 percent under the Foreign Exchange Regulation Act; grant of automatic permission of the facility to specified list of hi-tech and high-priority industries; automatic approval of foreign collaborations in high priority industries up to 5 percent of domestic sales or 8 percent of export sales or up to a limit of Rs. 10 million; and reduction of political and bureaucratic control and influence through measures such as : (a) removal of the requirement of prior clearance from the government for the location of projects except in the case of large cities; (b) allowing small scale enterprises the option to offer up to 24 percent of equity in large scale undertakings while still retaining their small scale status; (c) removal of the mandatory requirement that loan agreements of financial institutions with private firms formally provide for the conversion of loans into equity (convertibility clause); and (d) the liberalization of procedure for foreign exchange remittances.

Financial Reforms

Since the globalization policy will open up the Indian economy, changes in the EXIM policies and Convertibility of the Rupee have been effected. The new credit policy announced by the RBI aims at increasing the supply of money in the financial market which was subjected to liquidity crunch.

Considering South East Asia currency turmoil (slide) involving devaluation of the currencies and collapse of the share markets and the resultant political crisis (e.g. Thailand) India should not rush for full convertibility of the capital account even though one of the conditions for full convertibility i.e. inflation has been brought down to 3.75%. India should wait till her fiscal deficit falls to 3% of GDP.

Removal of Import-Export Curbs

Government of India has further liberalized the import of gold a few days ago. Eleven agencies have been permitted to import unlimited quantities of the precious metal for sale in the domestic market as well as for export of gold jewelry which will generate a lot of foreign exchange for the country besides preventing smuggling of gold.

Economic Growth

It has been argued that liberalization and globalization will open up the Indian economy thereby facilitating faster rate of economic growth, the fruits of which will trickle down to the poor. According to the present estimate the growth rate has shot-up to

6.5% thanks to the reforms vis-a-vis 3.5% before the reforms. However, economits say that India will not be able to sustain the 7% rate for long. The governor of the RBI feels that India has the potential to reach 7% growth rate.

India has already started experiencing the inevitable negative consequence of liberalization namely the trade cycles. Since the economy has been hit by a sharp industrial slow down, low business confidence and sluggish investment, private sector magnates have urged the Government to increase public expenditure to shore up demands in the economy. The recession of the economy is bound to increase the unemployment in the country as the private entrepreneurs resort to the EXIT policy.

Subsidy

The policy of the Government towards subsidy has been denounced by both internal and external critics. While the latter (World Bank & IMF) advise the government to completely stop the subsidies so that the government can reduce is fiscal deficit, the domestic detractors have questioned its basic approach to the subsidy question which is based on a particular conceptualisation of merit and non-merit goods resulting in skewed subsidies. All merit goods are entitled at present to automatic subsidy. Under this policy Government has brought primary education and R&D under merit good entitled to subsidy and education beyond primary level under non-merit good and therefore no subsidy. R&D is entitled for subsidy but not higher/university education. In a developing country like India with one-third of people living below the poverty level, the "social safety net" and the "human face" of the new policy taking the form of subsidies to the Public Distribution System and to small, marginal farmers, agricultural farmers, subsidy given to Social services should continue. Recently the government hiked subsidy on some renewable energy programme with special focus on SCs and STs and poor.

Weaker Sections

Several "human face" measures have been taken up by the Government. Thanks to the reservation policy the proportion of SC and ST in Central Government Services has gone up to 16.90 percent and 5.48 percent in 1994 respectively. Their literacy rate has also gone up to 37.41 percent for SC and 28.6 for the ST. A five member National Commission for Backward Classes has been established under the 1993 Act. Pre-examination coaching classes for OBCs and facilities for their economic development under National Backward Classes Finance and Development Corporation with a capital of Rs.156.9 million to provide loans have been created recently.

Till the end of 1995-96, the National Scheduled Caste Finance and Development Corporation established in 1989 to provide support to economic development programmes of the SC has distrbuted about Rs.3000 million. The state level bodies established for the same purpose have disbursed to 87 lakh beneficiaries in 1994-95. To remove the indignity of the lowest caste and promote its liberation a National Commission for Safai Karamcharis (Cleaning Staff) has been created in 1992. A National Minority Commission has been established to take care of the interest of the minorities.

Corruption

The protagonists of liberalization do not hesitate to condemn public administration as the most inefficient and corrupt one. But there is a growing evidence to show that corruption is built into the market economy. In their study on Liberalization and Corruption, Barbara Harves White and Gordon White of the Institute of Development Studies, London question the assumption that corruption can be rolled back by eliminating the State through privatization and deregulation. The privatization of the Telecommunication Sector alone resulted in scams involving Rs. 1750 million, the resignation of a Cabinet Minister and bureaucrat.

Privatisation of Public Sector

The Government of India's decision to grant increased financial and operational autonomy to select PSUs that have been brought under the Navratna scheme is laudable. The disinvestment and privatisation of the PSU shares should be slowed down as efficiency and accountability will go up with the new policy. The decision of the Government not to off load the shares of PSUs (GAIL & MTNL in the context of the global financial crisis is a wise one.

Unequal Treatment at International Trade

As long as the global economy is characterized by inequalities, international trade which is based on the principle of mutual interest of the partners cannot bring benefits to the weaker partners i.e. the developing countries like India. India's trade deficit during 1995-96 stood at $ 4,056.62 million as against $ 1,837.41 million during 1994-95. The recent decision taken by India, Malaysia etc. at the Common Wealth Heads of Government Meet and the Group-15 nations that a second round of trade negotiations at the WTO should be avoided and developing nations should not submit to the procedures of globalization devised by the advanced industrialized nations are correct.

Unemployment, Poverty, Illiteracy and Inequality

Economic liberalization involving anti-labor and anti-poor exit policy, fierce foreign competition from MNCS and emphasis on profit maximizing has resulted in the creation of greater unemployment and poverty in the country than before. Thanks to SAP, *"jobless growth"* has taken place in India as elsewhere. *Not only unemployment and poverty but also inequality and corruption have increased. India's debt - burden has increased.* The private entrepreneurs - domestic and foreign alike do not want to invest in infrastructural (power/road) projects as these entail huge capital investment and long gestation period. *Privatization has led to undesirable consumerism and cultural invasion of the country.* In the social sector the cost of education and medical treatment and care provided by the private sector have increased enormously to the determented of the interest of the weak and poor.

India is destined to march into the new millennium with the largest number of illiterates in the world. Both the win-win policies have not resolved the problem of illiteracy in the country as they have failed to provide the most basic of human rights-education. While 30 million have no access to schooling, out of the 14 million who are enrolled, only two-third complete the primary stage. Of the remaining, only half reach the eighth standard. The majority of the drop outs are girls.

According to **UN World Development Report,** 1997 India's vital development/welfare indices read as follows:

India continues to be a Low Income Country (LIC) with a population of 929.4 million in 1995; a GNP per capita of $ 340; average annual growth percentage of 3.2 during 1985-95; 52.5 percent poverty- ridden people living on less than $ one a day (PPP), life expectancy at birth 62; adult illiteracy 48 percent; Central Government's current deficit/surplus as percentage of GDP minus 1.6; average annual lending rate 16.3 percent; average inflation 9.8 percent in 1985-95; Current Account Balance minus 1.8; and net present value of external debt 23 percent of the GDP.

To sum up, the debit side of the economic liberalization policy weighs more heavily than its credit side. Dissatisfaction with the new policy is growing among different sections of the people for different reasons. The small indigenous industralists, business community and farmers who have contributed their mite to the economic/industrial development for the last 50 years after India's independence are now faced with the threat of extinction-the big fish swallowing the small ones in the face of fierce competition from powerful monopolist foreign companies/MNCs. In all fairness the Government has to provide a *level-playing field* to the Indians through protection and concessions while simultaneously motivating them to modernize their enterprises with the latest technology which will help them and the country in the long run.

CONCLUSION

Under Win-win policy model II, though the State activities in the Indian economy have shrunk, it does not mean that government has rolled back or it has no function to perform. Under the impact of the new economic reforms, the Indian bureaucracy has to bring about debureucratisation, deregulation, delicensing and decentralisation of development administration. However, its performance in this regard has been far from satisfactory. India's main development goal of building a Welfare State is still a distant goal. The new economic reforms have not been able to make a dent on unemployment, poverty and inequality in the country. The gap between rich and poor and crime and violence are increasing. Agriculture, the back bond of the Indian economy has been neglected under the new regime of economic liberalization. The recent shortage of essential commodities and mismanagement of this sector by the Union Government is a pointer to the poor performance of the second win-win model of development in force in the country since 1991.

REFERENCES

Adiseshiah, Malcolm (1970), "Planning and Development" in S.K. Sharma, ed., *Dynamics of Development*, Vol.2.

Adiseshiah, Malcolm (1970), "Development As People: The Total Approach", The Second Devlopment Decade, Kuruskhetra, November 12.

Austin, Granville ( ) *The Indian Constitution: The Cornerstone of a Nation.*

Bava, Noorjahan (1996), "Welfare State and Liberalization", *The Indian Journal of Public Administration*, Special Number on Liberalization Policy and Social Concerns, Vol. X<II.

Bava, Noorjahan (1993), *Development and the Social Science Method: An Interdisciplinary and Global Approach*, New Delhi, Uppal Publishers.

Furniss Norman and Tilton Timothy (1977), *The Case of the Welfare State from Social Security to Social Equality* Bloomington, Indiana University Press.

Islam Nasir and Henault George M. (1979), "From GNP to Basic Needs, A Critical Review of Development and Development Administration", *International Review of Administratie Sciences*, Vol. VI, No.3.

Lin, Paul (1976), `Development Guided by Values' in Rajni Kothari, *State and Nation Building*, New Delhi, Allied publishers.

Lipset, Martin Seymour (1972), *Politics and the Social Sciences Method*: New Delhi, Wiley Eastern Pvt. Ltd.

Marshall, T.H. (1963), *Sociology at the Crossroads.*

Mukheswaran and Kotwal Ashok (1994), *Why Poverty Persists in India*, Bombay, Oxford.

Nagel, S. Stuart (1984), *Contemporary Public Policy Analysis*, Alabama, the University of Alabama Press.

Nagel, S. Stuart (1995), "Win-Win Policy" *Public Studies Journal*, 23:1, Spring 1995.

Nagel, S. Stuart (1995), "Universal Values and Win-Win Policy", *Policy Studies Journal*, 23:2, pp. 3-6.

Nagel, S. Stuart (1980), *The Policy Studies Handbook*, Lexington, D.C. Health and Comp.

Robson William (1976), Welfare State and Welfare Society: *Illusion and Reality*, London, George Allen and Unwin.

Sen, Amartya (1986), "The Concept of Well-being" in S. Gulshan and Manu Shroff, eds., *Essays on Economic Progress and Welfare*: In Honour of I.G. Patel, Bombay, Oxford.

Streeton, Paul et all, (1981) *First Things First*: Meeting *Basic Needs in Developing Countries*, New York, Oxford.

Titmus Richard M. (1976) *Talking About Welfare: Readings in Philosophy and Social Policy*, London, Routledge and Kegal Paul.

Titmuss Richard M. (1958), *The Welfare State*, London, George Allan and Unwin Novel Timms and David Watson, (eds.)

Toye, John (1995), *Structural Adjustment and Employment Policy: Issues and Experience*, Geneva, ILO.

Weber, Max (1949) Objectivity in Social Science and Social Policy, *The Methodology of the Social Sciences*, New York, Free Press.

Wilensky, Harold L. (1976) *The New Corporation, Centralisation, and Welfare State*, London, Sage Publications.

INDEX

A

B

C

D

E

F

G

H

I

J

K

L

M

N

O

P

Q

R

S

T

U

V

W

Z